MANUAL OF STYLE
AND USAGE

The New York Times
MANUAL OF STYLE AND USAGE

A Desk Book of Guidelines
for Writers and Editors

Revised and Edited by

LEWIS JORDAN
News Editor, The New York Times

Times
BOOKS

Library of Congress Cataloging in Publication Data

Jordan, Lewis.
    The New York Times manual of style and usage.

    1. Journalism—Handbooks, manuals, etc.
2. Printing, Practical—Style manuals.   I. New
York Times.   II. Title.   III. Title: Manual of
style and usage.
PN4783.J6   1975   651.7′ 402   75-8306
ISBN 0-8129-0578-4 (hardcover)
ISBN 0-8129-6316-4 (paper)

Manufactured in the United States of America

10   9   8

Acknowledgments

The present revision and enlargement of this manual could not have been accomplished without the help given by members of the news, Sunday and editorial departments of The New York Times. Their contribution is typified by the work of Allan M. Siegal, an assistant foreign editor. He participated in all stages of the revision, wrote or suggested useful new entries and was throughout a perceptive and constructive editor. Eileen M. Butler and Jeffrey H. Schmalz also gave much valuable aid in research and editing, in addition to managing with sureness a manuscript containing thousands of entries.

L.J.

Foreword

Here is a new and enlarged edition of the desk book of guidelines compiled for those who write and edit The New York Times. Many of the entries that have been added concern language usage rather than printing style—so many, indeed, that the title of the book has been changed to add the word *usage* and thus more accurately describe the contents.

"Style," as it is used in the title, is not literary style; it is a set of rules or guides intended to assure consistency of spelling, capitalization, punctuation and abbreviation in printing the written word. There is little difference between a Martini and a martini, but unless there is a style rule the word may be capitalized in one instance and lower-cased in another. Such untidiness must be avoided, in matters small or large, because it detracts from even the best of writing. Rules are especially needed when many very different people write and edit a publication that has an identity of its own. For examples of the style guidelines in this self-indexing book, see these alphabetical entries: **abbreviations; Bishop; capitalization; comma; company and corporation names; Mr., Mrs. and Miss; numbers; President, president; years, decades, centuries.**

"Usage" is something else. In this manual, it means the manner in which words are employed—or, most often, the preferred manner of using them when a choice can be made. The intent is to give preference to that which safeguards the language from debasement: to maintain, for instance, distinctions like that between *imply* and *infer;* to avoid faddish neologisms like the verbs *host* and *author,* while also avoiding a cliché like *crying need;* to shun slang and colloquialisms in inappropriate contexts, but to use them without self-consciousness when the context is appropriate. For examples of usage entries, see these: **adverb placement; allude, refer; clichés; fewer, less; fused participles; hopefully; like, as; O, oh; oral, verbal; sequence of tenses; that, which; who, whom.**

This edition of the manual also contains brief entries defining terms that sometimes require definition in news stories. These entries provide a ready source of reference as deadlines near. See, for example, **Abstract Expressionism; Anglican Communion; bug, tap; debentures; hurricanes; ketch; metric system; nolo contendere;**

pulsar; relativity, theories of; State University of New York.
Still other entries explain certain matters of policy and objectives of
The Times that members of its news staff are asked to keep especially
in mind. The subjects dealt with include these: **corrections; datelines, integrity of; fairness and impartiality; obscenity, vulgarity, profanity; opinion polls; products and purposes;
sources of news; women.**

The manual is easy to use. As already stated, it is self-indexing. A
boldfaced word or phrase that appears without discussion in the alphabetical listings should be so spelled and capitalized in a normal
sentence. Many compound words are listed under their prefixes and
suffixes. Abbreviations are listed separately, followed by the spelled-
out forms. These listings are not intended to encourage the use of
abbreviations, which in profusion are unsightly. Titles of all sorts
appear separately, and the forms for first and subsequent references
are shown by example. A title that is abbreviated before a name is
listed under the abbreviation. General subjects are also listed alphabetically, with cross-references to specific listings.

If an answer to a question of style or usage cannot be found in the
manual, the answer may sometimes be reached by analogy. For example, if a word or a class of words listed in the book is capitalized, it
is reasonable to capitalize similar words that are not listed.

The dictionaries to be used as authorities for spelling and definitions
are Webster's New World Dictionary of the American Language (Collins-World), to be consulted in the first instance, and the more comprehensive Webster's Third New International Dictionary of the English
Language (Merriam), for words not to be found in the New World
Dictionary. For definitions, New World will in most instances be ade-
quate; if more information is needed Webster's Third will often provide it. But New World provides a great deal more information concerning whether a word is slang, informal, colloquial, substandard or
vulgar. New World also contains much useful biographical and geographical information.

The chief authority for the spelling of geographic names is the
Columbia Lippincott Gazetteer of the World. Exceptions to the style
of this gazetteer include *St.* and *Ste.*, which should usually not be
spelled out in place names. The exceptions also include place names
in some countries in Southeast Asia that are to be spelled in the style
of the Official Standard Names Gazetteers of the United States Board
on Geographic Names, but with accent marks omitted. See **geographic names.**

In cases of conflict, the forms listed in this manual take precedence
over the styles given in the dictionaries or the gazetteers.

L.J.

MANUAL OF STYLE
AND USAGE

Style rules should be extensive enough to establish the desired system of style, but not so extensive as to inhibit the writer or the editor. The rules should encourage thinking, not discourage it. A single rule might suffice: "The rule of common sense will prevail at all times."

—Foreword, *The New York Times Style Book for Writers and Editors*, 1962.

A

---

a, an. The indefinite article *a* is used before words beginning with a consonant sound, including the aspirate *h: a car, a hotel, a historical.* It is also used before words like *union, euphonious, unit.* The indefinite article *an* is used before words beginning with a vowel sound: *onion, uncle, honor.* The choice of article before an abbreviation or a numeral or other symbol also depends upon the sound: *an N.Y.U. student, an 11-year-old girl.* See **articles** and **the.**

A.A. for Alcoholics Anonymous; also for an athletic association: *the Boston A.A.*

A.&P. for the Great Atlantic and Pacific Tea Company.

A.B. or **B.A.** for Bachelor of Arts. Also: *a bachelor's degree.*

A.B.A. for the American Banking Association, the American Bar Association or the American Booksellers Association. In headlines, the abbreviation should be used only when the context is unmistakable.

abbreviations. Commonly used abbreviations are listed separately and alphabetically.

Points are usually used in abbreviations of the names of governmental bureaus and agencies, well-known organizations, companies, etc.: *F.C.C., N.A.M., A.&P.* But to avoid inconsistencies, points are omitted in abbreviations of the names of the broadcasting networks and their subsidiaries. (See **television networks** and **ABC, BBC, CBC, CBS, NBC** and **PBS.**)

If an abbreviation has become a recognized word and is pronounced as a word, the points are omitted and the word may be set either caps and lowercase (the usual style for an acronym formed from a company name) or all caps: *Alcoa, NATO, UNESCO.* To avoid confusion, points are required in the cases of some abbreviations that spell actual words: *W.H.O., C.A.B., A.I.D.*

In company and corporation names, points should be omitted when an abbreviation that formerly required points has been adopted without points as the official name: *the RCA Corporation.*

When letters within a single word are used as an abbreviation, they are capitalized but do not take points: *DDT, TB, TV.* But *V.D.* requires the points because it stands for two words.

Abbreviations may be used more freely in headlines than in stories. Certain titles spelled out in stories before last names may be contracted in headlines: *Gen. Jones, Gov. Brown, Rep. Smith,* etc. Place designations may also be abbreviated in headlines: *Fifth Ave.,*

3

Fordham Rd., Patchin Pl., Brooklyn Hts. Department (which see) may be abbreviated in headlines when it is part of a name *(State Dept.)*, but other such abbreviations, like *Comm.*, are not permitted. *Bros., Co.* and *Corp.* are acceptable in company names in headlines.

Even freer use of abbreviations is permitted in tabular matter to conserve space and keep listings within one line so far as possible. All the standard abbreviations may be used, as well as coined contractions, provided the item can be understood.

The main considerations in using abbreviations in stories and headlines are to avoid obscure contractions like *N.R.D.G.A.* (National Retail Dry Goods Association) and to avoid creating a typographical mess by excessive use of abbreviations. There is no reason to inflict on the reader a sentence like this: *The U.A.W. and the U.M.W. supported the complaints made by the W.H.O., UNICEF and the F.A.O., but A.F.L.-C.I.O. leaders did not.*

See **acronym** and **company and corporation names** and **state abbreviations.**

ABC for the American Broadcasting Companies (note the plural). ABC News, ABC Radio and ABC-TV are the full names of ABC divisions. Any of these names, as well as ABC, may be used in first references, depending on context, and ABC alone may be used in subsequent references. ABC alone is preferable in some first references, especially when the networks are mentioned together in a lead: *ABC, CBS and NBC will televise President Manley's address to the nation tomorrow night.*

A B C's (the alphabet or rudiments).

able-bodied.

ABM('s) for antiballistic missile(s).

A-bomb may be used in stories or in headlines, but in both cases *atomic bomb* or *atom bomb* is preferred. In cap-and-lowercase headlines, the *b* is capitalized: *A-Bomb.*

aboveboard.

absolve. Use preposition *from* or *of.*

Abstract Expressionism. The painting style of a group of American artists (Jackson Pollock, Mark Rothko and others), dating from the 1940's, in which pigment is applied in a free, often improvisatory manner to depict either abstract or highly subjective motifs. See **styles and schools in the arts.**

A.C. for an athletic club in subsequent references and in headlines: *the Downtown Athletic Club, Downtown A.C.*

academic degrees and titles. Joan Manley, Doctor of Philosophy (or Ph.D.); Dr. Joan Manley, Dr. Manley (if the doctorate is earned and the title used; see **Dr.**); Prof. John P. Manley, Professor Manley, the professor. Also see separate and alphabetical listings.

academic departments. Lowercase *department of natural history, department of English literature,* etc., whether in school, college or university.

Academy. Capitalize in second references to the French Academy, the National Academy of Sciences and the United States Military, Naval and Air Force Academies: *the Academy.* But: *the service academies.*

a cappella.

accent marks are to be used in ordinary reading matter in certain words of languages developed from the Latin and in German words. Some words have lost their accents through frequent use in English: *cafe, facade*, etc. Words that have lost their accents and words that require accents are listed separately and alphabetically. These include some exceptions to dictionary style, but in general dictionary style should be followed.

The most frequently used accents are the grave accent *(è)*, the acute accent *(é)* and the circumflex *(â): cause célèbre, raison d'être.*

The cedilla *(ç)*, used in French and other languages to denote a soft *c*, is also available and should be used in words requiring it: *garçon, François, français*, etc.

The tilde *(ñ)*, which in Spanish and Portuguese has a marked effect upon the pronunciation, should also be used when required: *vicuña, mañana, São Paulo.*

The German umlaut *(ä)*, like the other accents, is to be used in stories but not in headlines. In some publications, an *e* is added to the vowel when the umlaut is omitted. But to add an *e* in the head would create more of a discrepancy than would the absence of the umlaut. The difference between, say, *Düsseldorf* and *Dusseldorf* is so slight that any misunderstanding is unlikely. The slight disadvantage is outweighed by the advantage of more familiar spellings in stories: *Dürer, Tannhäuser.*

In the Latin languages, the dieresis, also consisting of two dots, is used to indicate that two adjacent vowels are pronounced separately *(Citroën, Noël)* or that a normally silent final consonant is pronounced *(Saint-Saëns).*

In general, we do not use the accent marks in other languages—the Scandinavian languages and Hungarian, for example—whose accenting systems are so unfamiliar to us as to invite error.

accommodate.

accountable. Use preposition *to* or *for.*

accouterment.

accuse. Use preposition *of.* And after *charge*, use *with.*

acknowledgment.

acquit. Use preposition *of.*

acre. Equal to 43,560 square feet or 4,047 square meters. The metric hectare is equal to 10,000 square meters or 2.47 acres.

acronym. An acronym is a word formed with the first letter or letters of each of a series of words: *NATO* from *N*orth *A*tlantic *T*reaty *O*rganization, *radar* from *ra*dio *d*etecting *a*nd *r*anging. *ABM* is not an acronym because it is not a word; it is merely an abbreviation. See **abbreviations.**

Acting. John P. Manley, Acting Secretary of State; the Acting Secretary. Whenever it becomes part of a title that would ordinarily be capitalized, *Acting* is also capitalized. But: *the acting chairman of the committee*, etc.

acts, amendments, bills and laws. Capitalize the name of an act or a law when the full official title is given or when using a title by which an act or a law is most commonly known: *Sherman Antitrust Act, Social Security Act, Taft-Hartley Act, Multiple Dwelling Law*, etc. But lowercase *act* when it stands alone or in shortened titles or general descriptions: *the antitrust act, the housing act*, etc.

A legislative measure is a bill until it is enacted; it then becomes an act or a law. Bills and proposed constitutional amendments not yet enacted into law should be lowercased *(equal rights amendment, food-stamp bill)* except for words in the description that would normally be capitalized *(Taft-Hartley bill)*.

An enacted and ratified amendment to the United States Constitution is capitalized when its formal title (including the number) is used: *the Fifth Amendment, the 18th Amendment.* But lowercase informal titles of amendments *(the income tax amendment)* unless they include words that are capitalized in their own right *(the Prohibition amendment).*

acute accent. See **accent marks.**

ad (for *advertisement*). The use of this most useful colloquialism cannot be denied to headline writers, and it is appropriate in informal references in news stories. But use *advertisement* in ordinary contexts.

A.D. for anno Domini. Since it means *in the year of the* [or *our*] *Lord,* the abbreviation should be placed before the year: *The town was founded in A.D. 73.* It may also be used to refer to a century; then, however, it is *fourth century A.D.* But *B.C.,* for *before Christ,* always follows the date: *founded in 128 B.C.* or *The town dates its origins from the second century B.C.*

adapted. Use preposition *to, for* or *from.*

addresses. See **streets and avenues** and **ZIP code.**

Addressograph (trademark).

adjutant. Like *adjutant general* (which see), this is a duty assignment, not a rank, and should not be abbreviated and used as a title:

Capt. John P. Manley, the battalion adjutant. But not *Adjt. John P. Manley.*

Adjutant General. It is *Maj. Gen. John P. Manley, the Adjutant General,* when referring to the officer in charge of personnel records and administration in the main headquarters of a country's army or armed forces. In second references, it is *the Adjutant General* or just *General Manley, the general.* That capitalization also applies to the commander of a state's National Guard if, as in most cases, he bears the title Adjutant General. (But in New York State the corresponding title is Chief of Staff to the Governor.) Lowercase uniformly when referring to the adjutant general of a lesser command, such as a division, a brigade, etc.: *Lieut. Col. John P. Manley, the division adjutant general; Colonel Manley; the colonel.* The plural is *adjutants general.*

Adm. John P. Manley, Admiral Manley, the admiral.

Administration. Capitalize when referring to a specific Presidential administration of the United States Government: *the Manley Administration, the Administration.* Lowercase when referring to national administrations of other countries and to all state or city governments: *the Smith administration, the Walker administration.*

administrative law judge. This Federal title should be used in lowercase after the name: *John P. Manley, administrative law judge.* A holder of this position was formerly known as a hearing examiner. In second references: *Judge Manley, the judge.*

Administrator John P. (or Joan P.)

Manley (for the head of a governmental agency so titled), Administrator Manley, the Administrator, Mr. (or Mrs. or Miss) Manley.

Admiral of the Fleet (in the British Navy). This rank, unlike the similar American rank (see **Fleet Adm.**), cannot properly be shortened to *Admiral* in second references. But British holders of the rank usually have other titles by which they can subsequently be called: *Admiral of the Fleet Earl Mountbatten of Burma, Earl Mountbatten, Lord Mountbatten.*

admissible.

A.D.R.('s) for American depository receipt(s).

Adrenalin, adrenaline. Use *adrenaline* (or a synonym, *epinephrine*) in references to a hormone produced by the adrenal gland, or in figurative contexts: *A good fight made their adrenaline flow.* But capitalize the trademark *Adrenalin* when the reference is to a synthetic or chemically extracted product.

adverb placement. An adverb used with a compound verb should normally be placed between elements of the verb, as it is a few words back in this sentence and in the following example: *He will usually take the opposing side.* The split infinitive (which see) is another matter.

adverse (opposed to or unfavorable to), **averse** (unwilling to or reluctant to).

adviser.

Aer Lingus, the Irish national airline. While *Aer Lingus* will suffice in some first references, the identification should appear somewhere in the story.

Aeroflot (Soviet airline).

Aeromexico (airline), formerly Aeronaves de Mexico.

Afars and Issas. See **Territory of Afars and Issas.**

affect, effect. The verb *affect* means to influence, change or otherwise have effect *(Her attitude affected the outcome);* to like to do, wear or use *(He affected cowboy boots and spurs);* to pretend *(He affects erudition that few scholars can match).* The verb *effect* means to accomplish, complete, cause, make possible, carry out *(They effected changes in important statutes).* The noun is almost invariably *effect (One effect was a hurried rewriting of the textbooks). Affect* as a noun is another, psychological matter; it is rarely used.

affiliate (v.). Use preposition *with* or *to.*

Afghan(s). The people of Afghanistan. The adjective is *Afghan.*

Afghan hound.

aficionado(s).

A.F.L.-C.I.O. for the American Federation of Labor and Congress of Industrial Organizations, the merged labor movement. The abbreviation suffices for almost all first references. Also in most instances, the full name need not be used even subsequently in an article (especially if the article is short). Care should be taken, however, that articles are not peppered with the abbreviation, which is unsightly to begin with and especially so in profuse repetition. There are other ways of managing subsequent references.

African Methodist Episcopal Church.

African Methodist Episcopal Zion Church.

Afro-. Avoid the prefix in references to the relations of African nations with countries on other continents: *African and Asian* or *African-Asian*, not *Afro-Asian; African-Chinese*, not *Afro-Chinese*. But, in quoted matter or in the names of organizations, publications, etc., *Afro-American* is often correct. Also see **black** and **ethnic background of an American in the news.**

after is almost always better than the preposition *following*, as in *He went home after the game.*

after-. afterbeat, afterdeck, after-dinner (adj.), aftereffect, aftermath, after-mentioned, after-theater, afterthought.

afterward, not *afterwards.*

AFTRA for the American Federation of Television and Radio Artists.

Agence France-Presse. In news stories, it is Agence France-Presse, without an article. A translation or explanation, such as *the French press agency*, should not be used either in place of the name or along with it. In datelines: PEKING, Oct. 12 (Agence France-Presse)—etc. Use a centered credit line in 5-point Regal type on undatelined articles and on page 1 stories:

By Agence France-Presse

It is *the agency* in subsequent references. In quoted matter, *A.F.P.* may be used.

agenda. It is now construed as a singular: *The agenda was adopted.* The plural is *agendas.*

ages and eras of history. Capitalize *Stone Age, Bronze Age, Iron Age, Dark Ages, Middle Ages, Age of Discovery, Christian Era, Renais-*

sance, etc., but not *ice age.* Also: *atomic age, missile age, rocket age, space age.*

ages of people and animals should be given in figures: *Caroline Smith, 25 years old; a 7-year-old boy; 3-month-old daughter; 4½-year-old son; a race for 2-year-olds.* In a story giving the ages of more than one person, use *years old* only with the first age given. In giving ages of inanimate objects or other things, spell out through nine and use figures above nine: *two-year fight, a house eight years old, 10-year fight, a house 20 years old.* Use numerals in referring to the ages of people by decades: *He is in his 60's.*

aging.

ahold, aholt. Do not use except in quoted matter.

A.I.D. for the Agency for International Development. But after the full title has appeared in a story, *the aid agency* is an acceptable reference, as is *the agency.*

"Aïda," Aïda. The title is quoted, the character is not.

aide (assistant).

aide-de-camp.

air(-). air base, airborne, airbus, air-condition, air-conditioned, air-conditioner, air-conditioning, aircrew, airdrop, air express, airfield, air force (which see), airfreight, airlift (n., v., adj.), airline, airmail (n., v., adj.), airman, air-minded, airplane, air raid (n.), air-raid (adj.), airship, airspace, airtight.

air base, Air Force base. There is a difference. See **military bases.**

Air Canada, formerly Trans-Canada Air Lines.

Air Chief Marshal Sir John Manley, Sir John, Air Chief Marshal Manley. This and other British Royal Air Force ranks cannot properly be shortened.

aircraft names are printed in regular body type without quotation marks: Air Force One (the President's jetliner), the Spirit of St. Louis, Concorde, Boeing 707, DC-9, HueyCobra, A-4 Skyhawk, F-4 Phantom II, F-86 Sabre, F-100 Super Sabre, MIG-21. In first references, the model number or name of a well-known aircraft can appear without the name of its manufacturer or designer: DC-10, MIG-21, Phantom. The best source for names and model numbers is Jane's All the World's Aircraft. For plurals, use the apostrophe: MIG-17's, B-52's, A-4H's. Use a hyphen before the numeral, but not after it: DC-6B. In some cases, Western military authorities have agreed on designations for Soviet aircraft: Bison (the TU-22), Foxbat (the MIG-25); if such expressions are used in stories, their origin should be specified.

Airedale terrier.

Air Force. Capitalize in *United States Air Force, Royal Air Force, Soviet Air Force,* etc. It is *the Air Force* in subsequent references to that of the United States, but lowercase such references to any foreign air force. It is also *Air Force* in references to United States Air Force Academy sports teams. There is a distinction between *Air Force bases* and *air bases;* see **military bases.**

Air Force Academy, the Academy.

Air Force One. The Presidential jetliner.

Air Force ranks are listed separately and alphabetically, in full or by abbreviations. Also see **enlisted men's ranks.**

Air France.

Air-India.

airline(s). That is the usual spelling, but follow the lines' style in proper names: Delta Air Lines, American Airlines. Lines are listed separately and alphabetically. In some cases, the names are followed by abbreviations that may be used in subsequent references.

Airman John P. Manley (or Joan Manley), Airman Manley, the airman. Also: Airman 1st Class (or 2d Class, etc.) John P. Manley (or Joan Manley).

airmobile. A military designation for ground troops transported by air. Also: *the First Cavalry Division (Airmobile).*

Air National Guard.

Air New England.

airplane names. Do not quote them. See **aircraft names.**

airport names are listed separately and alphabetically. They are almost never preceded by *the: Kennedy International Airport.*

akvavit. Use *aquavit* instead.

Ala. for Alabama after cities and towns.

Alabamian(s).

à la carte.

à la mode.

Alaska. Do not abbreviate after cities and towns, even in datelines.

Alaska Airlines.

Alaskan(s).

Alaska native(s). Aleuts, Eskimos and Indians of Alaska use this term with pride in referring to themselves. Thus it does not have the offensive connotation that *the natives* often has in other contexts.

Alberta (Canadian province). Do not abbreviate after cities and towns, even in datelines.

Albertan(s). The people of Alberta.

albino, albinos.

Alcan Aluminium Ltd. But the company's United States subsidiary is the Alcan *Aluminum* Corporation.

Alcoa for the Aluminum Company of America.

Al Fatah, a Palestinian guerrilla organization. To avoid redundancy, drop *Al* if the name must be preceded by *a* or *the: a Fatah leader.* In headlines: *Fatah.*

Algerian(s). The people of Algeria.

alibi must be used with care. It is acceptable, colloquially, as meaning not only a mere excuse but sometimes also an excuse fabricated to avoid responsibility. The original meaning, in law, is a plea of having been at a place other than the scene of an act at the time of its commission.

Alice Tully Hall (at Lincoln Center).

Alitalia Airlines.

Allegany. Counties in New York and Maryland.

alleged is properly used when referring to accusations or suspicions of undesirable behavior or traits. When that is not the intended meaning, *ostensible, reported, reputed, apparent, seeming* or some similar word should be used: *his alleged dishonesty,* but *his ostensible friends; alleged stinginess, reputed generosity; alleged guilt,* *seeming innocence; alleged machinations, apparent high motives.*

Alleghany. County in Virginia.

Alleghany Corporation.

Allegheny. This is the spelling for the mountains and for the river, city and county in Pennsylvania. The plural for Allegheny Mountains is Alleghenies, an exception to the rule that, for example, makes Germanys the plural of Germany.

Allegheny Airlines.

Allegheny Ludlum Industries. Its principal subsidiary is the Allegheny Ludlum Steel Corporation.

allies, allied. Do not capitalize in references to post-World War II alliances, including the alliance of the United States, Canada and the West European powers. The members of the North Atlantic Treaty Organization are *NATO allies, Atlantic allies, Western allies* or, if the context has been established, *allies.* Capitalize *Allies* and *Allied* in references to the World War I and World War II alliances and any similar alliance that includes *Allies* or *Allied* in its primary name.

allot, allotted, allotting.

all right (never *alright*).

all-round (adj.). Not, for example, *all-around quarterback.* Also, note that *round* does not take an apostrophe; it is a word in its own right. See **round.**

all-time. As an adjective applied to sports, weather and other records it is imprecise and superfluous.

allude, refer. To allude to something is to speak of it without direct mention; to refer to it is to mention directly.

ally (v.). Use preposition *to* or *with.*

alma mater.

almanacs. Do not quote their titles; capitalize principal words.

aloof. Use preposition *from.*

alphabetizing names. When dealing with *Mc* or *Mac,* alphabetize by the second letter: *Mabley, Mac-Adam, Maynard, McNeil.* In a listing, if family names are printed before given names, the expression *Jr.* (or *Sr.,* or *3d,* etc.) comes last: *MANLEY, John P. Jr.,* not *MAN-LEY Jr., John P.*

Alsatian wolfdog.

also-ran (n.).

aluminum, not *aluminium,* except in *Alcan Aluminium Ltd.*

Aluminum Company of America (Alcoa).

alumna (fem.), **alumnae** (fem. pl.), **alumnus** (masc.), **alumni** (masc. pl., or a mixed group).

Alyeska Pipeline Service Company.

A.M. (time). Capitalize: *10:30 A.M. yesterday.* Avoid this redundancy: *10:30 A.M. yesterday morning.* Also: *10 A.M.,* not *10:00 A.M.* See **time.**

A.M.A. for the American Medical Association.

Ambassador, ambassador, ambassadorial. Ambassador John P. (or Joan) Manley; John P. Manley, Ambassador to France; the Ambassador; Mr. (or Mrs. or Miss) Manley. But: *an ambassador* or *an ambassador of good will; the ambassadors* (for capitalized plural exceptions, see **titles**). Lowercase *ambassadorial* in all contexts.

In news articles, for simplicity and quick comprehension, the title *Ambassador* should be applied only to a diplomat heading an embassy in a foreign country. An official who is not so assigned, but who nevertheless possesses the personal rank of ambassador, should ordinarily be styled *Mr., Mrs., Miss* or *Dr.,* not *Ambassador.* And an envoy to an international organization or conference should preferably be called *delegate, chief delegate, representative* or *chief representative* (all of which see), but not *permanent representative* (which see). Also see **High Commissioner.**

Ambassador at Large. No hyphens. Capitalize when referring to a specific person holding a governmental position so titled.

Ambassador to Britain. Another title, Ambassador to the Court of St. James's, may also be used, but reserve it for instances in which that flavor is desirable.

A.M.C. for the American Motors Corporation.

amendments, legislative. See **acts, amendments, bills and laws.**

amendments to the Constitution. Capitalize when referring to a specific amendment: *the Fifth Amendment.* Spell out ordinals through the ninth and use figures for 10th and above: *First Amendment, 14th Amendment.* Lowercase general descriptions of amendments: *income tax amendment.* See **acts, amendments, bills and laws.**

America, American(s), Americas. America is not only the United States but also North America or South America. Although citizens of the United States are not the only Americans, the word is often reserved for them. But the words America, American and Americans may be used in all their senses if the context makes the meaning apparent. The countries of the Western Hemisphere are, collectively, the Americas.

Americal Division (United States Army).

-American. Hyphenate *Italian-American, Japanese-American, Irish-American, Polish-American* and similar nouns and adjectives denoting ethnic background. But: *French Canadian, Latin American.* See **ethnic background of an American in the news.**

American Airlines.

American Baptist Churches, the. Formerly the American Baptist Convention.

American Broadcasting Companies (note plural). See **ABC.**

American Export Lines.

American Federation of Labor and Congress of Industrial Organizations. For guides to dealing with this cumbersome name, see **A.F.L.-C.I.O.**

American Geographical Society. Do not confuse with the National Geographic Society.

American Lutheran Church.

American Motors Corporation (A.M.C.).

American President Lines.

American Revolution, the. Also: the Revolutionary War, the Revolution.

American Stock Exchange. In second references: *the American Exchange, the Amex, the exchange.*

American Telephone and Telegraph Company (A.T.&T.).

America's Cup (yachting), **Americas Cup** (golf).

Amex, or *the American Exchange,* in second references to the American Stock Exchange.

amid, not *amidst.*

amidships.

among, not *amongst.*

among, between. In general, *between* applies to two things, and *among* to more than two. But *between* is correct in reference to more than two when the items are related severally and individually: *The talks between the three powers ended in agreement to divide the responsibility among them.*

ampersand (&). In company and corporation names, an ampersand should not be used in place of *and* except when the company's name is composed of personal names *(the Procter & Gamble Company)* or when the *and* appears directly before *company* or an equivalent term *(J. P. Morgan & Company).* Certain railroads are exceptions to this rule; they are listed separately and alphabetically.

An ampersand should be used in place of *and* in the names of partnerships, such as law firms, accounting firms, brokerages, etc., whose names are composed of personal names: *Paul, Weiss, Rifkind, Wharton & Garrison.*

When abbreviations are used in second references to company names, an ampersand should generally be used in place of *and* *(A.T.&T., C.&O.,* etc.).

The symbol should not otherwise be used in place of *and* in either stories or headlines. See **company and corporation names**

Amtrak may be used in first references instead of *the National Railroad Passenger Corporation,* with which it is synonymous. If the meaning of *Amtrak* is clear, the longer name may on occasion be omitted entirely. (*Amtrak* is an acronym extracted from the first, second and fourth words of *American travel by track*, but the less said about that the better.)

AMVETS for American Veterans of World War II, Korea and Vietnam.

an. See **a, an.**

analogy. Use preposition *between* or *with.*

and. See **ampersand.**

and/or. Avoid except in quoted matter.

anemia, anemic.

anesthetic.

Angeleno(s). The people of Los Angeles.

Angkor, not *Angkor Wat,* for the temple complex in Cambodia. Angkor Wat is a single temple in the complex.

angles (mathematical). Following are some of the angular measurements:
DEGREE—one-360th of a circle.
MINUTE OF ARC—one-sixtieth of a degree.
SECOND OF ARC—one-sixtieth of a minute of arc.
RADIAN—an angle at the center of a circle subtending an arc of the circle equal to the circle's radius. Equal to roughly 57 degrees.

Anglican Church may be used in second references to the Church of England (which see), but *the church* will almost always suffice.

Anglican Communion. It comprises the Church of England and episcopal churches that are informally and traditionally related to it in matters of doctrine and ritual.

This association of independent churches includes not only other churches in Britain, but also the Anglican Church of Canada, the Episcopal Church in the United States and others elsewhere in the world. The administrative arm is the Anglican Consultative Council. Every 10 years the bishops of the Anglican Communion gather for the Lambeth Conference. See **Church of England** and **Episcopal Church.**

Anglo-. Anglo-Saxon, Anglo-Catholic. But: Anglophile, Anglophobe. Use *English* or *British* in adjectival references to two countries: *British-French trade, English-Irish cultural rivalry.* Not *Anglo-French* or *Anglo-Irish.*

angry. Use preposition *at* or *with.*

angstrom or **angstrom unit.** One ten-billionth of a meter. It is the shortest widely employed unit of length, and is used in particular to measure wavelengths of light and other forms of electromagnetic radiation.

Angus (sing. and pl.) for the cattle. Also: *Black Angus* and *Red Angus.* In almost all cases, *Angus* alone means Black Angus.

animals. Do not use a personal pronoun in referring to an animal unless its sex has been established or it has been personalized with a name: *The dog was lost; it howled. Rover was lost; he howled. The dog, which was lost, howled. Rover, who was lost, howled. The bull tossed his horns.* Ages of animals are given in figures: *a race for 3-year-olds.*

annoyed. Use preposition *by, at* or *with.*

13

ANTA for the American National Theater and Academy.

Antarctic (n., adj.). Antarctic Circle, Antarctic continent, Antarctica.

ante-. ante-Babylonian, antebellum, antedate, antepenultimate.

antecedents, missing. See **pronouns and missing antecedents.**

anthems. Quote their titles: "The Star-Spangled Banner." Lowercase *the national anthem.* See **songs.**

anti-. antiaircraft, anti-bias, anti-inflation, anti-intellectual, antimatter, antiparticle, antiproton, antislavery, antisocial, antitrust. But: anti-American, anti-Communist, anti-Freud, anti-Semite. An exception: Antichrist.

Anti-Defamation League, a division of B'nai B'rith.

antipathy. Use preposition *to, toward* or *against.*

antitrust division of the Justice Department.

any(-). anybody (pron.), anyhow, any more (something additional), anymore (adv.), anyone (pron.), any way (in any manner), anyway (in any event), anywhere.

apathy. Use preposition *toward.*

apogee. It is the highest altitude of an orbiting space vehicle or other object in relation to the earth. The word also has the general meaning of highest or farthest point. See **perigee.**

apostle(s). Generally lowercase: *the apostles of Jesus, an apostle, the apostle.* But: *the Twelve Apostles, the Apostle Thomas, the Apostles' Creed.*

Apostolic Delegate. Bishop (or Archbishop) John P. Manley, the Apostolic Delegate; the Delegate. But: *an apostolic delegate; apostolic delegates* (for capitalized plural exceptions, see **titles**). An apostolic delegate is a Roman Catholic diplomat designated by the Pope as his envoy to the church in a foreign country with which the Vatican does not have formal diplomatic relations. He is not a nuncio, an envoy accredited to a foreign government with which the Vatican has a treaty. See **Papal Nuncio.**

apostrophe. The apostrophe is used to indicate the possessive case of a noun *(man's)*, to denote a contraction or omission of letters or numerals *(it's* for *it is, '64* for *1964)*, and to form the plurals of letters or numerals *(p's and q's, size 7's, B-52's).*

The singular possessive is formed with *'s (boy's coat)* and the plural with *s' (boys' coats, the Manleys' car).*

For a plural that does not end in *s (women, children)*, the possessive is formed with *'s: women's, children's.*

Sometimes a singular idea is expressed in words that are technically plural; in such a case, the plural form of the possessive is used: *United States', General Motors', Lehman Brothers'.* Never *United States's,* etc.

Almost all singular words ending in *s* require another *s* as well as the apostrophe to form the possessive: *James's, Charles's, The Times's.* But the *s* after the apostrophe is dropped when two or more sibilant sounds precede the apostrophe: *Kansas' Governor, Moses' behalf.* It is also dropped in certain expressions in which the word following the apostrophe begins with *s: for conscience' sake, for appearance' sake, for goodness' sake.*

When a name ends with a sibilant

letter that is silent, the possessive is formed with *'s: Arkansas's, Duplessis's, Malraux's.* By custom, however, the possessive of an ancient classical name is formed with an apostrophe only: *Achilles' heel, Euripides' dramas.*

The apostrophe is used in expressions like *60 days' notice* and *20 years' confinement.* But: *a 60-day warning period, a 20-year sentence, a sentence of 20 years.* Also: *a million dollars' worth of publicity, two cents' worth.* But, with figures: *$5 million worth.*

The apostrophe is used when *Mc* or *Mac* occurs in a name in a headline that is to be set in uppercase: *M'CLELLAN, M'ARTHUR,* etc. If the setting is caps and lowercase, use *c* and *ac.* Set *c* and *ac* in small caps when caps and small caps are specified.

Apostrophes are omitted in names of many organizations: *Citizens Union, Doctors Hospital, Teachers College,* etc. But if the word is plural before the addition of an *s,* the apostrophe is used: *Young Men's Christian Association, Children's Court.* Also: *The Ladies' Home Journal.*

In contractions that have come into common usage, the apostrophe is not used: *cello, cellist, copter, chutist, phone, plane.* The apostrophe is used in abbreviations and contractions like *O.K.'d.*

appall.

Appellate Division.

apprehensive. Use preposition *of* or *for.*

April. Do not abbreviate.

apropos. Use preposition *of* or no preposition.

aquavit (not *akvavit*).

Arab Emirates. See **United Arab Emirates.**

Arabian American Oil Company (Aramco).

Arabic numerals. Capital *A.* See **Roman numerals.**

Arabic terms in place names include the following: Ain (spring), Bab (gate), Bahr (sea, lake and sometimes river), Bir (well), Birket (pond), Burj (tower), Dahr (mountaintop), Dar (abode of), Deir (monastery), Jebel (mountain), Jisr (bridge), Kafr (hamlet), Khan (caravanserai), Marj (meadow), Nahr (river), Naqb (pass), Qasr or Kasr (castle), Ras (promontory, cape), Suq (market), Tell (hill), Wadi (dry riverbed, ravine).

In Egyptian usage, the standard Arabic *j* is pronounced as a hard *g.* Thus Burg, Gebel, Gisr and Marg appear in Egyptian place names instead of Burj, Jebel, Jisr and Marj.

French modes of transliteration have become standard usage for North African names; thus Djebel and Ouadi instead of Jebel and Wadi. But in all cases gazetteer spelling is to be followed.

Arabist.

Arab names and titles. Arab names are usually Arab words governed by grammatical rules. Many of them incorporate the definite article *al.* The vowel may appear as *a, e* or *u,* or disappear entirely as a result of elision. The *l* may appear as *d, dh, n, r, s, sh, t, th* or *z.* The definite article may be joined with the preceding or the following word, or both. Except where other usage has become established (Abdel Nasser, Abdullah) use *al* hyphenated with the following word: al-Sabah, al-Azhar. Many Arabs prefer to drop the definite article from their names in English: Ismail Fahmy, not *al-Fahmy*. Omit the definite article in personal names after first reference: Anwar el-Sadat, Mr. Sadat. (But capitalize the definite article in publication titles and omit the hyphen: Al Ahram.)

Compound names should be left intact. The commonest are composed with the word *Abd* (Worshiper of): Abdullah (Worshiper of God), Abdel Nasser (Worshiper of the Victorious One), Abdur Rahman (Worshiper of the Merciful One).

Another compound is completed by *al-Din* (the Religion), which may appear in such forms as *ed-Din, eddine, uddin*, etc.: Kamal ed-Din (the Perfection of the Religion), Nureddin (the Light of the Religion), Allah-ud-Din or Aladdin (the God of the Religion).

Allah or *ullah* (God) completes such compound names as Jad-Allah (God giveth), Nasrullah (the Victory of God). *Abu* (Father of) and *Ibn, bin* or *ben* (Son of) combine in such names as Abulhuda, Abubakr, Abul Zalaf, Ibn Saud. Do not capitalize *ibn* when it is preceded by first or middle names.

A Moslem Arab has at least three names—the given name, the father's given name and the grandfather's given name. The permanent family name, if there is one, follows. Use whichever family name the subject seems to prefer. Otherwise, in second references use *Mr.* or the official title before the last name and treat it as a family name. When in doubt, repeat the name in full in second references.

The Arab titles Pasha and Bey, both of Turkish origin, have been abolished. Royal titles, as in English, are used with the first name: Abdel Faisal ibn King Aziz al-Saud, King Faisal. Sheik is the title of the rulers of the Persian Gulf principalities: Sheik Abdullah al-Salem al-Sabah, Sheik Abdullah. The title and the first name alone suffice in first references to rulers (kings, imams, emirs and sheiks) unless it is necessary to give the full name to distinguish between two persons with the same title and the same first name.

Aramco for the Arabian American Oil Company.

arboretums, not *arboreta.*

Arc de Triomphe (in Paris), the arch. In quoted matter, *the Arch of Triumph* is acceptable.

arch-. archangel, archbishop (which see), archdiocese, archduke, archenemy, archfiend, archrival. The primary meaning of this prefix is chief or principal. But it is sometimes defined as meaning extreme, and in that sense must be used with great care. For example, words like *archconservative, archradical, archliberal, arch-Protestant* and *arch-Republican* are best avoided as pejorative. See **ultra-.**

Archbishop. In accordance with the current tendency in the Roman Catholic Church, omit *the Most Rev.* before the name: *Archbishop John P. Manley of Hartford, Archbishop Manley, the Archbishop.* Or: *the Archbishop of Hartford, John P. Manley.* But: *an archbishop, the archbishops* (for capitalized plural exceptions, see **titles**). *The Most Rev.* is used before the names of the superiors general of some Catholic orders and the name of the Anglican prelate who is the Archbishop of Canterbury. See **Canterbury, Archbishop of; Superior General; Bishop; Rev.; Most Rev.; Rt. Rev.; Very Rev.**

archeology. Also: archeological, archeologist.

16

archetype.

architecture. See **styles and schools in the arts.**

Arco for the Atlantic Richfield Company.

Arctic (n., adj.). Arctic Circle, Arctic Ocean, Arctic Current, Arctic zone, arctics (overshoes).

area code. See **telephone numbers.**

Argentine(s). The people of Argentina. The adjective is *Argentine.*

Ariz. for Arizona after cities and towns.

Arizonan(s).

Ark. for Arkansas after cities and towns.

Arkansan(s).

Armed Forces Day.

Armistice Day is now Veterans Day.

Army. Capitalize in *United States Army, British Army, Soviet Army,* etc. It is *the Army* in subsequent references to the United States Army, but lowercase such references to any foreign army. It is also *Army* in reference to United States Military Academy sports teams.

Army corps. A United States Army corps is designated by Roman numerals: *XVI Corps.*

Army ranks are listed separately and alphabetically, in full or by abbreviations. Also see **enlisted men's ranks.**

art. See **styles and schools in the arts.**

Art Deco (architecture and interior design). This 1920's and 1930's style, sometimes called style moderne or jazz modern, is noted for frequent setbacks and zigzag forms and other ornament symbolizing modernism. In architecture, Radio City Music Hall and the Chrysler Building are well-known New York examples. See **styles and schools in the arts.**

articles. See **a, an** and **the.** Avoid the faddish practice of dropping *A* or *The* when it begins a sentence. If several consecutive paragraphs of a story begin with the same article, recast enough of the first sentences of the paragraphs to break up the monotony.

The article should appear before each of the coordinate nouns in a series or a pair: *He was helped by a policeman, a fireman and a doctor. The hero and the heroine received medals.* An exception is made if the nouns convey a single idea: *They found a bow and arrow.*

Art Nouveau (architecture and interior design). A decorative style common in the 1890's and the early 20th century that made use of undulating, flowing forms and often took its inspiration from nature. See **styles and schools in the arts.**

as. See **like, as.**

ASCAP for the American Society of Composers, Authors and Publishers.

Ascension. Capitalize when the reference is to Jesus.

Asian, Asiatic. Use the noun *Asian* or *Asians* when referring to people. *Asiatic,* in this sense, is regarded by some Asians as offensive.

as if is preferred, but *as though* is not incorrect.

as much as. Write *as much as if not more than,* not *as much if not* *more than.* Even better: *He earns as much as an Army colonel, if not more.*

aspire. Use preposition *to, after* or *toward.*

aspirin.

Assembly. Capitalize in *United Nations General Assembly, the State Assembly,* etc. In second references: *the Assembly.* But it is *state assembly, state assemblies, an assembly,* etc., when the reference is not specific.

Assembly districts. Capitalize in specific references: *First Assembly District, 11th Assembly District.*

Assemblyman, Assemblywoman. Assemblyman John P. Manley, Assemblywoman Joan Manley. In second references, Assemblyman or Assemblywoman Manley, the Assemblyman or Assemblywoman, Mr., Mrs. or Miss Manley. Also: *an assemblyman, an assemblywoman, assemblymen, assemblywomen* (for capitalized plural exceptions, see **titles**). Also see **women.**

assistant. Some subordinate titles containing the word *assistant* are not capitalized, except before names, in references to specific individuals: *The assistant district attorney* [or *the assistant United States attorney*] *spoke briefly.* This applies especially in cases where the subordinate rank is shared by several persons. It does not apply to positions of major importance: *the Assistant Secretary of State.* See **Deputy, deputy.**

Assistant Bishop. See **Bishop.**

Assistant Chief John P. Manley (police), Chief Manley, the chief. In the New York City police, never *Assistant Chief Inspector.*

Associated Press, The. It is *The Associated Press* in news stories. *A.P.* is the abbreviation, except in datelines: RECIFE, Brazil, June 10 (AP) —etc. Use a centered credit line in 5-point Regal type above the dateline on page 1 stories and, when needed, on undatelined stories inside the paper:

By The Associated Press

Associate Justice John P. Manley (of the Supreme Court of the United States), the Associate Justice, Associate Justice Manley (or Justice Manley), the Justice.

association. Capitalize when part of the name of an organization, but not when standing alone. Also capitalize in *Association football* (British).

astronaut. The Russian term is *cosmonaut,* but use that only in quoted matter that was originally spoken or written in English.

astronomical unit. This unit of length used in astronomy is the mean radius of the earth's orbit around the sun. It is approximately equal to 93 million miles.

Astroturf (trademark).

A.T.&T. for the American Telephone and Telegraph Company.

Atchison, Topeka & Santa Fe Railway, the Santa Fe; a subsidiary of Santa Fe Industries.

Athabasca (with a *c,* not a *k*) for the town, lake, mountain, pass and river in Canada. Also, *Athabasca Oil Sands.*

Athenian(s). The people of Athens.

Atlantan(s). The people of Atlanta.

Atlantic. The actual shoreline of the Atlantic Ocean is the Atlantic *coast;* the region of the United States lying along the shoreline is the Atlantic *Coast* or the Atlantic *Seaboard.* It is *the coast* in all second references. Only the West Coast is referred to as *the Coast.* Also: *North Atlantic, South Atlantic, Atlantic Coast States.*

Atlantic alliance, or just *alliance,* may be used as well as *NATO* in subsequent references to the North Atlantic Treaty Organization. These alternates are preferred to repeated uses of *NATO,* which is typographically obtrusive. *Atlantic alliance* may also be used occasionally in a lead sentence, to prevent awkward constructions or excessive length, provided the full name of the alliance is given soon afterward.

Atlantic Container Line Ltd.

Atlantic Richfield Company (Arco).

at large. Do not hyphenate *ambassador at large, councilman at large, delegate at large, representative at large.* But hyphenate adjectival forms: *the councilman-at-large election.* Capitalize in all references to a person holding a governmental position that has *at large* in its title: *John P. Manley, Councilman at Large.*

atmosphere (unit of pressure). See **bar.**

atomic age.

Atomic Energy Commission. It was replaced in 1975 by the Energy Research and Development Administration and the Nuclear Regulatory Commission.

atomic mass, atomic mass unit, atomic weight. Atomic mass is the weight of a specific isotope, or form, of an element expressed in atomic mass units. The atomic mass unit is one-twelfth the weight of the car-

bon 12 atom. Atomic weight is the average weight of atoms of a given element expressed in atomic mass units. See **mass number.**

atomic number. The number of protons in an atomic nucleus, which is also the number of positive charges in the nucleus and which therefore defines the chemical properties of the atom.

attaché. Col. John P. Manley, military attaché; the attaché.

Attorney General John P. Manley, the Attorney General. Plural: *attorneys general.*

attribution. See **parenthetical attribution;** also **quotations** and **sources of news.**

Aug. for August before numerals: *Aug. 16.*

author, co-author. Do not use either word as a verb except in quoted matter.

authoress. Use *author.* See **women.**

autobahn (sing.), **autobahns** (pl.).

automatic pistol. This hand weapon, designed for automatic or semiautomatic firing, is not a revolver. The automatic's cartridges are held in a magazine, the revolver's in chambers in a cylinder that revolves. Both are properly called pistols.

automobile racing and rallies. Times of races are given in figures: *His time was 2 hours 13 minutes, an average speed of 97 miles an hour.*

Many racing cars are variations of models sold by automobile dealers. The variations should be specified: *Cooper Climax, birdcage Maserati, 1975 Ford with a 1973 Thunderbird engine,* etc. Some races are conducted for cars similar in engine size. These sizes are known as formulas: *Formula One, Formula Junior, Formula Libre,* etc.

In auto rallies, drivers must cover specified road courses at specified speeds. Such events should not be referred to as races.

Auto-Train Corporation.

autumn (also *fall*).

Auxiliary Bishop. See **Bishop.**

avant-garde (n. and adj.), **avant-gardism, avant-gardist.**

Ave. may be used for *Avenue* in headlines with the name of the avenue.

Avenue of the Americas (Manhattan), not *Sixth Avenue.* In headlines, *Ave. of Americas.* But *the Sixth Avenue subway* is acceptable, especially when juxtaposed with such expressions as *the Eighth Avenue subway.* In an especially difficult headline, *6th Ave.* may be used, provided the article mentions, gracefully, that Sixth Avenue is the former name of the Avenue of the Americas.

avenues. See **streets and avenues.**

averse (unwilling to or reluctant to), **adverse** (opposed to or unfavorable to).

Avery Fisher Hall, formerly Philharmonic Hall (at Lincoln Center).

aviatrix is seldom seen these days, but when it is written, use *aviator* instead, unless there is a historical context requiring *aviatrix.* See **women.**

awe-struck.

a while, awhile. *He plans to stay for a while. He plans to stay awhile.*

AWOL for *absent without leave.*

ax.

Axis. The German-Italian-Japanese alliance of World War II.

B

B.A. or **A.B.** for Bachelor of Arts. Also: *a bachelor's degree.*

baby-sit, baby-sitting, baby sitter.

baccalaureate.

bachelor's degree. But: *Bachelor of Arts* or *Science,* etc. Also: *A.B.* or *B.A., B.S.,* etc. See **academic degrees and titles.**

back(-), -back. backache, backbone, backfield, backfire, background, backhand, backlog, back room (n.), back-room (adj.), back seat (n.), back-seat (adj.), back stairs (n.), backstairs (adj.), backstop, backstretch, backstroke, backwoods, backyard. Also (all n.): comeback, flareback, halfback, rollback, setback, throwback.

back of, in back of. *Behind* is better: *the tree behind the barn.*

backward, not *backwards.*

Baghdad.

Bahamas, the. Lowercase *the,* even in datelines.

Bahamian(s). The people of the Bahamas.

Bahrain, not *Bahrein,* for the group of islands in the Persian Gulf.

bail. A defendant may be *freed on bail* or, for example, *freed on $10,000 bail.* But if the defendant fails to produce cash or a bond in the amount determined by a judge who

has *set bail,* the defendant is *held in bail* or *in $100,000 bail.*

baked alaska.

ball(-). ball-bearing, ball boy, ballcarrier (sports), ball club, ball game, ball handler, ball park, ballplayer, ball-point (adj.), ballroom.

Baltimore & Ohio Railroad, the B.&O.; a subsidiary of the Chessie System.

Baltimorean(s). The people of Baltimore.

Band-Aid (trademark).

bandanna(s).

Bangladesh, formerly East Pakistan. Use also as the adjective.

Bangladeshi(s). The citizens of Bangladesh. But use *Bengali(s)* for the ethnic group in Bangladesh or in the Indian state of West Bengal.

Bangor & Aroostook Railroad, a subsidiary of the Amoskeag Company.

Banjul (Gambia), formerly Bathurst.

BankAmerica Corporation, the parent company of the Bank of America. Also: *BankAmericard.*

Bankers Trust New York Corporation, the parent company of the Bankers Trust Company.

bar (unit of pressure) is used chiefly in meteorology. An atmosphere is the unit used in high-pressure engineering. One bar and one atmosphere, while differing slightly, are roughly equal to air pressure at sea level. Weather maps often show pressure in millibars. (A millibar is one-thousandth of a bar.)

bar-. barkeeper, barmaid, barman, barroom, bartender.

Barbados.

barbecue (n. and v.).

Barclays Bank.

bar mitzvah (for a boy), **bas mitzvah** (for a girl).

Baron. *Lord,* not *Baron,* is the customary form in Britain: *Lord Manley.* In other foreign countries, *Baron* is used.

Baroness. *Lady,* not *Baroness,* is the customary form in Britain, although *Baroness* may be used in the first reference to a woman who holds the title in her own right: *Baroness Manley, Lady Manley.* In other foreign countries, *Baroness* is used.

baronet (British rank). See **Sir.**

Baroque, baroque. Capitalize in references to a style of painting, sculpture and architecture developed in Rome in the 17th century and influential throughout Europe immediately afterward. The principal characteristic of Baroque style is a vividly achieved harmony of an elaborately wrought configuration of dramatic detail. Also capitalize *Baroque* in references to music composed between 1600 and 1750, beginning with Monteverdi and ending with Bach and Handel; the era saw the rise of opera and oratorio. Lowercased, *baroque* refers to any style in which there is a tendency to dramatic and highly formal resolution of abundant and elaborate detail. See **styles and schools in the arts.**

baseball. Scores are given in figures: *The Giants won, 12 to 6* (or *12-6*). Numbers of runs, hits and innings below 10 are spelled out: *They scored three runs in the seventh inning. In the 10th inning, they got their 12th hit.*

Capitalize *All-Star Game, World Series* and *Little World Series.*

Avoid tired words and phrases like *all-time, autumn classic, annex* (as a verb), *frame, nightcap, Pale Hose, win* (as a noun), *winless,* etc.

Basel (Switzerland).

Basenji (dog).

bases. See **military bases.**

basis, bases.

basis point. A basis point is one-hundredth of 1 percent. It is used most often to describe changes in yields on bonds, notes and other fixed-income securities. Thus, if the yield on a bond issue moved from 8 percent to 8.15 percent, the yield would have increased 15 basis points. Basis points should always be given in figures, not spelled out. See **percent, percentage.**

basketball. Use figures for points and scores: *He scored 8 points in two minutes. They won, 99 to 98* (or *99-98*). Spell out the number of baskets below 10: *He made only four baskets in the first half, but shot 17 in the second.* Also: *24-second rule.*

Basotho (sing. and pl.). The people of Lesotho. The adjective is *Basotho.*

bas-relief.

basset hound.

Bastille.

bath(-). bathhouse, bath mat, bathroom, bath towel, bathtub.

Bathurst (Gambia) is now Banjul.

bathyscaph for the deep-sea diving craft.

Batswana (sing. and pl.). The people of Botswana. The adjective is *Botswana*.

battalion. Capitalize in names: *Third Battalion, 10th Battalion.*

battle(-). battle-ax, battle cry, battle fatigue, battlefield, battlefront, battleground, battle(s) royal, battleship, battle station(s).

bavarian cream (a dessert).

Bayreuth (Germany).

BBC for the British Broadcasting Corporation. The full name should be used more frequently in first references than is the case with the networks in the United States. But in many instances *BBC* will suffice.

B.C. As an abbreviation for *before Christ*, it follows the year or the century: *The town was founded in 73 B.C. The town dates its origins from the second century B.C.* But *A.D.*, for *anno Domini* or *in the year of the* [or *our*] *Lord*, is placed before the year *(in A.D. 73)* and after the century *(in the second century A.D.)*.
B.C. is also used for *boat club* in second references: the *Schuylkill B.C.*

beagle.

Beaux-Arts. Capitalize when referring to the French Ecole des Beaux-Arts, which had a significant effect on American architecture, and when referring to the style itself. The Beaux-Arts style is elaborate and formal, with great amounts of sculpture and much symmetry. Grand Central Terminal and the Public Library are two examples of this style in New York. See **styles and schools in the arts.**

bed(-). bedchamber, bedclothes, bedfast, bedfellow, bed jacket, bed linen, bedpost, bed rest, bedridden, bedroll, bedroom, bedside, bedspring, bedtime.

Bedlington terrier.

Bedloes Island was renamed Liberty Island in 1956.

before is better than the stilted *prior to.*

beforehand.

Beirut (Lebanon).

Belize, formerly British Honduras. The capital is Belmopan.

Belizean(s). The people of Belize, formerly British Honduras. The adjective is *Belizean.*

Bellerose (Queens and L.I.).

Bellmore (L.I.).

benediction.

benefited, benefiting.

Benelux. Belgium, the Netherlands and Luxembourg.

Bengali(s). Ethnic group in Bangladesh and India. See **Bangladeshi(s).**

Ben-Gurion International Airport at Lod, Israel, serves Jerusalem and Tel Aviv. In subsequent references: *Ben-Gurion Airport* or *Lod airport.*

Benzedrine (trademark).

Bergdorf Goodman. No hyphen.

Bering Sea.

Berlin. Do not use in datelines; use *West Berlin* or *East Berlin.*

Berliner(s). The people of Berlin.

Berlin wall, the wall.

Bermudian(s). The people of Bermuda.

Bermuda shorts.

Bern (Switzerland), not *Berne.*

beside (at the side of), **besides** (in addition to).

besiege.

bessemer converter.

best(-). best-dressed, best-informed, best-liked, best man, best-paid, best seller, best-selling.

In general, the hyphens are omitted when the compound adjectives follow the nouns they modify: *A survey found newspaper readers best informed.*

better half (meaning a spouse) is offensive in almost all contexts, and should be avoided. See **women.**

bettor.

between. See **among, between.**

Bev. See **Gev** and **Mev.**

Bhutanese (sing. and pl.). The people of Bhutan.

bi-. biangular, biannual, bicameral, bicentennial, biennial, bilateral, bilingual, bimonthly, bipartisan, bistate, biweekly, bizonal. Also see these separate entries: **biannual, biennial; semiannual, semiyearly; bimonthly; semimonthly; biweekly; semiweekly.**

biannual, biennial. *Biannual* means twice a year; so do *semiannual* and *semiyearly*. Every two years is *biennial*. To aid comprehension, avoid the prefix forms when possible and write *twice a year* or *every two years.*

Bible, biblical. Capitalize *Bible* (but not *biblical*) if the reference is to the Old Testament or the New Testament. But: *The style manual is their bible.* See **Gospel(s), gospel** and **Scripture(s), scriptural, scriptural citations.**

Bible Belt. Use with care; in certain contexts it can give offense.

Big Three (or *Four, Five,* etc.). Construe as a plural. Numerals may be used in headlines: *Big 3.*

bikini (bathing suit).

billion is used in the American sense of 1,000 million, rather than in the British sense of one million million. See **numbers** and **numbers, round** and **dollars and cents.**

Bill of Rights. The first 10 amendments to the Constitution of the United States. Do not shorten to *the bill* in subsequent references. Also capitalize the Bill of Rights enacted in Britain in 1689.

bills, legislative. See **acts, amendments, bills and laws.**

bimonthly means every two months; twice a month is *semimonthly*. To aid comprehension, avoid the prefix forms when possible and use *every two months* or *twice a month.*

bird's-eye (adj.).

Bishop. Following, by church or denomination, are guides to style for references to bishops of various kinds. In every case, the titles should be lowercased in the general sense *(a bishop)* and in most plural instances: *the bishops.* But capitalize a plural reference to a small number of bishops individually and specifically identified in the story: *the Bishops of Hartford and Topeka, the two Bishops, the Bishops.*

EPISCOPAL

The Episcopal Church has bishops (who head dioceses and hold other posts), suffragan bishops (who assist bishops of dioceses), bishops coadjutor (who are suffragans with the right of succession) and assistant bishops (usually retired bishops who perform duties for bishops of dioceses but who are not formally installed).

In accordance with the current tendency in the Episcopal Church, omit *the Rt. Rev.* before the names of bishops. In first references, use the titles given in the previous paragraph: *Bishop John P. Manley of New York, Suffragan Bishop John P. Manley of New York.* Also: *the Bishop of New York, John P. Manley* (or *the Suffragan Bishop of,* etc.). In subsequent references, a full dual title *(Suffragan Bishop)* may be used with the last name or, in all cases, simply *Bishop Manley* or *the Bishop.*

The Episcopal Church is headed by the Presiding Bishop. In first references: *Presiding Bishop John P. Manley of the Episcopal Church.* In subsequent references: *Presiding Bishop Manley, the Presiding Bishop, Bishop Manley, the Bishop.*

LUTHERAN

Lutherans in the United States rarely use the term Bishop, but when they do, this is the first-reference style: *the Rev. John P. Manley, Bishop of Missouri.* Subsequent references: *Bishop Manley, the Bishop.*

METHODIST

In the United Methodist Church, the first-reference style is *Bishop John P. Manley of Massachusetts.* Subsequent references: *Bishop Manley, the Bishop.*

MORMON

Mormons also have bishops, who head wards: *Bishop John P. Manley of the Manhattan Ward, Bishop Manley, the Bishop.*

ORTHODOX

The style for bishops and archbishops of the Eastern Orthodox Church is similar to the first- and second-reference style for other churches. In many instances, however, a prelate adopts an ecclesiastical name and that name alone is used after the title in first references: *Archbishop Makarios (Makarios* means *Blessed).* The church also uses the titles *patriarch* and *metropolitan* (which see).

ROMAN CATHOLIC

The Roman Catholic Church has archbishops (who normally head archdioceses), bishops (who normally head dioceses) and auxiliary bishops (who assist archbishops or bishops). In accordance with the current tendency in the Catholic Church, *the Most Rev.* is omitted before the name in almost all cases: *Archbishop John P. Manley of Hartford; Bishop John P. Manley of,* etc.; *Auxiliary Bishop John P. Manley of,* etc. Also: *the Bishop of Hartford, John P. Manley* (or *the Archbishop of,* or *the Auxiliary Bishop of,* etc). Subsequent references: *Archbishop Manley, the Archbishop; Bishop Manley, the Bishop; Auxiliary Bishop* [or *Bishop*] *Manley, the Auxiliary Bishop* or *the Bishop.* But *the Most Rev.* is used before the name of superiors general of certain Catholic orders.

Also see **Archbishop, Canon, deacon, Dean, Most Rev., Rev., Rt. Rev., Superior General, Very Rev.**

Bishop Coadjutor. See **Bishop** (EPISCOPAL).

bivouac, bivouacking.

biweekly means every two weeks. It can also mean twice a week, but not in this book. For twice a week use *semiweekly.* To aid comprehension, avoid the prefix forms when possible and use *every two weeks* or *twice a week.*

black (n., adj.). In general, use *black(s)* and *black* as noun and adjective rather than *Negro(es)* and *Negro,* although the latter are acceptable in many contexts, both current and historical. The race of a person figuring in the news should be specified only if it is truly pertinent. The same stricture applies to ethnic and religious identifications.

black(-). blackjack, blacklist, blackmail, blackout, black tie (n.), black-tie (adj.), blacktop.

Black Panther Party. Lowercase titles of officers of the party: *John P. Manley, minister of information of the Black Panther Party.* Use *Black Panther(s)* in reference to members.

blame on. This is to be avoided: *The wreck was blamed on carelessness.* Since the wreck is not the target of the blame, it should be: *Carelessness was blamed for the wreck. The wreck was attributed to carelessness.*

blast off (v.), **blastoff** (n.). Use only in references to rocketry.

Bleecker Street (in Greenwich Village).

blitz, blitzkrieg.

blizzard. Do not call a storm a blizzard unless it meets the specifications set by the National Weather Service: winds of at least 35 miles an hour; temperature of 20 degrees or lower; considerable falling snow or considerable snow picked up from the ground and blown about to an extent greatly reducing visibility. Also, *a severe blizzard:* a great density of falling snow or snow picked up from the ground; winds of 45 miles an hour or more; temperature of 10 degrees or less.

blockfront.

blond, blonde; brunet, brunette. Use the nouns *blond* and *brunet* for boys and men, and the nouns *blonde* and *brunette* for girls and women. Use the adjectives *blond* and *brunet* for people of both sexes, and for inanimate things.

bloodhound.

blowout (n. and adj.), **blow out** (v.).

blue line (hockey).

BMT for Brooklyn-Manhattan Transit, a division of the Metropolitan Transportation Authority. Also: *the N train* (or *line*), *the RR train.*

B'nai B'rith, Bnai Zion. Note that one of these Jewish organizations does not punctuate its name. Do not use *the* before either name. The Anti-Defamation League is a division of B'nai B'rith.

board. Capitalize only when part of a name. Do not abbreviate, even in headlines.

board chairman and **chairman of the board.** Always lowercase. Do not use *chairlady, chairwoman* or *chairperson.* See **women.**

Board of Regents, the Regents.

Boardwalk (Coney Island, Atlantic City).

boat(-). boathook, boathouse, boatload, boatman, boat race.

Boeing Company, formerly the Boeing Aircraft Company.

bogey (n. and v.) for one over par in golf and for making such a score: *He scored a bogey. He bogeyed the third hole.* The plural is *bogeys.* Also see **bogy.**

Bogotá (Colombia).

Bogotano(s). The people of Bogotá.

bogy. A bugbear or a goblin or an evil spirit. The plural is *bogies.* Also see **bogey.**

bona fide.

bondholder.

bond ratings. The two most widely followed companies that judge the investment risk of bonds are Moody's Investors Service Inc. and the Standard & Poor's Corporation.

Moody's uses nine ratings: *Aaa, Aa, A, Baa, Ba, B, Caa, Ca* and *C.*

Those rated *Aaa* are judged to be of the best quality and those rated *C* are regarded as extremely poor prospects. Standard & Poor's has seven main grades: *AAA, AA, A, BBB, BB, B* and *D.* It also sometimes uses a plus or minus sign on grades from *AA* through *BB.*

bonds (financial). Bonds are interest-bearing certificates issued by governments and corporations when they borrow money. Bonds are generally long term, coming due in eight years or more. See **debentures** and **notes.**

booby trap (n.), **booby-trap** (v.).

book(-), (-)book. bookbinder, bookcase, book club, book dealer, bookend, book jacket, bookkeeper, bookmaker, bookmark, bookmobile, bookseller, bookshelf, bookshop, bookstore. Also: bankbook, checkbook, notebook, pocket book (a small book), pocketbook (a billfold, purse or handbag), reference book, schoolbook, storybook (n. and adj.), textbook.

Book of Common Prayer.

books. In ordinary matter, quote their titles and capitalize principal words. But do not quote titles of standard reference works like dictionaries, encyclopedias, gazetteers, etc.

boost, booster. Acceptable uses include these: *boost* [n. or v.] *over a wall, civic booster, morale booster, booster rocket.* But avoid such trite phrases as *boost wages, boost taxes, boost a bill's chances.*

border terrier.

"Boris Godunov" (the opera).

Borough President John P. Manley of Queens (etc.), the Borough President, but never *the President.*

borscht.

Börse (German exchange).

Bosporus, the, not *Bosporus Strait.*

Boston & Maine Railroad, the B.&M.; a subsidiary of the Boston and Maine Corporation.

Boston Stock Exchange.

Boston terrier.

Botanical Garden, New York (in the Bronx). But: *the Brooklyn Botanic Garden.*

Botswana. Its people are Batswana (sing. and pl.). The adjective is *Botswana.*

Boulevard. Spell out and capitalize in ordinary reading matter when part of a name: *Bruckner Boulevard.* The abbreviation *(Bruckner Blvd.)* may be used in headlines and in agate and other special matter.

-bound. Africa-bound, eastbound, muscle-bound, northbound, snowbound, vacation-bound.

Bourse (French exchange).

boutonniere.

bowl games. Capitalize: *Rose Bowl, Cotton Bowl, Orange Bowl,* etc.

box(-). boxcar, boxholder, box kite, boxlike, box lunch, box office (n.), box-office (adj.), box score, box seat, box spring (n.), box-spring (adj.), box supper, boxwood.

boxing. Spell out the number of rounds below 10 and use figures for the time within a round: *2:03 of the sixth round.* Also use figures for the knockdown count: *a count of 8.*

boyfriend, girlfriend. Despite the wide currency these objectionable colloquialisms have attained, they should not be used until it has been definitely established that no other term or description will suffice. They are especially distasteful, as well as imprecise, in references to adults.

Boy Scout, a Scout, the Scouts.

brackets. See **parentheses and brackets.**

Brahman, Brahmin. Use *Brahman* for the priestly Hindu caste, or for a member of that caste. Use *Brahmin* in general references to aristocracy: *a Boston Brahmin.*

brand-new.

Braniff Airways.

Brasília, the capital of Brazil.

brassiere. No accent.

brazil nut.

bread(-). bread and butter (n., in the sense of livelihood), bread-and-butter (adj.), breadbasket, breadboard, breadbox, bread crumbs, breadfruit, bread line, breadstick, breadwinner.

break-. breakdown (n.), breakoff (n.), breakthrough (n.), breakup (n.), breakwater.

breast-stroke.

breechloader.

bribe-. bribegiver, bribegiving, bribetaker, bribetaking.

bric-a-brac.

bride. When the wedding bells have stopped ringing, avoid expressions like *his bride* when *wife* is the intended meaning: *John P. Manley and his wife attended the convention.* Better still: *John and Joan Manley attended, etc.* See **women.**

bridge. See **contract bridge.**

briefcase.

Brig. John P. Manley, Brigadier Manley, the brigadier.

Brig. Gen. John P. Manley, General Manley, the general.

bring, take. *Bring* denotes movement toward the speaker or writer; *take* denotes movement away from the speaker or writer, or any other movement that is not toward him.

Thus it would be incorrect, in a dispatch from any city except Detroit, to write that the Canadian Prime Minister was *bringing* a group of industrialists to a conference in Detroit. Since headlines are unaffected by datelines, the word *bring* in a headline in The Times will usually refer to movement toward New York, or toward the United States from abroad.

Britain, not *Great Britain.* Do not use *Britain* after cities and towns when a locating word is required. Use *England, Scotland, Wales* or *Northern Ireland.* See **datelines.**

British, Briton(s). The people of Britain; this group includes the English, the Scottish, the Welsh and in some general contexts the Northern Irish. The more specific terms should be used when they apply. Do not use *Britisher(s).*

British Airways is the successor to both British European Airways and the British Overseas Airways Corporation.

British Broadcasting Corporation. See **BBC.**

British Caledonian Airways.

British Columbia. Do not abbreviate after cities and towns, even in datelines.

British Columbian(s). The people of British Columbia.

British Commonwealth is now simply the Commonwealth (which see).

Britisher(s). Do not use in place of *Briton(s)* or *the British.*

British Guiana is now Guyana.

British Honduras is now Belize. The capital is Belmopan.

British Leyland Ltd.

British Petroleum Company (B.P.).

British titles are listed separately and alphabetically.

British West Indian Airways (B.W.I.A.).

broadcast (past tense). Never *broadcasted.*

broad jump (track) is now called the long jump.

Bronx Zoo. This informal name, used even by the zoo's management, is appropriate in most references. Occasionally, in an especially detailed story about the zoo, it may be appropriate to use the full official name, the New York Zoological Park. The zoo is operated by the New York Zoological Society.

Bronze Age.

Brookings Institution.

Brooklyn-Battery Tunnel.

Brooklyn Botanic Garden. But: *the New York Botanical Garden* (in the Bronx).

Brooklyn Heights, the Heights. In first references, there is no article before *Brooklyn.* In headlines: *Brooklyn Hts.*

Brooklyn Navy Yard. The official name of this former installation, New York Naval Shipyard, was almost never used.

Bros. Spell out *Brothers* (or *Brother*) in company and similar names in news stories. It may be abbreviated to *Bros.* (or *Bro.*) in headlines and tabular material when used with the name of a company. See **company and corporation names.**

brunet, brunette. See **blond, blonde; brunet, brunette.**

Brünnhilde.

brussels carpet.

Brussels griffon (dog).

brussels sprouts.

B.S. for Bachelor of Science. Also: *a bachelor's degree.*

B.T.U.('s) for British thermal unit(s). A B.T.U. is the amount of heat needed to increase the temperature of a pound of water by one degree Fahrenheit. It is equal to approximately 252 gram calories. See **calorie.**

Budapest.

Budget Message. The President's.

bug (as a synonym for *insect*). Do not use except in special contexts (humorous, for instance).

bug, tap. Bugging is the use of concealed listening devices to pick up sounds in a room, an automobile, etc. Tapping, a different practice, is the use of listening devices attached to a telephone circuit to pick up conversations on that circuit. Do not quote *bug, bugs, bugged, bugging* in the sense of electronic spying, or recording conversations secretly.

building names. Capitalize the names of governmental buildings, churches, office buildings, hotels, specially designated rooms, etc.: *the Capitol* (state or national), *Criminal Courts Building, First Presbyterian Church, Empire State Building, Inter-Continental Hotel, Grand Central Terminal, Oak Room, Ohio State Penitentiary,* etc.

buildup.

bulldog, bull terrier.

bullet. It is the bullet, not the cartridge, that is discharged from the muzzle of a gun. The cartridge is a case that, before firing, contains an explosive charge and the bullet.

bullfight, bullfighter.

bull pen (baseball).

bull's-eye (when the reference is not to the eye of a bull).

bunsen burner.

Bureau, bureau. Capitalize in names of government agencies

(Bureau of Indian Affairs) and private agencies *(Newspaper Advertising Bureau)*, but not in references to newspapers' news bureaus *(the Washington bureau of The New York Times).*

burglarize. Do not use.

burglary, larceny, robbery, theft. Legal definitions of *burglary* vary among localities, but it must involve entering a building (not necessarily breaking and entering) and remaining unlawfully with the intent to commit a crime. *Larceny* is the wrongful taking of property (the equivalent, in nonlegal terms, of *theft* or *stealing*). *Robbery*, in its legal sense, is a larceny carried out through the use or threat of violence. In a broader sense, *to rob* means to plunder or rifle or loot. Thus, a safe may be *robbed*, as a person is *robbed*. An object that is taken away is *stolen*. Also see **mugging.**

Burlington Northern, the B.N.; the railroad subsidiary of Burlington Northern Inc.

Burmese (sing. and pl.). The people of Burma.

Burmese names. When used in full on first reference, a Burmese name includes an honorific that is considered an essential courtesy: *U* for a man, *Daw* for a married woman, *Mah* for an unmarried woman, *Maung* or *Ko* for a young man or a boy. Thus a newspaper article should normally refer to a Burmese man, the first time he is mentioned, as *U*; for example, *U Kyaw Myint.* When possible, a governmental or professional title (such as *President, Gen.* or *Dr.*) should be used in first reference, and the *U* should be dropped. On subsequent reference, a Burmese man without such a title should be called *Mr.: Mr. Kyaw Myint.* Similarly, a woman without a title should be called *Mrs.* or *Miss*

on second reference. Burmese can have either one name *(U Nu, U Lwin)* or two *(U Kyaw Soe, Dr. Hla Han);* if two, both names must be used on second reference: *Mr. Kyaw Soe, Dr. Hla Han.*

bus, bused, buses, busing (all v.) for transporting by bus(es).

bushel. Four pecks or eight gallons. The United States bushel is equal to 35.24 liters; the British imperial bushel, 36.37 liters.

business directories and guides. Do not quote their titles; capitalize principal words.

businessman, businesswoman. But: *small-business man.* See **compound words.**

by-. by-election, bylaw, byline, bypass (n., v.), bypath, byplay, byproduct, byroad, bystander, byword.

bylines. In the news sections of The Times, bylines are to be set as follows, in boldface caps:

By JOAN P. MANLEY

When the news article has a dateline, a credit line in 5-point Regal follows the byline:

By JOHN P. MANLEY Jr.
Special to The New York Times

The style is the same in the rare instances when a byline is used over a news agency dispatch or one from The Times of London. Then the byline and the credit line would, for example, read:

By REGINALD ARMSTRONG
Dispatch of The Times, London

or

By MARIANNE JONES
The Associated Press

Note, in the second example above, that the word *by*, which appears in the byline, is not repeated in the 5-point credit line.

Also see **credit lines.**

C

C.A.B. for the Civil Aeronautics Board.

cabby, cabbies for taxicab driver(s). Especially useful in headlines.

cabdriver. But: *gypsy-cab driver.*

Cabinet, cabinet. Capitalize when the reference is to a group of officials of a national or state government formally so designated: *the Cabinet, President Manley's Cabinet, a Cabinet minister, Cabinet ministers.* The plural is capitalized when it refers to a small number of cabinets specifically identified in the story: *the French and British Cabinets, the two Cabinets.* Otherwise: *cabinets, a cabinet, trying to form a cabinet;* and, figuratively: *His friends made up a kind of cabinet.*

cabinet lists are set hanging indent in 8½-point or 7-point:

Prime Minister — Francisco Largo Caballero, Socialist.
Agriculture—Vincent Uribe, Communist.
Air and Marine—Indalecio Prieto, Socialist.
Foreign—Julio Alvarez del Vayo, Socialist.
Interior—Angel Galarza, Socialist.
Public Works — José Antonio Aguirre, Basque Nationalist.

cabinet titles, both United States and foreign, are capitalized: *Secretary of Labor Helen Manley, Minister of Justice,* etc.; *the Secretary, the Minister.* But: *a secretary, a minister, the secretaries, the ministers* (for capitalized plural exceptions, see **titles**).

caddie (golf), **caddy** (tea).

Cadet John P. Manley, Cadet Manley, the cadet.

cafe.

Cairene(s). The people of Cairo.

Cairn terrier.

caliber (of weapons). Figures are used in giving the calibers of guns and ammunition: *.22 rifle* (or *.22-caliber rifle*), *.38-caliber revolver, .410* (or *.410-bore*) *shotgun* (the only shotgun so measured), *7.3-inch gun, 11-inch cannon, 8-pound gun, 8-pounder, 105-millimeter gun, 7.62-millimeter ammunition.* Shotguns, except for the .410, are not measured in inches: *10-gauge shotgun, 12-gauge,* etc. The abbreviation for *millimeters (mm.)* may be used in headlines and in tabular or other special matter.

Calif. for California after cities and towns.

calorie. A *gram calorie* is the amount of heat required to raise one gram of water one degree centigrade under standard conditions. A *large calorie* is equal to 1,000 gram calories, and is the unit used to express the energy value of food. In that context, use the single word *calorie(s)* without the preceding *large*.

Cambodia, Cambodian(s). But in references to Cambodia's language, *Khmer* may be used, and in discussion of the country's predominant ethnic group, the people may be called Khmer(s).

Cambodian names. Because of differences in their ethnic backgrounds, Cambodians' names assume a variety of forms. In news stories, for the sake of consistency and certainty, use full names in all references: *Foreign Minister Long Boret; Mr. Long Boret.* In headlines, however, if it is known without doubt that part of the name is a surname, or is used alone by Cambodians, that part may stand alone: Prince Norodom Sihanouk may be referred to as *Sihanouk.*

Cameroon, not *Cameroons* and not *Cameroun.*

Cameroonian(s). The people of Cameroon.

camp(-). camp chair, camp cot, campfire, campground, campsite, campstool.

Canada goose, not *Canadian goose,* for the common wild goose of North America.

Canadian Arctic Gas Pipeline Ltd.

Canadian National Railways.

Canadian Pacific Steamships.

Canadian provinces are listed separately and alphabetically. Do not abbreviate their names after cities and towns, even in datelines.

canal. Lowercase *the canal* in subsequent references to the Panama Canal, the Suez Canal and others.

Canal Zone (Panama), the zone. Do not abbreviate after cities and towns, even in datelines.

cancel, canceled, canceling, cancellation.

Candia (Crete) is now Herakleion.

candle-. candleholder, candlelight, candlepower, candlestick.

cannot.

Canon is an Episcopal clergyman connected with a cathedral or assigned to a bishop: *Canon John P. Manley, Canon Manley, the Canon.* But: *a canon, the canons* (for capitalized plural exceptions, see **titles**).

Cantabrigian(s). The people of Cambridge in England or students or graduates of Cambridge University.

cantaloupe.

Canterbury, Archbishop of. The Most Rev. John P. Manley, Archbishop of Canterbury; Archbishop Manley; the Archbishop of Canterbury; the Archbishop. See **Most Rev., Rt. Rev.**

canto, cantos.

canvas (cloth), **canvass** (to survey, poll or solicit).

Cape Breton Island.

Cape Canaveral (Fla.), formerly Cape Kennedy, remains the home of the John F. Kennedy Space Center. The related installation at Houston is the Lyndon B. Johnson Space Center.

Cape Town (South Africa).

Cap-Haïtien.

capital (city), **Capitol** (building). Lowercase for a city that is the seat of national or state government: *the capital, the national capital, the* *state capital, the capital city* or *Trenton, the capital of New Jersey.* Capitalize all references to a specific national or state building: *the Capitol.* Also: *Capitol Hill, the Hill.*

capitalization. Style for capitalization is given throughout this manual in separate and alphabetical listings. A word, phrase or abbreviation that is listed but not discussed is to be used in a normal sentence as it appears in the listing, capitalized or not capitalized.

In cap-and-lowercase headlines, capitalize nouns, pronouns and verbs, and all other words of four or more letters. Capitalize *No, Nor, Not, Off, Out, So, Up,* etc. Lowercase *a, and, as, at, but, by, for, if, in, of, on, or, the, to,* except when they appear at the beginnings of lines in the tops of heads, at the beginnings of banks, and immediately after dashes in banks. Some of the foregoing words are also capitalized when connected with the preceding word, as in *Mayor Drops In* and *Cared For by His Mother.* Note that the expressions *Call on* and *Call for,* when followed by objects, do not fall into that category, and the prepositions remain lowercase: *Mayor Calls on President to Yield; Senator Calls for Decision.* Set infinitive as follows: *to Be, to Do, to Go,* etc.

When the preposition *for* substitutes for a verb meaning *supports* or *advocates,* it is capitalized: *Mayor For Health Insurance Plan.*

Capitalize both parts of a hyphenated compound in headlines if both are actual words: *Cease-Fire, Able-Bodied, Sit-In, Make-Believe.* Fractions are an exception *(One-fifth),* as numbers like *Twenty-three* would be if the style did not

call for *23.* In sums of money: *$7 Million, $34 Billion.* Lowercase after the hyphen in a headline word formed with a prefix that is not itself an actual word: *Re-elect, Re-entry, Pre-emptive.* But capitalize if the word after the prefix is a proper noun, adjective or name: *Pre-Roman.* Capitalize both parts of *Teen-Age* or *Teen-Ager.*

Always capitalize the first word of the second or third line of a headline (though not necessarily of a bank). Also capitalize the principal words in side headings and the headings of tables, lists, etc., in tabular matter.

Capt. John P. Manley, Captain Manley, the captain. This applies to military, naval, maritime, fire and police captains.

Caraqueño(s). The people of Caracas.

carat. A unit of weight used for gemstones. It is equal to 200 milligrams, or about 3 grains. See **karat** (a unit measuring the fineness of gold).

Cardinal (Roman Catholic). John Cardinal Manley, Cardinal Manley, the Cardinal. First names should be used in first references, even to the Cardinal who is Archbishop of New York. Capitalize in the official name of a group: *the College of Cardinals.* But: *a cardinal, the cardinals* (for capitalized plural exceptions, see **titles**).

CARE may be used in all references to the Cooperative for American Relief Everywhere. Articles dealing with the agency in detail should mention its full name.

care-. carefree, caretaker, careworn.

careen, career. *Careen* means to tilt or be tilted or to heel over (as a ship). The verb *career* means to move at high speed, to rush wildly.

caret (writers' and proofreaders' mark). Also see **carat** and **karat**.

cargo, cargoes.

Caribbean Sea, the Caribbean.

carload.

Carnegie Institute (Pittsburgh), **Carnegie Institution** (Washington).

Carolina. *N. Carolina* and *S. Carolina* may be used in headlines when necessary to avoid the ambiguity of *Carolina* alone.

carte blanche.

cartridge. A cartridge for a gun is a case that contains an explosive charge and a bullet or shot. The gun discharges only the bullet or shot.

case(-). casebook, case history, caseload, casework, caseworker.

cashmere (wool).

casket. Use *coffin* instead for the box in which a corpse lies.

cast-. castaway (n.), castoff (n. and adj.).

caster (roller).

castor (oil).

casualty lists are set hanging indent in 7-point, with a full-measure 8½-point italic introduction. The last name is given first in light caps, and the names are alphabetized. Use P heads or G caps for categories.

Following is a list of the dead and injured in the plane crash yesterday:

Dead
ROE, Richard Jr., 22 years old, Garden Grove, Calif.

Injured
DOE, John 3d, 48, Los Angeles, the pilot.

catalogue.

catboat. A sailboat having one mast, far forward, and one sail.

catcall.

Cathedral of St. John the Divine. Not *Cathedral Church*.

Catholic. It does not necessarily mean *Roman Catholic*. If that is meant, use *Roman Catholic* in first references and, when necessary to avoid confusion, in subsequent references also.

cat's-paw(s). A person who is a dupe or a tool.

cause célèbre.

cave-in (n.).

CBC for the Canadian Broadcasting Corporation.

CBS. The full name is *CBS Inc.*, not *the Columbia Broadcasting System*. The full names of CBS divisions include *CBS News, CBS Radio* and *CBS-TV*. Any of these, as well as *CBS*, may be used in first references, and *CBS* alone may be used in subsequent references. *CBS* alone is preferred in some first references, especially when the networks are mentioned together in a lead: *ABC, CBS and NBC will televise President Manley's address to the nation tomorrow night.*

C.C.N.Y. No longer used. See **City College**.

cease-fire (n. and adj.).

cedilla. See **accent marks**.

celebrant, celebrator. The distinction is worth preserving: *celebrant* of a religious rite, such as a mass; *celebrator* of, for example, an anniversary or some other special occasion, often festive.

cellist, cello.

cement. There are many kinds of cement, which is a binding agent. One kind is among the ingredients of the artificial stone called concrete. Thus: *The wall was built with concrete* [not *cement*] *blocks.*

center(-). centerboard, center field, centerpiece.

center around. Avoid the expression. Use *center on, center in* or *revolve around.*

Centereach (L.I.).

Centerport (L.I.).

centigrade, Celsius. The temperature scale used in the metric system. In it, zero represents the freezing point of water, and 100 degrees is the boiling point at sea level. To convert to Fahrenheit, multiply by 9, divide by 5 and add 32.

Celsius was the name of the Swede who invented the centigrade system, and there is a growing movement to designate the system by his name. But *centigrade* (lowercase *c*) is still more common and thus preferred. The abbreviation for either name is capital *C: 20°C* (without a period). See **Fahrenheit** and **Kelvin** and **temperature.**

CENTO for the Central Treaty Organization.

Central Conference of American Rabbis. A Reform group.

Central Intelligence Agency (C.I.A.), the agency. It is headed by the Director of Central Intelligence; his title does not include the word *agency.*

Central Railroad Company of New Jersey, the Jersey Central.

central standard time (C.S.T.). See **time.**

Centre Street (Manhattan).

cents. See **dollars and cents.**

centuries. Lowercase and spell out through the ninth: *the eighth century, the 12th century.* Hyphenate the adjectival form: *18th-century poet.* Also, in almost all contexts, *the 1700's,* not *seventeen-hundreds,* and *mid-ninth century, mid-16th century, mid-1890's.* See **years, decades, centuries.**

Ceylon is now Sri Lanka. Its people may still be referred to as *Ceylonese* (n. or adj.), or *Sri Lanka* may be used as an adjective. The language is *Sinhalese.*

chair (v.). Avoid in the sense of serve as a chairman.

chairlift.

chairman, chairmen. Use for both men and women. Also: *board chairman* and *chairman of the board.* Do not use *chairlady, chairwoman* or *chairperson.* See **women.**

Chairman of the Joint Chiefs of Staff. Capitalize the title, but do not use it in front of a name, except when separated by a comma: *the Chairman of the Joint Chiefs of Staff, Gen.* [or *Adm.*] *John P. Manley; Gen.* [or *Adm.*] *John P. Manley, Chairman of the Joint Chiefs of Staff; General* [or *Admiral*] *Manley; the Chairman.* In headlines or subsequent references, *the Joint Chiefs* or *the Chiefs* is acceptable.

Chamber of Deputies, the Chamber.

champagne. The wine from the Champagne region of France, or any similar wine.

Champs-Elysées.

Chancellor John P. Manley (the head of a government, a governmental agency or a school system), Chancellor Manley, the Chancellor, Mr. Manley. Also: *School Chancellor, Chancellor of the Exchequer.* But: *John P. Manley, the chancellor of Queens College* (or *of New York University*, etc.), *the chancellor.*

Channel 2 (television), Channel 13, etc. Also: WCBS-TV, WNET, etc.

characters in books, plays, etc. Do not quote their names: *He played Hotspur.*

charge. Use preposition *with.* (But after *accuse*, use *of.*) In stories about arrests and criminal proceedings, the word *charge* should be used with care: Ideally it is the formal allegation submitted to a court by a prosecutor or (in the case of an indictment for a serious crime) by a grand jury; at a minimum, *charge* may refer to the official allegation lodged by the police at the time of booking. But the informal, usually imprecise account given by officers at the scene of a crime should not be called a *charge* or introduced by the verb *charged.* Thus: *The police accused Mr. Wilson of having thrown a brick through the supermarket window and having threatened the manager with a pistol.*

chargé(s) d'affaires.

Charles de Gaulle Airport (at Roissy-en-France, north of Paris).

Charleston (West Virginia capital and South Carolina seaport), **Charles Town** (also in West Virginia), **Charlestown** (part of Boston).

Charter New York Corporation, the parent company of the Irving Trust Company.

Chase Manhattan Corporation, the parent company of the Chase Manhattan Bank.

chassis (sing. and pl.).

chateau (sing.), **chateaus** (pl.).

cheerleader.

cheese(-). cheeseburger, cheesecake, cheesecloth, cheese spread.

chef(s)-d'oeuvre.

chemical elements and formulas. Do not capitalize the name of an element, even when used with the mass number (which see): *carbon 14, strontium 90, uranium 235.* Chemical formulas are set thus: H_2O, CO_2.

Chemical Mace (trademark). Use *Mace* in second references. Do not use *Mace* or *mace* as a verb: *The police Maced* [or *maced*] *the crowd.*

Chemical New York Corporation, parent company of the Chemical Bank.

Chesapeake & Ohio Railway, the C.&O.; a subsidiary of the Chessie System.

chess. The names of the pieces are spelled out, lowercase, in stories and columns reporting and analyzing games: *king, queen*, etc. In notation, the abbreviations are *K* (king), *Q* (queen), *R* (rook), *B* (bishop), *N* (knight) and *P* (pawn). Openings and major variations are capitalized, but subvariations are not, except for proper nouns: *King's Indian Defense, Dragon Variation*, but *Maroczy bind, exchange variation.*

Black and *White* are capitalized as nouns but not as adjectives: *With*

8 P-K4 White seized the initiative.
But: *The white pieces were cramped.* The words *kingside* and *queenside* are lowercased as nouns or adjectives.

In stories and columns, black and white moves are separated by commas, pairs of moves by semicolons: *5 P-B3, P-B4; 6 B-B4, Q-Q2.* A black move standing alone or at the start of a sequence is preceded by an ellipsis: *3 . . . B-N2.*

Punctuation marks connoting criticism—such as *!*, *?* or *!?*—are permissible in analyses but not in game scores. In game scores, words and abbreviations are lowercase and not separated from the move: *18 PxPe.p., 14 QxRch, 42 Q-N8mate.*

The slash mark is used for queening and to clarify ambiguous moves: *44 P-B8/Q, 16 N/3xP.* Names of files and pawns are abbreviated in stories and columns: *White was unable to defend his KBP. Black brought pressure on the QN file.*

In the chess column, *Mr.* need not be used before the last names of men. In news stories, however, *Mr.* should be used except when actual play is being reported.

Chessie System, parent company of the Baltimore & Ohio Railroad, the Chesapeake & Ohio Railway and the Western Maryland Railway.

chesterfield (overcoat).

Chevy, not *Chevie* or *Chevvy.* This nickname for Chevrolet should be used only in special contexts (an informally written feature, for example) or in quoted matter.

Chiang Kai-shek.

Chicago Board of Trade.

Chicago Board Options Exchange. Not *Board of.*

Chicago Mercantile Exchange.

Chicago, Milwaukee, St. Paul & Pacific Railroad, the Milwaukee Road; a subsidiary of the Chicago Milwaukee Corporation.

Chicago, Rock Island & Pacific Railroad, the Rock Island.

Chicano(s) may be used when appropriate in references to United States citizens or residents of Mexican descent.

Chief John P. Manley (police), Chief Manley, the chief. But if the title is held by the head of a city or town police force: *the Chief.* In the New York City police, never *Chief Inspector.*

chief delegate (to an international organization). Lowercase and use the preposition *to: Joan Manley, chief United States delegate to the United Nations Educational, Scientific and Cultural Organization; Mrs. Manley; the chief delegate.* Also see **representative, chief representative.** In news stories, avoid substituting *Ambassador* or *permanent representative* (both of which see).

Chief Judge John P. Manley (of the Court of Appeals in New York State, and of the state itself), Judge Manley, the Chief Judge.

Chief Justice John P. Manley, Chief Justice Manley, the Chief Justice. It is Chief Justice *of the United States,* not *of the Supreme Court.*

Chief of Staff, chief of staff. In the military sense, capitalize only when the reference is to an officer in a very high post—the top man in an army, for example, or the leader of a nation's armed forces: *Gen. John P. Manley, Chief of Staff; the Chief of Staff; the general.* Lowercase when the reference is to some lesser command, such as chief of staff of a division. Also lowercase civilian references: *John P. Manley, the White House chief of staff.*

Chief Petty Officer John P. Manley, Mr. (or Chief Petty Officer) Manley, the chief petty officer.

Chief Rabbi John P. Manley of Britain (or any country where the title is used); *John P. Manley, Chief Rabbi of Britain; the Chief Rabbi; Rabbi Manley; the rabbi.* Also: *a chief rabbi, the chief rabbis* (for capitalized plural exceptions, see **titles**). Note that in Israel, Sephardic and Ashkenazic Jews have separate chief rabbis. Follow the same styles for *Grand Rabbi* in countries where that title is used.

chief representative (at an international organization or conference). Lowercase: *John P. Manley, chief representative of Britain at the United Nations conference on the law of the sea; Mr. Manley; the chief representative.* Also see **delegate** and **chief delegate.** In news stories, avoid substituting the expression *Ambassador* or *permanent representative* (which see).

Chief Warrant Officer John P. Manley, Mr. (or Chief Warrant Officer) Manley, the chief warrant officer.

chili, chilies.

China. Standing alone, it means the mainland nation and is to be used instead of *People's Republic of China* except in texts or quoted matter. Ordinarily do not use *Communist China* (which see). Also see **Nationalist China** and **Taiwan.**

chinaware.

Chinese (n., sing. and pl.; also adj.). The people are always *Chinese;* never use the disparaging *Chinamen* or *Chinaman,* except in direct quotation.

Chinese names. A modified form of the Wade-Giles system is to be used in the transliteration of Chinese names. The apostrophe and the two dots *(ü)* that are traditionally part of this system are not to be used: Chiang *Kai*-shek, not *K'ai*-shek. Note that the name following the hyphen is not capitalized. In Chinese names, the family name ordinarily comes first: *Chou* in Chou En-lai, *Chiang* in Chiang Ching; the second reference is *Prime Minister Chou* or *Mr. Chou* (without the *En-lai*), or *Miss Chiang.* Some Chinese (usually overseas or on Taiwan) have westernized their names, putting their given names or initials first: *Dr. Tsing-fu Tsiang, K. C. Wu.*

chinese red (color).

chitchat.

chock-full.

Chock Full o'Nuts.

choirmaster.

Cho Lon, the Chinese section of Saigon.

chord (music, mathematics), **cord** (vocal).

chow chow (dog).

Christ. See **Jesus.**

Christchurch (New Zealand).

Christian Church (Disciples of Christ). The parentheses and the words they surround are part of the official name and must be used in first references. In subsequent references: *the Christian Church.*

Christian Era.

Christian Methodist Episcopal Church.

Christian Science. The name of the denomination is the Church of

Christ, Scientist. Members belong to branch churches (for example, *the Fourth Church of Christ, Scientist*) and may also hold membership in the First Church of Christ, Scientist, which is in Boston and is known as the Mother Church.

There are no clergymen in the church; thus *the Rev.* should never be used. Members are elected for designated terms to fill the posts of *first reader* and *second reader* in local congregations and the Mother Church. There is also a president of the denomination. The church supports *lecturers*, who speak about Christian Science throughout the world.

Christmas. Never abbreviate to *Xmas* or any other form.

Church, church. Capitalize when used in the name of an organization *(the Roman Catholic Church, the Episcopal Church)* or a building or congregation *(the First Presbyterian Church)*. But: *a Roman Catholic church, an Episcopal church.* In all second references: *the church.*

church and state. Do not capitalize when used in this sense: *conflict between church and state, church-state issue.*

churches and other religious organizations are listed separately and alphabetically.

Churches of Christ. One of the major Protestant denominations in the United States.

churchgoer.

Church of Christ, Scientist. See **Christian Science.**

Church of England. This episcopal church is the established church of England, and it is headed by the sovereign. Its primate is the Archbishop of Canterbury. In second references, *the Anglican Church* may be used, but *the church* will almost always suffice. See **Anglican Communion; Canterbury, Archbishop of; Episcopal, episcopal.**

Church of Jesus Christ of Latter-day Saints. In first and subsequent references it may be called by its less formal name, the Mormon Church, so long as the full title appears at least once in any story that substantially deals with that church. See **Mormon Church.**

Church of the Brethren.

Church of the Holy Sepulcher (Jerusalem).

chute and **chutist** may be used in headlines for *parachute* and *parachutist.*

C.I.A. for the Central Intelligence Agency. It is headed by the Director of Central Intelligence. Note that this title does not include the word *agency.*

cigarette.

circumflex. See **accent marks.**

Citibank, Citicorp (without a preceding *the*), formerly the First National City Bank and its parent company, the First National City Corporation.

Citroën. The dieresis is standard equipment.

City, city. Capitalize when it is an integral part of an official or other regularly used name, or of a nickname: *New York City* (the preferred form when *New York* does not suffice), *the City of New York* (the official, corporate name), *Kansas City, Mexico City* (not the official *Mexico, D.F.*), *Windy City, City of Light.* Also capitalize when, to avoid ambiguity in stories, it is sometimes necessary to add the word to a name: *Panama City* and *Guatemala City,* for example. (When the ambiguity does not exist, *Panama* and *Guatemala* are to be used as the names of the cities as well as the countries.)

When there is a possibility of confusion with the state, *New York City* rather than *New York* alone should be used, just as *New York State* should be used in such situations. Also capitalize *City* when used with the name of a New York City agency or with an official title (*the City Planning Commission, City Comptroller John P. Manley*) if the context requires the specification.

The word *city* should be lowercased in forms like *city of Boston,* except in certain rare legal contexts calling for a corporate name: *The chief complainant in the suit was the City of Boston* [or *the City of New York*]. But when the word is used alone in such instances, this is correct: *The city sued the state.* Also lowercase *city* in all references, first or subsequent, like these: *the city, city government,* etc.

City Charter (New York City's), the Charter.

City College, formerly the City College of New York, is no longer known as C.C.N.Y. The college is a part of the City University of New York (which see).

City Council, the Council.

City of London (financial district), the City.

City University of New York. The system of higher education oper-ated by the Board of Higher Education in New York City. It consists of two-year and four-year colleges and graduate and professional programs. Individual institutions or campuses such as City College are units of the City University. The acronym *CUNY* should be restricted in general to quoted matter. In second references, *the City University* or *the university* is fine, and *City University* or *City U.* suffices for headlines. See **State University of New York** and **University of the State of New York.**

citywide.

Civil Service.

Civil War for the war between the Union and the Confederacy, which was officially called the Confederate States of America. Also: *the War Between the States.* And: *the Spanish Civil War, the civil war.*

-clad. copper-clad, half-clad, ironclad, snow-clad, steel-clad.

claptrap.

Claridge, Claridge's. It is *the Hotel Claridge* in Paris, and *Claridge's Hotel* in London.

class(-). class book, class day, classmate, classroom. Also: *class of 1943* (or *'43*).

classical (architecture). A general term for Greek and Roman architecture. For more recent buildings that are classical in spirit it is best not to use the term standing alone. See **styles and schools in the arts.**

Classical, Classicism (music). The capitalized terms generally refer to Viennese music in a period covering roughly 1770 to 1840, especially the works of Haydn, Mozart and Beethoven. The period was characterized by the stabilization of sonata and symphonic forms. See **styles and schools in the arts.**

clean-. clean-cut, cleanup (n.).

clear-. clear-cut, clear-eyed, clearheaded, clear-minded, clearsighted.

clerical titles are listed separately and alphabetically.

Clevelander(s). The people of Cleveland.

clichés. They are all things to all men. Many are beneath contempt, but some are all to the good; they lend a helping hand and add insult to injury. But they are, regrettably, never in short supply. They come in two categories: the ones that have attained a ripe old age, like those already mentioned here, and the overnight stars, like *ambience, charisma, dialogue, dichotomy, game plan, life style, orchestration, polarization, scenario, stonewalling* and *think tank*, to name a few of the many that truly need no introduction.

Some of the oldies assay as golden, and the language would be poorer if they were proscribed. They have survived not only because they are apt, but also because they have flavor and style that consciously devised replacements cannot match. It is hard to improve on *labor of love, sour grapes, dog in the manger, Achilles' heel, spill the beans, tip of the iceberg* and even *foregone conclusion* if they are properly used. But *armed to the teeth, crying need, flat denial, floral tribute, last sad rites, in this day and age, leaps and bounds, wee small hours* and even a single word like *massive* in some contexts are better left unsaid.

As for the overnight stars, they do have this distinction: They require virtually no time at all to become tiresome and trite. That is because faddishness, in writing as in raiment, is so hard to resist. But it must be resisted, just as clichés with older and more respectable qualifications must be carefully examined to determine whether their use can be justified. Most often the answer will be no.

clientele.

climax (v.). Avoid as trite.

clinch (v., sports). It is not a synonym for *win*. It is appropriate only for the point when, although play will continue, the outcome has been determined.

clock time. See **time.**

clockwise, counterclockwise.

close-up (n., adj.).

cloture, not *closure,* for the parliamentary procedure for closing debate in the United States Senate.

club(-). club car, clubhouse, clubman, club owner, clubroom, club sandwich, clubwoman.

club officers. Do not capitalize titles.

clue.

clumber spaniel.

co-. co-author (n.; never a verb), co-chairman, co-defendant, coed (which see), coeducation, coequal, coexist, coexistence, co-op (which see), cooperate, cooperation, cooperative (n., adj.), coordinate, coordination, co-owner, co-partner, co-pilot, co-star, co-worker.

Co. Spell out *Company* in names in news stories. It may be abbreviated to *Co.* in headlines and tabular material when used with the name of a company. See **company and corporation names.**

coast. Lowercase when referring to an actual shoreline: *Atlantic coast, Pacific coast, east coast, west coast,* etc. Capitalize when referring to certain specific regions of the United States lying along such shorelines: *Atlantic Coast, Pacific Coast, Gulf Coast, West Coast, East Coast.* Do not capitalize when reference is to lesser regions: *the Jersey coast* (but: *the Jersey Shore*). Capitalize *Coast* standing alone only when the reference is to the West Coast.

Coast Guard (United States). Members are *coastguardsmen.* Capitalize only before a name: *Coastguardsman John P. Manley.*

Coca-Cola, Coke (trademarks).

cocker spaniel.

cocksure.

coco (a palm tree), **coconut.** But: *cocoa* (the chocolate drink).

c.o.d. for cash, or collect, on delivery.

codes. Lowercase *steel code, oil code, penal code, building code,* etc. Capitalize such titles as *Code of Civil Procedure, Code Napoléon.*

coed (n. and adj.). As a noun meaning woman student in a coeducational institution, it seems timeworn and should be avoided in almost all instances, as can easily be done. But the adjective *coed,* a shortened form of coeducational, continues to be useful, especially in headlines. See **college boy, college girl** and **women.**

coffee(-). coffee break, coffeecake, coffee hour, coffeehouse, coffee mill, coffeepot, coffee table. But: *kaffeeklatsch,* not *coffee klatch.*

coffin. Use this word, not *casket,* for the box in which a corpse lies.

cognoscente (sing.), **cognoscenti** (pl.).

Col. John P. (or Joan) Manley, Colonel Manley, the colonel.

cold-blooded.

cold war.

collarbone.

collectible.

college boy, college girl. Use only in feature contexts. Otherwise use *college man, college woman* or *college student.*

College of Cardinals.

collide, collision. There is a collision only when both bodies are in motion. If the phrase *collided with* seems to fix blame, it can be avoided by using this construction: *An automobile and a bus collided.* The phrase *were in collision* accomplishes the same purpose, but is stilted and should be avoided.

collie.

colloquialisms. Use only when the context justifies them. Do not quote. See **slang and colloquialisms.**

Colo. for Colorado after cities and towns.

colon. The colon is used as a mark of introduction to a word, phrase, sentence, passage, list, tabulation, text, textual excerpts, etc. It is also used in giving clock times *(10:30 A.M.)* and, in sports, the times of races *(2:55, 4:10:23).*

As a mark of punctuation within the sentence the colon can be effective: *Today is the dead center of the*

year, or as near dead center as one
can conveniently get: 182 days
gone by, 182 to come.

In ordinary writing, the first word
after a colon is not capitalized if
what follows is not a complete sentence: *There were three considerations: expense, time and feasibil-
ity.* But: *He promised this: The
company will make good all the
losses.*

While a comma suffices to introduce a direct quotation of one
sentence that remains within the
paragraph, the colon should be used
to introduce longer quotations.

Do not use a dash with a colon.

Coloradan(s).

color-blind.

Columbia Broadcasting System is
the former name of CBS Inc. See
CBS.

Columbusite(s). The people of the
various Columbuses in the United
States.

combated, combating.

combined words are listed separately and alphabetically.

Comdr. John P. Manley, Commander
Manley, the commander.

comeback (n.).

Comecon for the Council for Mutual
Economic Assistance. Its members
are the Soviet Union, Poland, Czechoslovakia, East Germany, Hungary,
Rumania, Bulgaria, Cuba and Mon-
golia.

comedian (masc. or fem.), **comedienne** (fem.). *Comedian* may be
used in most references to a woman
entertainer, but *comedienne* may
sometimes be better. Also see
women.

Comédie Française.

come to a head. Avoid as trite.

comma. In general, do not use a
comma before *and* in a series unless the other elements of the series
are separated by semicolons: *Au-
tomobiles, buses and trains were
stalled. Jack Jones, the manager;
Jeff Stone, the coach; Dick Smith,
a player, and Harry Roberts, an
umpire, were arrested.* But use a
comma in sentences like this to
avoid confusion: *A martini is made
of gin and dry vermouth, and a
chilled glass is essential.*

Commas are also to be used in
compound sentences before *and,
but* and *for: They left early, and
their mother said they would ar-
rive before lunch. The track was
slow, but the betting was fast.
He was impatient, for his dismissal was due any day.* When the
clauses are exceptionally short,
however, the comma may be omitted: *Nero fiddled and Rome
burned.* Also: *The comma is small
but mighty.*

Use commas to set off a nonrestrictive clause: *The house, which
was 100 years old, was still in good
condition.* Do not use the comma
after an identifying noun used in
the restrictive sense: *The painter
Van Gogh had a hard struggle.*
The absence of commas in *His
brother George was best man*
means that the bridegroom has
more than one brother. If there is
only one brother, *George* should be
set off by commas. Thus a monoga-
mous society must be well supplied
with commas: *His wife, Nancy, was
not there.*

Between adjectives in a series
or a pair, use a comma if the adjectives are of equal significance—
that is, if they could sensibly
be connected by *and: a tired,
disillusioned politician; quick,*

easy solutions. But: *a gray iron cot; a wiry old carpenter.*

The comma may also be used to introduce a quotation: *He said, "I will be back."* For quotations of more than one sentence use the colon (which see). In attributing quoted matter, put the comma before the quotation mark: *"I am ready," he said.*

A comma may also introduce a paraphrase similar in form to a quotation but lacking quotation marks: *The question is, How high will prices rise? He said, Yes, he would accept the job.* But: *He said yes. She said no.*

In general, use the comma when giving figures in thousands *(1,250 miles, $12,416.22).* But do not use it in designations of years, street numbers, box numbers, room numbers or telephone numbers.

In financial matter, precise use of the comma is often needed to avoid confusion: *The stock advanced 3 points, to 21.* The comma makes it clear that the range of advance was not between 3 and 21, but from 18 upward.

Do not use a comma before an *of* indicating place or position: *George H. Brown of Brooklyn. President John P. Manley of Ghana.* In ages, heights, distances, times, etc., expressed in the following form, the comma is omitted: *4 years 9 months 21 days; 6 feet 3 inches tall; 2 hours 15 minutes 10 seconds.*

Commas are not used in names like these: *John P. Manley Jr.* (or *Sr.*), *John P. Manley 3d.*

Commas are used when constructions like this cannot be avoided: *the Salem, Ore., public schools; a Columbus, Ohio, newspaper.* (But *public schools of Salem, Ore.,* is preferred.) In proper names, use parentheses to indicate that what is enclosed is not part of the name:

The Columbus (Ohio) Citizen. See **parentheses and brackets.**

In dates giving the month and the year but not the day, the comma should not be used between month and year: *He said he left Boston in April 1975 and never returned.* But when the day is given, a comma is used between day and year, and a comma or some other punctuation mark must always be used after the year. A construction like this is not acceptable: *He said that May 5, 1969 was not a happy day for him.*

commander. See **Comdr.**

Commander in Chief. No hyphens. Capitalize in specific references to the President of the United States or to the highest officer of a country's army or armed forces. Lowercase in a reference to an officer so titled at the head of a lesser command: *Adm. John P. Manley, commander in chief of Pacific forces.*

commission. Capitalize only when part of a name. Do not abbreviate, even in headlines.

Commissioner, commissioner. Capitalize when referring to the head of a governmental agency: *Commissioner John P. Manley, the Commissioner.* This also applies to forms like *Police Commissioner.* But lowercase references to members of a commission such as the City Planning Commission: *a commissioner, the commissioner.*

commitment.

committee. Capitalize only when part of a name. Do not abbreviate, even in headlines. See **Congressional committees and subcommittees.**

Commodity Exchange. The one in New York.

common(-). common law (n.), common-law (adj.), commonplace,

44

common sense (n.), common-sense (adj.), commonweal, commonwealth.

Common Market. This unofficial designation for the European Economic Community may be used in first references, but the official name should be used at least once in every news story. In subsequent references, use *Common Market* rather than *E.E.C.* except in quoted matter and other special contexts. Also, *the market.* See **Nine.**

Commonwealth, the, formerly the British Commonwealth. It is a free association of sovereign states joined in recognizing the British sovereign as head of the Commonwealth, though not in all cases as the head of their states. The members are Australia, Bangladesh, Barbados, Botswana, Britain, Canada, Cyprus, Fiji, Gambia, Ghana, Guyana, India, Jamaica, Kenya, Lesotho, Malawi, Malaysia, Malta, Mauritius, New Zealand, Nigeria, Sierra Leone, Singapore, Sri Lanka, Swaziland, Tanzania, Tonga, Trinidad and Tobago, Uganda, Western Samoa and Zambia. Nauru is a special member, participating in certain activities but not in meetings of government heads.

Communications Satellite Corporation (Comsat).

communiqué.

Communism, communism. Capitalize when referring to the Communist Party movement and philosophy. Lowercase in a general sense: *The residents of Brook Farm sought to achieve communism.*

Communist. Capitalize as a noun for a member of the Communist Party and as an adjective referring to the party or its philosophy.

Communist China. Do not use as the name of the country, which is simply China. The full official name, *the People's Republic of China,* should be used only in texts or quoted matter. *Communist China* is acceptable only when making a special point—a contrast, for example—or in direct quotations.

Communist Party.

company (military). Capitalize only when part of a name: *Company A, Company H, Service Company, the company.* Do not use nicknames for companies (*Charlie Company,* for instance), except in quoted matter or feature contexts.

company and corporation names. In stories, always spell out *Company, Corporation, Industries, Brothers, Associates,* etc., when they are part of a name. The full name of the company should generally be used in first references. In the case of some major corporations, where common usage has made the name a household term (*General Motors, General Electric),* the terms *Company, Corporation,* etc., may be dropped on first reference but should be worked in later. When *Company* or *Corporation* is used with the full name, the name should normally be preceded by the article *the.*

Inc. or an equivalent foreign abbreviation (*Ltd., S.A., S.p.A., G.m.b.H., N.V.,* etc.) should not be used in the name of any company that has some other company term in its name (*Company, Corporation, Industries,* etc.). When it is used, *Inc.* or an equivalent foreign abbreviation should not be set off by commas *(Time Inc.).*

In headlines, the abbreviations

Bros., Co. and *Corp.* may be used in the names of firms, companies and corporations. In listings of companies in body type, the terms *Company, Corporation*, etc., may be dropped. If the company's name appears later on, the full name should then be used.

The ampersand *(&)* should be used in place of *and* only when the company's name is composed of personal names *(the Procter & Gamble Company)* or when the *and* appears directly before a company term *(J. P. Morgan & Company)*. Certain railroads are exceptions to this rule and are listed separately and alphabetically. When abbreviations are used in second references, an ampersand should generally be used in place of *and*, as in *A.T.&T., C.&O.*, etc.

In second references, points should be used in abbreviations when the initials stand for words *(I.B.M.* for the International Business Machines Corporation). If a company has changed its name to just initials, however, no points should be used *(the RCA Corporation)*. Where corporate acronyms are used in second references, they should in general be set caps and lowercase, not all uppercase *(Alcoa* for the Aluminum Company of America).

Contrived spellings in which letters are capitalized in the middle of company names should not be used unless the second portion of the name is a proper noun *(Pepsico*, not *PepsiCo; Teleprompter*, not *TelePrompTer;* but *the BankAmerica Corporation* or *the SmithKline Corporation)*.

The term *firm* applies to partnerships and should not normally be used for corporations. An exception to this rule is stockbrokerage houses, which are *member firms* of a stock exchange whether or not they are incorporated.

Company and corporation names, some of which are exceptions to these rules, are listed separately and alphabetically.

company officers. Do not capitalize titles: *He was elected president of the company. They complained to the treasurer, Joan P. Manley.*

compare. Use preposition *to* or *with.* In the sense of likening, use *to: He compared the quarterback's role to that of a company's vice president for operations.* Use *with* in the sense of examining for similarities or differences: *They compared Mrs. Jones's record as a forecaster with Mr. Smith's, and found Mrs. Jones's more accurate.*

compound words are listed separately and alphabetically. To avoid confusion, and sometimes absurdities, compound nouns that are usually solid words should be separated when the first part of the compound is modified by an adjective: *businessman, small-business man; sailmaker, racing-sail maker.*

The usefulness of the hyphen in forming compounds that serve as adjectives before nouns is demonstrated in the entries **ill-** and **well-**. An example: *He wore a well-tailored gray suit.* But the hyphen is omitted when the words follow the noun they modify: *The suit was well tailored.*

In cap-and-lowercase headlines, capitalize each of two actual words joined by a hyphen: *Governor-Elect, Cease-Fire, Sit-In.* Also: *Teen-Age, Teen-Ager.* But in combinations that include a prefix or a suffix that is not an actual word, capitalize only the first part: *Re-elect.* See **capitalization.**

comprise means to include or contain; the whole comprises the parts: *The system comprises 35 formerly independent rail and bus lines.* Not: *Thirty-five lines comprise the system.* And not *comprised of.* See **include.**

Comptroller should be used for a financial official of a government if that is the official title or the title includes that word. It is *comptroller* in the Federal Government (*Comptroller General* and *Comptroller of the Currency*) and in New York State and New York City (each has a comptroller). Capitalize in all references to a specific person (*Comptroller John P. Manley, the Comptroller*), but lowercase *the comptrollers.* For the financial officer of a business, use *controller.*

Comsat for the Communications Satellite Corporation.

concerto. Capitalize in a title: *Mozart's Piano Concerto in E flat (K. 271), Mozart's "Coronation" Concerto.* But: *the concerto.* Also: *concertos* (pl.), but *concerti grossi.*

Concorde, not *Concord,* the British-French supersonic airliner.

concrete. See **cement.**

Con Ed or **Con Edison** for the Consolidated Edison Company.

Confederate States of America, the official name of the Confederacy. See **Civil War.**

conference (sports). Capitalize in names: *Western Conference.* But: *the conference.*

Conference Board, the. A nonprofit, business-sponsored research organization.

confidant (n. masc.), **confidante** (n. fem.).

confrère.

Congo. Use, without a preceding *the,* instead of the full name, *the People's Republic of Congo.* The capital is Brazzaville. See **Congolese;** also **Zaire** and **Zairian(s).**

Congolese (sing. and pl.). The people of Congo (capital: Brazzaville). See **Zaire** and **Zairian(s).**

Congo River, not *the Zaire.* But when appropriate, stories can mention that Zaire, the country on one of its banks, calls the river the Zaire.

Congregational. This denominational name did not disappear when the Congregational Christian Churches joined in a merger forming the United Church of Christ (which see). The name *Congregational* is still used by many individual churches, and news stories may reflect that fact.

Congressional. Capitalize only when the reference is to the United States Congress.

Congressional committees and subcommittees. Capitalize committee names: *Ways and Means Committee, Appropriations Committee.* But: *the committee.* The word *subcommittee* is usually lowercase: *Foreign Affairs subcommittee, Appropriations subcommittee.* But capitalize if a subcommittee has a name of its own: *Senate Permanent Subcommittee on Investigations.*

Congressman, Congresswoman. These words are usually used to mean *member of the House* rather than *member of Congress.* Thus *Representative* or *member of the House* is more precise, and the style for all first references is *Representative Joan Manley.* But thereafter *the Congresswoman* or *the Congressman* is acceptable when the context is clear.

Conn. for Connecticut after cities and towns.

Connecticuter(s). For smoothness, it is preferable to say *citizen(s)* or *resident(s)* of Connecticut, or something similar.

conscience(-). conscienceless, conscience money, conscience-stricken.

-conscious. air-conscious, class-conscious, clothes-conscious, music-conscious, self-conscious (and: un-self-conscious), style-conscious, unconscious.

consensus, not *concensus.* Also, not the redundant *consensus of opinion* and not *general consensus.*

conservative. Capitalize as noun or adjective only if the reference is to a political party or movement with *Conservative* in its name or to a member of such a group.

Conservative Judaism.

Conservative Party.

consistory (religious).

Consolidated Edison Company (Con Ed or Con Edison).

Consolidated Rail Corporation (Conrail).

Constable John P. Manley, the constable.

Constitution. Capitalize when referring to the specific constitution of a nation or a state. But: *constitutional, unconstitutional.*

constitutional amendments. Capitalize amendments to the United States Constitution when referred to by their formal titles (which include the numbers): *Fifth Amendment, 15th Amendment.* But lowercase informal titles *(the income tax amendment)* unless such titles include words that are capitalized in their own right: *the Prohibition amendment.* See **acts, amendments, bills and laws.**

Consul (or **Consul General**) John P. Manley, Consul (or Consul General) Manley, the consul (or consul general).

consulate (or **consulate general**). Lowercase when standing alone. But: *the United States Consulate, the French Consulate General.*

Consultation on Church Union, the. An organization working for the merger of several major Protestant denominations in the United States.

Consumer Price Index, the price index, the index. Do not describe it as a cost-of-living index.

contact (v.). Although it has gained acceptance, it remains. graceless and has also achieved triteness. On those grounds, avoid it where possible.

container ship (freight), **container port.**

continent. Lowercase after a name: *African continent, North American continent, European continent,* etc. Capitalize *the Continent* and *Continental* only when Europe is meant.

Continental Air Lines.

Continental Divide (Rocky Mountain watershed), the divide.

Continental Oil Company (Conoco).

continental shelf, continental slope. Also: *outer continental shelf.*

continual (over and over again), **continuous** (unbroken).

48

contract bridge. Capitalize *North, East, South, West.* Lowercase *spades, hearts, diamonds, clubs* and *no-trump*, which is both singular and plural: *one no-trump, three no-trump.*

Also lowercase names of cards and spell them out when they appear singly: *ace, king, queen, jack, ten, nine, eight, seven, six, five, four, three* (never *trey*), *two* (or *deuce*). Use initials and numerals hyphenated, for two or more cards in combination: *He led into South's A-9* (not *ace-nine*). Use lowercase *x* as a symbol substituted for a numeral: *His holding in diamonds might have been K-x-x.*

Use numerals for all points above one in counting the value of a hand: *His hand was worth only 3 points. He had a 3-point hand. He had only one point.* Also use numerals for all match points or international match points except *one.* In scoring, use numerals for all points except fractions that are not combined with a whole number: *370 points, 379½ points, 2½ points, one-half point, half a point.*

In giving the distribution or division of a bridge hand or suit, always use numerals with hyphens: *He had a 5-3-3-2 hand. They hoped the suit would be divided 3-1.*

Mr. need not be used before the last names of men in second references. But *Mr.* should be used in news stories except in passages where actual play is being reported.

contractions. In ordinary news copy, spell out such expressions as *is not, has not, have not, do not, are not, will not*, etc. But contractions are acceptable in quoted matter, in feature contexts and in headlines.

contrast. Use preposition *to* (something opposite) or *with* (something different).

controlled, controlling.

controller. Use *controller* for the financial officer of a business. But use *comptroller* for a government official who has that official title. See **Comptroller.**

convict (v.). Use preposition *of*, not *for*.

convince, persuade. Convince should be followed by an *of* phrase or a *that* clause, but not by the infinitive *to*. *Persuade* may be followed by any of them.

cookbook, cookhouse.

cookie, cookies.

coolly.

co-op. But: *a cooperative.* In cap-and-lowercase headlines, it is *Co-op* (second *o* lowercase) when *Cooperative* won't fit.

Copper Age.

copter (helicopter).

Coptic Church of Egypt. The principal Christian church in Egypt. It has its own patriarch. See **Oriental Orthodoxy.**

copy(-). copybook, copycat, copy desk, copy editor, copyright, copywriter (advertising).

cord (vocal), **chord** (music, mathematics).

CORE for the Congress of Racial Equality.

co-respondent (in a divorce suit).

Corn Belt.

cornerstone.

Corp. Spell out *Corporation* in company and similar names in news stories. It may be abbreviated to *Corp.* in headlines and tabular matter when used with the name of a company. See **company and corporation names.**

corporal. See **Cpl.**

corporations. See **company and corporation names.**

corps (military). Capitalize only when part of a name: *Marine Corps* (which see), *Artillery Corps, Signal Corps, Women's Army Corps, the corps.* For numbered corps use Roman numerals: *X Corps.*

corralled.

corrections. The Times's policy in this respect is simple: Errors occurring in news articles in The Times should be promptly and forthrightly acknowledged, and corrections of them should appear at a reserved place in the paper so that readers will know where to find them.

If a correction requires more space than can be given to it in the reserved place, then the error should be noted there briefly and the reader should be referred, for example, to a *corrective article* appearing on another page.

See **fairness and impartiality** and **sources of news.**

correspondent. But: *co-respondent,* in a divorce suit.

Corsica. Use instead of *France* after Corsican cities and towns. See **datelines.**

cortege.

Cortes (Spanish legislative body).

cosmonaut. Do not use for *astronaut* except in quoted matter that was originally written or spoken in English.

Costa Line.

Cotton Belt.

Councilman, Councilwoman. Councilman John P. Manley, Councilwoman Joan Manley; Councilman Manley, Councilwoman Manley; the Councilman, the Councilwoman. But: *the councilmen, the councilwomen* (for capitalized plural exceptions, see **titles**). The same style applies to *Councilman* [or *Councilwoman*] *at Large.* For a group consisting of both men and women, *Council members* is the preferred description. See **women.**

Council of Churches of the City of New York.

Council of the Organization of American States, the Council.

councilor (a member of a council), **counselor** (one who gives counsel; also, an embassy official).

counter-. counteralliance, counterargument, counterattack, counterbalance, countercharge, counterclaim, counterclockwise, counterculture, counterintelligence, counterirritant, countermeasure, counteroffensive, counterpart, counterplot, counterproductive, counterproposal, counterrevolution, counterspy.

Countess Manley, Lady Manley, the Countess. In Britain, the title denotes the wife of an earl or the female equivalent of an earl; in other countries, the wife of a count or the female equivalent of a count. If the title is territorial: *the Countess of Manleyford, Lady Manleyford.*

countries. See **geographic names** and **pronouns for countries.**

country(-). country-bred, country club, countryman, countryside, countrywide.

county. Capitalize when part of a

name: *Kings County, Ulster County.* But: *the county, the county government.*

County Clerk Joan P. Manley, the County Clerk.

coup d'état. *Coup* alone often suffices, and is sometimes better.

couple (n.). In the sense of two associated persons, the word should be construed as a plural: *The couple were married in 1952. The couple separated in 1960. The couple argued constantly; in fact, they* [not *it*] *never let up.* An exception: *Each couple was asked to give $10.*

court cases. Their names should be set roman, without quotation marks, and "versus" should be abbreviated v. rather than vs.: Manley v. the City of New York. In other contexts, the abbreviation vs. should be used. In cap-and-lowercase headlines, lowercase the abbreviations. See **versus.**

courthouse. Exception: *United States Court House* at Foley Square.

Courtlandt Avenue (the Bronx).

court-martial, courts-martial.

Court of St. James's, St. James's Palace. The United States Ambassador to Britain may also be called the United States Ambassador to the Court of St. James's. The briefer style is to be used, except in instances in which the flavor of the formal version is desirable.

courtroom.

courts. Capitalize the names of courts: *Appellate Division, County Court, Court of Appeals, Court of Claims, Court of Criminal Jurisdiction, International Court of Justice (the World Court), Supreme Court, Surrogate's Court,* etc.

Second references to a court as such, but not to its judge or other presiding officer, are lowercased: *the court.* There are two exceptions. It is *the Court* in such references to the Supreme Court of the United States and to the International Court of Justice. Also capitalize *Court* in direct references to the judge or other presiding officer of any court: *The Court ruled that the witness was out of order. The Court—The witness will proceed.*

The following terms and similar ones are to be lowercased: *administrator, appellant, coroner's jury, executor, grand jury, master, receiver, referee in bankruptcy.*

In the Federal court system, the appellate courts below the Supreme Court are the United States Courts of Appeals. These are circuit courts and should be referred to as *the United States Court of Appeals for the Fifth Circuit,* not *the Fifth Circuit Court of Appeals.* Below these courts are the United States District Courts. They may be referred to as *United States District Court* or *Federal District Court.*

Note that in the New York State system, the Supreme Court is not the highest court. It is outranked by the Appellate Division of the State Supreme Court and (at the highest level) by the Court of Appeals. Any article about the Appellate Division must specify prominently which judicial department is concerned; for example, the First Judicial Department (or First Department) covers Manhattan and the Bronx.

See **Associate Justice, Chief Justice, Chief Judge, Judge, Justice, Magistrate, Supreme Court, World Court.**

couturier is to be used for both men

and women who are designers in haute couture. A couturière is a "little" dressmaker.

cover-up (n. and adj.), **cover up** (v.).

C.P.A. for certified public accountant.

CP Air, formerly Canadian Pacific Airlines, a subsidiary of Canadian Pacific Ltd.

Cpl. John P. Manley, Corporal Manley, the corporal.

CP Rail, formerly the Canadian Pacific Railway; a subsidiary of Canadian Pacific Ltd.

crab(-). crab apple, crabgrass, crab meat.

crack-. crackbrained, crackdown, crackpot, crackup (n.).

crèche.

credit lines. Datelined articles by reporters for The Times that appear in the daily paper, on page 1 or inside, carry the following centered credit line in 5-point Regal type above the dateline, with or without a byline:

Special to The New York Times

News agency dispatches and other non-Times dispatches that appear on page 1 also carry 5-point Regal credit lines above the dateline:

By The Associated Press
By United Press International
By Reuters
By Agence France-Presse
Dispatch of The Times, London
The Globe and Mail, Toronto
The Washington Star

Credit lines may also be used on undatelined news agency stories inside the paper. Datelined agency stories on inside pages carry the credits—(AP), (Reuters), (UPI), for example—in the dateline: DE-TROIT, Jan. 16 (AP)—etc. The parenthetical style of credit is also used on page 1 in matter that follows a three-em dash.

Picture credits are normally set in 5½-point Times Gothic bold, indented one em from the right to align with the edge of the photograph, in any of the following styles:

The New York Times
Associated Press
United Press International
The New York Times/Carolyn J. Manley
Associated Press/Lee Brown

Map and chart credits, typographically similar to picture credits, carry the date of publication:

The New York Times/Jan. 24, 1975
The New York Times/John P. Manley/Jan. 24, 1975

crepe de chine.

crepe(s) suzette.

cricket. Runs are given in figures, but spell out the number of wickets under 10: *They scored 7 runs for two wickets.* There is a difference between a draw and a tie. A tied match, extremely rare, is one in which each team has the same score at the conclusion of play. A draw is a match that has been abandoned or not completed to a decision. *Innings* is both singular and plural.

Criminal Courts Building.

cripple(s) (n.), **crippled** (adj.). Whenever possible, avoid these cruel words in referring to the permanently handicapped. In some cases the solution may lie not in the mere substitution of a word like *handicapped,* but in a rephrasing that conveys the meaning.

crisis, crises.

crisscross.

criterion, criteria.

criticize.

crocus, crocuses.

cross(-). crossbar (sports), cross-bill (law), cross-country, crosscurrent, cross-examination, cross-examine, cross-examiner, crossfire, cross hair(s), crossover (n.), cross-purpose, cross-question (n., v.), cross-reference (n., v.), crossroad, cross section, crosstown, crossway, crossword puzzle.

crow's-nest (nautical).

crystallize.

Cubism. The style of painting and sculpture, created by Picasso and Braque from 1907 onward, in which forms are broken into fragments of cubelike shapes arranged to convey a many-sided view of the motif. See **styles and schools in the arts.**

cul-de-sac(s).

Cultural Revolution. The one in China that began in the 1960's. Also, in quoted matter or unusually formal contexts: *the Great Proletarian Cultural Revolution.* But: *a new cultural revolution; a cultural revolution.*

-culture. counterculture, subculture.

Cunard Line (Cunard Steam-Ship Company).

CUNY, but in general only in quoted matter, for the City University of New York (which see).

cup. Eight fluid ounces.

cupful, cupfuls.

cups (sports). Capitalize names of trophies: *America's Cup, Davis Cup.* See **America's Cup.**

Curaçao.

cure-all.

curriculums, not *curricula.*

Custom House.

cutoff (n.).

cutter. A single-masted yacht with two or more headsails. The mast is a little farther aft than in the sloop (which see). The distinction between cutter and sloop has almost disappeared. The word *cutter* is also used to designate a small Coast Guard vessel that is both powered and armed.

cyclone. This term for a spiraling wind system is used in parts of the United States for a tornado and in the Indian Ocean region for a hurricane. Because of ambiguity, the term is best avoided. See **hurricanes** and **tornado.**

Cypriot(s). The people of Cyprus.

Czar, czar, czarist. These more familiar spellings are to be used in preference to the *tsar* form—an exception to The Times's usual system of transliteration. Capitalize the title in all references to a specific Russian ruler: *Czar Nicholas, the Czar.* Lowercase *czar(s)* when the reference in a Russian context is not specific. Also lowercase all non-Russian references such as *baseball czar, economic czar,* etc. But use such terms sparingly. Lowercase *czarist(s).*

Czechoslovak(s). The people of Czechoslovakia. The adjective is *Czechoslovak. Czech* and *Czechs* may be used as synonyms in headlines only. When relevant, in headlines and stories, the distinction between Czech and Slovak should be made. Do not use *Czechoslovakian(s).*

D

D.A. for District Attorney, but only in quoted matter.

dachshund(s).

Dacron (trademark).

Dada. An art movement that emerged simultaneously in Zurich and New York during World War I. It was marked by an attitude of extreme dissent from established ways of creating works of art and thinking about them. Members of this movement are called Dadaists. See **styles and schools in the arts.**

Dakota. *N. Dakota* and *S. Dakota* may be used in headlines when necessary to avoid the ambiguity of *Dakota* alone.

Dalles, The (Ore.).

Dalmatian (dog).

Dame Margot Fonteyn, Dame Margot. A dame who marries retains her title unless her husband holds a higher rank: *Dr. Roberto Arias and Dame Margot Fonteyn de Arias.*

damn it. The expression is two words, but like other profanity it should not be used at all unless there is a compelling reason. See **obscenity, vulgarity, profanity.**

dance. Capitalize in a title: *Schubert's German Dances,* "Dance of the Hours," "Danse Macabre." Also: *a Chopin waltz, Chopin's Waltz in A flat.* Similarly treat *bourrée, gavotte, gigue, hornpipe, minuet* and *sarabande.*

Dandie Dinmont terrier.

Danzig. Use *Gdansk,* the Polish version, rather than this German version, except in historical contexts.

D.A.R. for the Daughters of the American Revolution.

Dardanelles. It is *the Dardanelles,* not *Dardanelles Strait.*

dark-. dark-eyed, dark-haired, darkroom (photography), dark-skinned.

Dark Ages.

dash. The dash is often misused for the comma: *John—who was badly hurt last year—was pronounced fit today. His friends—Mr. and Mrs. Jones—were late.* But the dash is properly used when what follows is a series punctuated by commas: *The Administration will face many problems—unemployment, school segregation, declining revenue and rising Government costs—during the present session of Congress.* Here the dash is also needed to avoid confusion: *The costs—taxes and lawyers' fees—were higher than expected.*

Another use of the dash is to

mark an abrupt change in continuity of expression: *"The balance of payments is—but you know all that."* A sudden interruption in dialogue or Q. and A. matter should be marked by a two-em dash:

"Your Honor," she said, "please let me finish my——."
"Overruled!" the judge shot back.

But a quotation that trails off indecisively is treated differently. See **quotations.**

The dash may also precede *namely, viz., i.e.* and similar words or abbreviations. Do not use a dash together with a comma, a semicolon or a colon.

In datelines the dash is used after the date: SCRANTON, Pa., March 12—etc.

data (pl.), **datum** (sing., but rare).

date (v.). The preposition *from* is preferred over *to: The ruins date from 2000 B.C.* Exception: *date back to.*

date line (international). It is two words.

datelines. Cities and towns are set all caps, followed in many cases by the country, state, province or region in caps and lowercase. Datelined stories by reporters for The New York Times always carry a credit line in 5-point Regal type above the dateline. Stories from other sources also carry such a credit when they appear on page 1; if they appear on inside pages, the credit is included in the dateline (see **credit lines**). Following are some examples of datelines:

Special to The New York Times
LAGOS, Nigeria, March 22—

By The Associated Press
LAGOS, Nigeria, March 22—

SUGAR HILL, N.H., July 16 (UPI)—

PALERMO, Sicily, June 14 (AP)—

ABERDEEN, Scotland, Dec. 4 (Reuters)—

HOBART, Tasmania, Feb. 16 (UPI)—

TAIPEI, Taiwan, Oct. 10 (UPI)—

ST. GEORGE'S, Grenada, Nov. 7 (Reuters)—

When a dispatch is so current that the dateline bears the same date as the issue of The Times in which it appears, name the day of the week to alert the reader:

CINCINNATI, Friday, Sept. 18 (AP)—

In shipboard datelines, include a locating phrase (but not an imprecise one, like *at Sea*):

Special to The New York Times
ABOARD U.S.S. KEARSARGE, off South Korea, July 16—

Datelines of dispatches sent from the United Nations enclave in New York City should include *N.Y.:*

Special to The New York Times
UNITED NATIONS, N.Y., Dec. 17—

The Soviet Union is the only foreign country whose name is abbreviated (U.S.S.R.) in a dateline. The abbreviations of states of the United States and some other abbreviations that are to be used in datelines are listed separately and alphabetically. When the names of the city and the country are identical, as in the cases of Guatemala and Panama, use only one.

Some major United States and foreign cities and some widely known smaller cities in the United States do not require the identify-

56

ing state or country in the dateline.
Here is a list of such cities: •

UNITED STATES

ALBANY	MIAMI BEACH
ANCHORAGE	MILWAUKEE
ATLANTA	MINNEAPOLIS
ATLANTIC CITY	NASHVILLE
BALTIMORE	NEWARK
BOSTON	NEW HAVEN
BUFFALO	NEW ORLEANS
CHICAGO	OKLAHOMA CITY
CINCINNATI	OMAHA
CLEVELAND	PHILADELPHIA
COLORADO	PHOENIX
SPRINGS	PITTSBURGH
DALLAS	RENO
DENVER	RICHMOND
DES MOINES	ROCHESTER
DETROIT	SALT LAKE CITY
EL PASO	SAN ANTONIO
FORT WORTH	SAN DIEGO
HARTFORD	SAN FRANCISCO
HOLLYWOOD	SEATTLE
HONOLULU	ST. LOUIS
HOUSTON	ST. PAUL
INDIANAPOLIS	SYRACUSE
IOWA CITY	TRENTON
JERSEY CITY	WASHINGTON
LOS ANGELES	WHITE PLAINS
MEMPHIS	YONKERS
MIAMI	

FOREIGN

ALGIERS	MADRID
AMSTERDAM	MANILA
ATHENS	MEXICO CITY
BERN	MONTREAL
BONN	MOSCOW
BRASILIA	NANKING
BRUSSELS	NAPLES
BUDAPEST	NEW DELHI
BUENOS AIRES	OSLO
CAIRO	OTTAWA
CANTON	PANAMA
CAPE TOWN	PARIS
COPENHAGEN	PEKING
DUBLIN	PRAGUE
EAST BERLIN	QUEBEC
EDINBURGH	RIO DE JANEIRO
FLORENCE	ROME
FRANKFURT	SAN SALVADOR
GENEVA	SHANGHAI
GLASGOW	SINGAPORE
GUATEMALA	STOCKHOLM
HAGUE, THE	TEL AVIV
HAVANA	TOKYO
HONG KONG	TORONTO
JERUSALEM	TUNIS
JOHANNESBURG	VENICE
LENINGRAD	VIENNA
LISBON	WARSAW
LONDON	WEST BERLIN
LUXEMBOURG	ZURICH

datelines, integrity of. The integrity of datelines in The New York Times should be unassailable. The dateline on a bylined or "special" dispatch must be warranty that a staff reporter or stringer was present in the town or city or other place of origin (a military base, for example) on the date given and provided the bulk of the information, in writing or by phone to a staff member in New York.

If publication is delayed, the original date should be retained unless the reporter or stringer is still at the place of origin and can file an updated lead and any needed revisions. If the dispatch is delayed a week or more, and cannot be updated as indicated, the date should be dropped from the dateline. For example, a dispatch dated CHICAGO, Feb. 1— is publishable in the papers of Feb. 2 through Feb. 8. In the paper of Feb. 9 or later, it would be simply CHICAGO—.

Roundups should follow a rule of reason. If they are written in New York with information from a variety of sources, they should be undated and the sources should be indicated. A roundup on a Middle Western or national subject written by a reporter in Chicago would properly take a Chicago date; one that had nothing to do with Chicago but was written there by a reporter who just happened to be there should be undated.

Occasionally an article concerning an event in one city may be more effectively written from another, or undated. For example, if a Cabinet officer gives an important speech in St. Louis, or even in New York, it may be effectively covered by a specialist writing in Washington on the basis of material made available there. This would happen only when the specialist was unable to cover the speech in the city where it was given, and care should be taken to verify the giving of the speech.

If a dispatch is actually sent from a military base in the United States, use the name of the base (FORT BENNING, Ga., for example) in the dateline. If a dispatch is actually sent from a base that is not well known, include high in the story a locating phrase, sentence or paragraph. If a dispatch concerning a base is sent from a nearby town or city, explain high in the story its geographical relationship to the base.

datelines, unfamiliarity of. An obscure dateline should be explained high in the story. A deft phrase will usually do: *... in Indian towns like this one in northern Argentina.*

dates. Numerals are used for days of the month when they follow the name of the month: *April 1, 1975.* In the rare instances, usually in quoted matter, when the day precedes the month, use this form: *on the 6th of January.* See **dates, punctuation in,** and **months** and **years, decades, centuries.**

dates, punctuation in. In dates giving the month and the year but not the day, the comma should be omitted between month and year: *He said he left Boston in April 1969 and never returned.* But when the day is given, a comma is used between day and year, and a comma or some other punctuation mark must always be used after the year. This construction is not acceptable: *The importance of the June 23, 1972 tapes was soon apparent.* Also see **dates** and **months.**

day(-). daybed, daydream, day letter, daylight, daylong, day room, day student, daytime.

daylight time. Do not capitalize: *9 A.M., Eastern daylight time.* Abbreviation: *E.D.T.*

days. See **dates.**

D.D. for Doctor of Divinity, an honorary degree that does not justify the use of *the Rev. Dr.* or *Dr.* with names. See **Dr.**

D.D.S. for Doctor of Dental Surgery.

DDT for the insecticide. The full name, ludicrously long, need almost never be used.

de (the particle). See **personal names and nicknames.**

deacon. Deacons are members of one of the three orders of Christian ministry; the two other orders are bishops and priests or ministers. In nonliturgical churches, deacons usually oversee the charitable activities of a congregation, and the post does not require any special theological training. In liturgical churches, the diaconate is one of the stages through which a candidate for the priesthood passes on the way to ordination and it requires completion of a course of study. In the Roman Catholic and Episcopal Churches, there are also, respectively, "permanent" and "perpetual" deacons for whom the diaconate is a final and usually part-time and nonstipendiary position. These deacons are entitled to perform most of the functions of a priest, such as distributing holy communion, but may not consecrate the elements of bread and wine or baptize.

The Episcopal form of address is *the Rev. John P. Manley, deacon of, etc.* In subsequent references, it is *Mr., Mrs., Miss, Dr.* or *the deacon,* but not *Deacon Manley.* For deacons of the Roman Catholic Church and other churches, use the following form: *John P. Manley, a deacon of, etc.,* with subsequent references as in the Episcopal style.

deaf and dumb, deaf-mute. Avoid these phrases. They are not precise, and they have cruel overtones. There are other ways of saying that a person cannot hear and speak.

Dean, dean. In the Episcopal Church, it is the title for the dean of a cathedral or, in some instances, the head of a seminary: *the Very Rev. John P. Manley, Dean of the Cathedral of St. John the Divine; Dean Manley; the Dean.* But: *the deans* (for capitalized plural exceptions, see **titles**). Also: *John P. Manley, dean of Harvard College* (or *dean of students*); *Dean Manley, Professor Manley* or *Mr. Manley; the dean.* See **Archbishop, Bishop, deacon, Canon, Most Rev.** and **Rt. Rev.**

death(-). deathbed, death knell, death rate, death's-head, deathtrap, deathwatch.

debacle.

debentures. Debentures are interest-bearing corporation certificates that, unlike bonds, are not backed by physical assets of the corporation. If a bond issue goes into default, the holder has some claim to the property of the issuer. If a debenture goes into default, the holder has no such claim. See **bonds** and **notes.**

debris.

debut.

debutante.

Dec. for December before numerals: *Dec. 17.*

decades should almost always be given in numerals: *the 1970's, the mid-1970's.* For a guide to the use of other forms, including *70's* and *mid-70's,* see **years, decades, centuries.** Also, for special designations of decades: *Gay Nineties, Roaring Twenties.*

decimals. Use figures for all numbers that contain decimals: *3.4 inches of rain, 22.25 inches of snow.* If the figure is entirely a decimal, use a cipher before the point: *0.3* (exception: *.22-caliber rifle*). See **fractions** and **numbers.**

décolletage (n.), **décolleté** (adj.).

décor.

Decoration Day is now called Memorial Day.

deductible.

deep-, -deep. deep-rooted, deep-sea (adj.), deep-seated, deepwater (adj.). Also: ankle-deep, waist-deep.

Deepfreeze (trademark). In general references to this type of equipment, *food freezer, home freezer* or *freezer* should be used. Something shelved or put off indefinitely may be said to be in the *deep freeze.*

Deep South.

deerhound.

defect (n.). Use preposition *in* (for a defect in a thing), but *of* for a person's shortcoming, as: *A defect of perception led him astray.*

defense. Do not use as a verb, even in sports contexts.

defensible, not *defendable.*

degrees. See **academic degrees and titles;** also **angles** and **temperature.**

deity. Capitalize all appellations such as *God, Holy Ghost* (or *Holy Spirit), Son of Man, the Supreme Being* (but: *a supreme being*). In references to *God, Jesus* or *Allah,* capitalize personal pronouns such as *He, Him, His, Thee, Thou,*

Thine, but not the relative pronouns *who*, *whom*, etc.

déjeuner.

Del. for Delaware after cities and towns.

Delancey Street (in New York City).

Delawarean(s).

Delaware & Hudson Railway, the D.&H.; a subsidiary of Dereco Inc.

delegate (to an international organization). Lowercase and use the preposition *to: Joan Manley, United States delegate to the United Nations Trusteeship Council; Miss Manley; the delegate.* Also: *chief delegate.* See **representative.**

delegate at large. No hyphens.

Delta Air Lines.

Delta Line (a subsidiary of Delta Steamship Lines).

deluxe.

demagogy.

démarche.

demi-. demi-Christian, demigod, demimonde, demitasse.

Democratic national (or **state** or **county**) **chairman.** John P. Manley, Democratic national (or state or county) chairman; the national (or state or county) chairman; the chairman.

Democratic National (or **State** or **County**) **Committee,** the national (or state or county) committee, the committee.

Democratic National (or **State**) **Convention,** the national (or state) convention, the convention.

Democratic Party.

denouement.

Denver & Rio Grande Western Railroad, the Rio Grande; a subsidiary of Rio Grande Industries.

Denverite(s). The people of Denver.

department. Capitalize when part of the name of an agency of government—national, state or municipal: *State Department, Conservation Department, Police Department.* For most departments of the Federal Government the form *State Department* is preferred to *Department of State.* Do not capitalize *department* in the names of academic departments: *physics department, English department, political science department.* The abbreviation *(Dept.)* may be used in agate and other special matter, but not in news stories. It may also be used in headlines, but only in a proper name of a governmental department: *Justice Dept., State Dept., Conservation Dept., Police Dept., Fire Dept.,* etc.

Depression. Capitalize when the reference is to the one that began late in 1929 and continued through the 1930's. It is also called *the Great Depression.*

Dept. See **department.**

Deputy, deputy. Capitalize when part of a title preceding a name: *Deputy Prime Minister* [or *Deputy Sheriff*] *John P. Manley.* Do not capitalize in second references unless the position so titled is major: *the Deputy Attorney General, the Deputy Mayor, the Deputy Prime Minister, the Deputy Ambassador,* etc. But: *the deputy sheriff.* Capitalize in a specific reference to a member of a foreign parliament whose title is *Deputy.* In general, plurals standing alone are lowercased (for capitalized plural exceptions, see **titles**). Also see **assistant**.

Deputy Chief John P. Manley (police), Chief Manley, the chief. In the New York City police, never *Deputy Chief Inspector.*

Deputy Inspector John P. Manley (police), Inspector Manley, the inspector. Some police precinct commanders in New York City hold this rank.

Dereco Inc., parent company of the Delaware & Hudson Railway. Dereco is controlled in turn by the Norfolk & Western Railway.

de rigueur.

desiccate.

-designate. Vice President-designate, Senator-designate, etc. Before names and in second references, capitalize the title before the hyphen if the office is governmental and the reference specific: *Vice President-designate John P. Manley, the Vice President-designate.* In cap-and-lowercase headlines, *Designate* is also capitalized.

détente, a diplomatic term that is useful both in news stories and in headlines, will become diplomatic jargon unless *relaxation of tension* or *easing of strain* or some other equivalents are also frequently employed. See **rapprochement.**

Detroiter(s).

Deutsche mark in quoted matter or special contexts, but ordinarily use just *mark* or, when clarification is needed, *West German mark.*

Devil. Capitalize if Satan is meant, but lowercase *devils* and *a devil.*

devotee.

devout. Use with care, to avoid cliché writing. Applied unthinkingly, as in the overworked phrase *devout Catholic,* the label may offend some readers by implying that there is something extraordinary about strong religious convictions.

DEW for distant early warning, as in *DEW line.*

Dexedrine (trademark).

dialect. Unless a reporter has a sharp ear and accurate notes he would do well to avoid trying to render dialect. Misspellings of words that do not alter their pronunciations—*pleez, sez, attenshun, kum* —will get him nowhere; they will not suggest dialect. Other misspellings may approximate but not render exactly a manner of speech by a minority. For example: *"Les get this straight—bagels and lox the Oil of Sanvich dint invent."* Two or three of those spellings are not quite on target. In general, a safer and less obnoxious way to get dialect across is to rely on the choice of words and the oddities of construction. Thus, with no trace of snobbery or condescension, that sentence could be written, *"Let's get this straight—bagels and lox the Earl of Sandwich didn't invent."*

diarrhea.

Diaspora.

Dictaphone (trademark).

dictionaries. Do not quote their titles; capitalize principal words. See **spelling.**

die-hard (n. and adj.).

die of, not *die from.*

dieresis. See **accent marks.**

diesel.

Diet. See **legislative bodies.**

dietitian, not *dietician.*

different from, different than. You can't go wrong with *different from;* you can, and almost always will, with *different than.*

dilemma does not mean simply a problem; it involves a choice between two alternatives, both unattractive.

dilettante(s).

dimensions, measurements, weights and proportion. When they consist of two or more elements, or when a decimal is used, they should be rendered in figures, even those below 10: *2 by 4, 7 feet 3 inches by 10 feet 5 inches* (no commas), *5 feet 10 inches tall, 6 years 5 months 13 days* (age), *8 pounds 3 ounces, 5 parts gin 1 part vermouth, 2 to 1, 50-50, odds of 4 to 3, 8-to-1 shot.* Also: *2½ by 4, 15½-foot boat.*

When a single dimension or measurement below 10 is given, it should be spelled out, even when it contains an ordinary fraction: *three and a quarter miles long, six feet tall, eight-pound baby,* etc. But when the fraction is given in decimal form: *6.5-inch snowfall.*

Diners' Club.

diphtheria.

Director, director. In contexts involving the Federal Bureau of Investigation or the Central Intelligence Agency, capitalize when the reference is to a specific individual: *John P. Manley, Director of the Federal Bureau of Investigation; the Director; Mr. Manley.* In the case of the C.I.A., note that it is headed by the Director of Central Intelligence; his title does not include the word *agency.* In general,

lowercase plurals: *the directors* (for capitalized plural exceptions, see **titles**). Lowercase *director* in all references to company officials, board members, educational officials, etc.

Director General John P. (or Joan) Manley, Director General Manley, the Director General. This is style for a person holding a high post so titled in a national government or an international organization. No hyphens in this or similar titles, like *secretary general.*

DISC for Domestic International Sales Corporation.

discothèque.

discus throw.

disinterested, uninterested. *Disinterested* means unbiased or impartial; do not confuse it with *uninterested,* which means bored or indifferent.

disk, not *disc.*

district. Capitalize when part of a name: *Second Election District, 10th Assembly District, 17th Congressional District, District of Columbia,* etc. The abbreviation *(Dist.)* may be used in agate and other special matter, but not in stories or headlines. *District* standing alone is capitalized only when the District of Columbia is meant.

District Attorney John P. Manley, District Attorney Manley, the District Attorney, Mr. Manley. But: *a district attorney; district attorneys* (for capitalized plural exceptions, see **titles**). Also see **assistant** and **D.A.**

dived, not *dove.*

division (corporate or governmental). Lowercase: *Chevrolet division of the General Motors*

Corporation, antitrust division of the Justice Department.

division (military). Spell out numerical designations through the ninth and then use figures: *Fifth Division, 34th Division; the division.* In subsequent references, the name of an infantry division may be informally shortened by dropping the word *infantry: First Division* instead of *First Infantry Division.* But never *the First Infantry,* without *Division.*

Divisionism (art). See **Neo-Impressionism.**

divorcée should be avoided. It has scarcely any usefulness as a principal identification and it still bears traces of a "gay sinner" connotation that is offensive. If the fact of divorce is pertinent, it should appear at a place in the story reflecting its relative importance. *Divorcée* and *divorcé* can easily be avoided by saying that the woman or the man has been divorced or that a previous marriage ended in divorce. A woman's divorce should not be mentioned in contexts where a man's would not be. See **women.**

D.M.D. for Doctor of Dental Medicine.

Dnepropetrovsk (U.S.S.R.).

Dneprostroy (U.S.S.R.).

Dobbs Ferry (N.Y.).

Doberman pinscher.

dock (n.). It is not a pier or a wharf, but the water between piers or wharves.

dock(-). dock hand, dockmaster, dockside, dockyard.

doctor. See **Dr.**

doctorates (earned and honorary). See **Dr.**

dog days.

dogs and dog shows. The breeds are listed separately and alphabetically. The dog singled out for top honors in an all-breed show is named best in show or gains the best-in-show award, but does not *win* the show.

dollars and cents. Sums of dollars and cents are usually set in figures: *5 cents, 25 cents, $10, $12.25, $10,629.* But: *$1 million, $3.63 million, $895 million, $1.5 billion,* etc. Also: *$3 million to $6 million,* not *$3 to $6 million;* and *$300,000 to $1 million.* In the simple adjective form, do not use a hyphen: *$2.5 million lawsuit.* But hyphens must be used in a modifier like this: *a $10-to-11-billion increase.*

When it is desirable to leave sums in the millions or billions unrounded, they are expressed in the ordinary way: *$1,913,658* or *$5,937,600,823.*

Although the forms above should be followed in general, it is sometimes appropriate to spell out indefinite and round sums: *a million-dollar suit; a million and a half dollars; half a million; a hundred dollars, more or less,* etc.

With dollars and cents, the rule of spelling out below 10 does not apply: *4 cents, $4.* The cent symbol *(3c, 26c)* may be used in headlines, financial quotations and tabular matter, but *cent* or *cents* should be spelled out in news stories: *9 cents apiece, 26 cents a dozen, 1-cent tax.* But: *He said he would not give them one cent.*

All these guides apply to sums of money not only in stories but also in headlines. But in headlines it is usually better to round off an uneven sum that appears in the story *($1.9 Million,* rather than *$1,913,658)* unless the exactness of the sum is important. The dollar sign may be omitted if absolutely necessary to save a good headline that otherwise would not fit: *4.9-Billion Budget.* (Note the hyphen, which is used in the adjectival form when the dollar sign is omitted.)

See **pounds and pence** and **money.**

Dolley Madison, wife of James.

Dominican(s). The people of the Dominican Republic. Also, members of the religious order. Provided the context is clear, these forms can also be used for the people of the island of Dominica.

door(-). doorbell, door key, doorknob, doorman, doorstep.

Dostoyevsky, Fyodor.

Douay Bible (Roman Catholic). Also called the Douay Version.

double(-). double-barreled, double-breasted, double-cross (n., v.), double-dyed, double fault (n.), double-fault (v.), doubleheader, double-quick.

doughnut, not *donut.*

Dowager Marchioness of Bute, the Lady Bute, the Marchioness. A dowager peeress in Britain is the earliest surviving widow of a holder of the title. A succeeding widow uses her given name before the title: *Alice Marchioness of Bute, Lady Bute, the Marchioness.*

Dow Jones & Company. The company publishes The Wall Street Journal, Barron's National Business and Financial Weekly, and The National Observer, and operates the Dow Jones News Service. It also compiles the Dow Jones industrial average, the Dow Jones transportation average, the Dow Jones utility average and the Dow Jones compos-

ite average. In second references, the industrial average may be referred to as *the Dow average* (not *index*).

down-. downcast, downhearted, downhill, downstairs, downtown, downtrodden.

Down East. The northeastern part of the United States, especially Maine.

Down Under. Australia, New Zealand and environs.

Dr. should be reserved, with scarcely any exceptions, for those with earned doctorates: *Dr. Joan Manley, Dr. Manley, the doctor* (usually medical in such a case). Some people with earned doctorates, such as Ph.D. degrees, prefer not to use the title. If The Times is aware of a preference regarding earned doctorates, it should be honored. As indicated, *Dr.* should not be used if the person in question has only an honorary doctorate.

draft. Use instead of *draught* for a current of air.

draft beer.

draft horse.

draftsman(men).

draperies, not *drapes.*

drop-kick (n., v., adj.), **drop-kicking.**

drought, not *drouth.*

drunk as an adjective is used only predicatively: *He was drunk.* But not *a drunk driver;* make it *a drunken driver.*

drydock. But it may be two words in some proper names.

Dubliner(s).

Duchess of Bedford, the; the Duchess. Never *Lady.*

dueling, duelist.

due to is properly used in the sense of *caused by* or *resulting from* when *due* is an adjective modifying a noun: *His dismissal was due to that single escapade.* (The modified noun is *dismissal.*) But *due to* should not be used when there is no modified noun: *He was dismissed due to that single escapade.* In this instance, *because of* solves the problem.

Duke of Bedford, the; the Duke. Never *Lord.*

dumbfound, dumbfounded.

du Pont, duPont, Du Pont. The full, formal name of the company is *E. I. du Pont de Nemours & Company.* In subsequent references, *the Du Pont Company,* or just *Du Pont.* In any article that deals with the company only peripherally, the shorter forms may be used even on first reference. The trademark for its products is *Du Pont.* The company was founded by Eleuthère Irénée du Pont. Many of his descendants spell their name *duPont.* In either form, the particle *du* in the personal name should be lowercased except when it begins a sentence or a headline. See **personal names and nicknames.**

Dupont Circle (Washington).

Düsseldorf.

Dutch. Dutch door, Dutch elm disease, Dutch oven, Dutch treat, Dutch uncle.

Dutch, Dutchman(men) and **Dutchwoman(women)** for the people of the Netherlands. Also *Netherlander(s),* but never *Hollander(s).* The adjectives are *Dutch* and *Netherlands.*

Dutchess County.

Dutch Guiana is now Surinam.

Dynel (trademark).

E

each other, one another. Two persons look at *each other;* more than two look at *one another.*

Earl Manley, Lord Manley, the Earl.

Earl of Manleyford, the; Lord Manleyford; the Earl.

earth, moon, sun. Lowercase, except in the rare instances when they are referred to as astronomical bodies, usually in conjunction with other such bodies and without a *the* preceding: *How do Mars and Earth fit into that pattern?* The absence of *the,* of course, is not the test for capitalization, as *down to earth* and *move heaven and earth* demonstrate.

earthquakes. See **Mercalli scale** and **Richter scale.**

earth satellites. Do not quote their names; use Arabic numerals in designations: Gemini 4, Skylab 2, Sputnik 5, etc. Lowercase *s* in *a sputnik, the sputnik.* See **rockets.**

East, east. Capitalize when referring to that geographic region of the United States, to the Orient or to the Communist side in the ideological division of the world. Lowercase as a point of the compass.

East Bank, West Bank (of the Jordan River). Continue to capitalize as long as the terms have political significance. Do not hyphenate when used as modifiers in that sense.

East Berlin, West Berlin. Use *East Berlin* or *West Berlin* in datelines, not *Berlin* alone.

Eastchester, N.Y.; East Chester, N.Y. Eastchester is in Westchester County, East Chester in Orange.

East Coast, east coast. Capitalize when referring to the region of the United States lying along the shoreline of the Atlantic Ocean; lowercase when referring to the actual shoreline. Use *the Coast* for the West Coast only.

East End (London or Long Island).

Eastern, eastern. Capitalize when referring to the East (geographic region) of the United States, to the Orient or to the Communist side in the ideological division of the world. But: *eastern New York, eastern France, eastern half,* etc.

Eastern Air Lines.

Easterner. Capitalize when referring to a person who was born in the East (United States only) or lives there.

Eastern Hemisphere, the hemisphere.

Eastern Orthodoxy. A branch of Christianity that came into being after the Great Schism of 1054. It consists of 14 autocephalous (autonomous) churches, organized mostly along national lines, that define themselves theologically by their recognition of only the first seven ecumenical councils (from 325 to 787). Examples include the Russian Orthodox Church, the Greek Orthodox Church and the Rumanian Orthodox Church. Each church has its own patriarch. The Ecumenical Patriarch in Istanbul is the leader of Eastern Orthodoxy. He convenes councils, but otherwise his authority is that of "first among equals." In the United States there is no single Orthodox church. Rather, there are several dozen separate ethnic churches, such as the Orthodox Church in America and the Greek Orthodox Archdiocese of North and South America. The 10 largest cooperate through the Standing Conference of Canonical Bishops. Also see **Eastern Rite** and **Oriental Orthodoxy.**

Eastern Rite (Roman Catholicism). A group of 22 ethnic churches that accept the ecclesiastical authority of the Roman Pope but follow an Eastern liturgy. Most have patriarchs. They operate with considerable independence, but any major decision, such as a change in canon law, requires papal approval. Examples include the Ukrainian Catholic Church, the Syrian Catholic Church, the Greek Catholic Church and the Melkite Church. Also see **Eastern Orthodoxy** and **Oriental Orthodoxy.**

Eastern Seaboard. The region of the United States lying along the Atlantic coast. Also: *the Atlantic Seaboard.*

Eastern Shore (region on Chesapeake Bay).

Eastern standard (or **daylight**) **time** (E.S.T., E.D.T.). See **time.**

East Germany. Use both words, not *Germany* alone, after cities and towns when a locater is required.

East Hampton (L.I.).

East Side. Capitalize when regularly used to designate a section of a city.

easygoing.

éclat.

Economic Message. The President's.

ecstasy.

Ecuadorean(s). The people of Ecuador.

ecumenical council. See **First Vatican Council** and **Second Vatican Council.**

Ecumenical Patriarch. See **Eastern Orthodoxy.**

edition(s), issue. Do not use the words *issue* and *edition(s)* interchangeably in references to The Times or other newspapers. An *issue* means all the copies printed on a specific day. When that is meant, say *the Nov. 5 issue of,* not *the Nov. 5 edition of,* or simply *The New York Times of Nov. 5.* It is proper to say *first edition* (or *City Edition*), *last edition, early editions, late editions* (or *Late City Edition*) and the like in referring to a portion or portions of the issue of a specific day: *some editions of the Nov. 5 issue; some copies of the first edition of the Nov. 5 issue.*

editorial, news. In references to a newspaper, reserve *news* for the news department, its employees and news articles; reserve *editorial* for the department that prepares the editorial page, its employees and an article that appears on the editorial page.

editor in chief. No hyphens.

E.E.C. for the European Economic Community, but use the abbreviation only in quoted matter or other special contexts. Use *Common Market* in subsequent references in articles; also, *the market* and (provided the context is clear) *the Nine. Common Market* may also be used in a first reference if the official name appears elsewhere in the dispatch.

effect, affect. See **affect, effect.**

egg roll, egg rolling. The food and the frolic.

Eglin Air Force Base, Fla. Not *Elgin.*

Egypt, no longer *United Arab Republic.*

E. I. du Pont de Nemours & Company. See **du Pont, duPont, Du Pont.**

eighteen-hundreds, 1800's, 19th century. In almost all contexts, use the numerals rather than the spelled-out words for centuries. Also: *mid-1800's, mid-19th century.* See **years, decades, centuries.**

El Al Israel Airlines.

élan.

-elect. President-elect, Vice President-elect, Governor-elect, etc. Before names and in second references, capitalize the title before the hyphen if the office is governmental and the reference specific: *Senatorelect John P. Manley, the Senatorelect.* In cap-and-lowercase headlines, *Elect* is also capitalized.

Election Day.

election districts. See **district.**

Electoral College. But: *electoral vote(s).*

electrical, electronic. The words should not be used interchangeably. An ordinary light bulb or a motor is electrical. A radio receiver, a television set or a computer is electronic, which means that the flow of electrons through it is controlled by vacuum tubes, or by transistors or other solid-state devices.

electron-volt. A unit used, for example, to define the energy in accelerator beams. See **Mev** and **Gev.**

elite, elitism, elitist. No accents.

ellipsis. See **textual excerpts.**

El Pasoan(s). The people of El Paso.

El Salvador. This style for the country helps to distinguish it from its capital, San Salvador. *Salvadoran(s)* should be used for citizens of the country.

Elysée Palace. Not *the.*

Embankment, the (London).

embarrassment.

embassy. Lowercase when standing alone. But: *the United States Embassy, the French Embassy.*

emeritus. It should be *Dr. John P. Manley, professor emeritus* [or *emeritus professor*] *of political science,* not *professor of political science emeritus.*

emigrate, immigrate. *Emigrate* (with preposition *from*) refers to leaving a country. *Immigrate* (with preposition *to* or *into*) refers to arriving in a country.

émigré (masc. and fem.).

emir. See **Arab names and titles.**

emirates. See **United Arab Emirates.**

Emperor Hirohito, the Emperor.

Empire State (New York State nickname).

employee(s).

emporiums, not *emporia.*

empty-handed.

enamored. Use preposition *of* or *with.*

enclose, enclosure, not *inclose* or *inclosure.*

encyclopedias. Do not quote their titles; capitalize principal words.

ended, ending. Use *ended* for the past, *ending* for the future: *the period ended* [last] *Jan. 15, the period ending* [next] *June 15.*

endorse, not *indorse.*

Energy Research and Development Administration (ERDA). This agency and the Nuclear Regulatory Commission (N.R.C.) replaced the Atomic Energy Commission in 1975.

enforce. But: *reinforce.*

English, Englishman(men) and **Englishwoman(women)** for the people of England, but not for the people of the United Kingdom. See **British, Briton(s).**

English setter.

English springer spaniel.

enlisted men's ranks are listed separately and alphabetically, in full or by abbreviations. The proliferation of such ranks during and since World War II has produced some titles, however, that resist logical and even reasonably attractive abbreviation. Some of the officially sanctioned abbreviations are all right for military record keeping, but hardly suitable in the ordinary news story. This is one: *Rdm3c.* Make it *Radarman 3d Class John P. Manley.* In some cases it is best to put the title after the name *(John P. Manley, a hospital corpsman*

second class), where it will be less formidable.

enormity, enormousness. *Enormity* refers to horror or great wickedness; *enormousness* refers to size: *the enormity of the crime, the enormousness of the national debt.*

enroll, enrollment.

Ens. John P. Manley, Ensign Manley, the ensign.

ensure. Use *insure* instead.

entr'acte.

entree.

entrepôt.

entrust.

envelop (v.), **envelope** (n.).

E.P.A. for the Environmental Protection Agency (Federal).

épée.

Episcopal, episcopal. The uppercase version is the adjective to use in references to the Episcopal Church, its doctrine and other matters concerning it, and to people: *an Episcopal minister. Episcopalian* should be reserved as a noun for a communicant of that church. In its lowercase form, *episcopal* means merely concerning bishops, of bishops or governed by bishops, as in *episcopal rank,* etc. When that is meant, it is often best to avoid *episcopal* for clarity: *A meeting of bishops,* etc. See **Anglican Communion.**

Episcopal Church, rather than Protestant Episcopal Church, is the preferred title, although the longer version is technically correct and is sometimes used. In referring to local churches, use this style: *Trinity Episcopal Church.* Also: *an Epis-*

copal church, *Episcopal churches*.
See **Anglican Communion**.

Episcopalian(s) for members of the Episcopal Church.

equaled, equaling.

equally as. Do not use the words together; one suffices.

Equator. But lowercase *equatorial*.

Equitable Life Assurance Society.

equivalent (adj. and n.). Use preposition *to* or *in* after the adjective; after the noun, use *of*.

eras. See **ages and eras of history.**

ERDA for the Energy Research and Development Administration (which see).

Erie Lackawanna Railway.

Erivan, the Armenian capital, is now Yerevan.

Eskimo, Eskimos.

Esmark Inc., formerly Swift & Company.

ESP for extrasensory perception.

Establishment, establishment. Be careful about capitalizing this word, as in *the Establishment* (of one kind or another). For example, the owners of the professional football teams and their league organizations constitute a *football establishment,* lowercase. But if in determining policy the owners were to act in concert with others interested in the business of football and profiting from it, *the football Establishment* might be justified in references to that complex of interests. Care must be taken in such cases because the act of uppercasing can sometimes result in disparagement.

esthetic.

etc. for et cetera. It has its uses in certain special matter (as in this book), but in general contexts it is a lazy way out of not-very-difficult problems and is best avoided.

Ethiopian names. Typically, an Ethiopian bears a given name followed by his father's given name. Endalkachew Makonnen was Endalkachew, son of Makonnen, and thus Mr. Endalkachew in subsequent references. But the name Haile Selassie meant *Holy Trinity* and did not follow the usual form. Thus: *former Emperor Haile Selassie* in first references and *Haile Selassie* (in full again) or *the former Emperor* in subsequent references. *Selassie* alone sufficed in headlines.

Ethiopian Orthodox Church. The established church in Ethiopia. It has its own patriarch, whose title is Abuna, and it should not be described by the term Coptic, which applies only to the Coptic Church of Egypt. See **Oriental Orthodoxy.**

ethnic. Use the word only as an adjective *(ethnic group)*, not as a noun *(white ethnics)*.

ethnic background of an American in the news. National origin or ancestry of an American should be specified in a news article only when it is clearly pertinent: *A Japanese-American, the Senator was not permitted to serve in the Pacific during World War II, but he earned the Silver Star in Italy.* Never this: *the Senator said with an Irish twinkle,* etc. The rule of pertinence applies also to racial and religious identifications of persons figuring in the news. Also see **-American.**

Eton collar, Eton jacket.

étude.

eucharist is a synonym for *holy communion* (which see). The adjective is *eucharistic*.

Euratom for the European Atomic Energy Community.

Eurocurrency, Eurodollar, Euromark and similar coinages like *Petrodollar* should be used only when their meaning is clear and their appearance unremarkable.

European Economic Community. Use *Common Market* rather than *E.E.C.* in subsequent references. Also, provided the context has been clearly established, *the Nine. Common Market* may be used in first references if the official name is used elsewhere in the article.

European Free Trade Association. It is no longer the Outer Seven. Do not use the unfamiliar abbreviation E.F.T.A. except in quoted matter. Do not capitalize the *a* in *the association*.

European Payments Union, the union.

evangelical. A term for conservative Protestants that is preferred to *fundamentalist*, which sometimes has pejorative connotations.

Evangelist(s), evangelist. In lowercase, it is a term for a preacher who makes a profession of seeking conversions. When capitalized, singular or plural, it is used only in references to Matthew, Mark, Luke and John, the Evangelists who wrote the Gospels.

even(-). even break, evenhanded, even money (n.), even-money (adj.), even-steven.

evensong, eventide.

ever-. everbearing, ever-faithful, evergreen, everlasting, evermore, ever-present, ever-ready.

every-. everybody, everyday (adj.), everyone (pron.), everything (pron.), everywhere. But, in some instances: *every one*. See **everyone, every one.**

everyone, every one. It is a solid word as a pronoun used in the sense of every person or everybody. But it is two words in the sense of every or each one (modified noun) of a group named: *Every one of his predictions came true. Every one of the defendants was heard.* But: *Everyone was there.* Also note that *everyone* (like *everybody*) is singular in form: *He wanted everyone to be a New Yorker.* Not: *to be New Yorkers.*

evildoer.

ex-. The hyphen is used in this form: *ex-champion, ex-President, ex-tennis champion.* In stories, the adjective *former* is generally preferred, but *ex-* is almost always used in headlines. Do not hyphenate *ex officio*, even in adjectival form *(ex officio chairman)*, or such expressions as *ex cathedra, ex dividend, ex parte, ex post facto.*

exam may be used for *examination* when the reference is to an academic or similar test. It should not be used for other examinations, such as a physical examination.

excerpt. Use preposition *from*, not *of*.

excerpts from texts. See **textual excerpts.**

exchanges. The principal stock exchanges and commodity exchanges in the United States are listed separately and alphabetically.

exclamation mark. It is rarely needed in news stories. The exceptions include quoted exclamatory phrases, often but not always of unusual strength, followed by vigorous verbs of attribution: *"Hang him!" the crowd shouted. "That is a monstrous lie!" he roared. "Resign! Resign!" came the cry from the opposition.* Omission of the mark in such cases would vitiate the intended effect. Depending on context, the mark is also properly used, inside quotation marks or not, in instances like these: *"Oh, what a vicious thing to say!" "Ouch!" How unfair was history's verdict! How ridiculous to call him "a second Babe Ruth"!* But, to repeat, the mark is seldom needed in ordinary news writing.

execute, execution. *Execute* means, among other things, to put to death in accordance with a sentence legally imposed; thus it should be avoided as a synonym for *kill, slay, murder, assassinate,* etc.

executive branch (of the United States Government). Also: *legislative branch, judicial branch.*

Executive Mansion.

executive order (by a President of the United States). But capitalize when citing a number: *Executive Order 39.*

executrix. Do not use. *Executor* is correct for a woman. See **women.**

exhilarate.

Export-Import Bank, the bank. *Ex-Im Bank* may also be used in quoted matter, but its use in unquoted subsequent references and in headlines should in general be confined to the financial pages.

exposé (n.).

Expressionism (art). In painting, a style that emerged in Germany in the 1900's, characterized by emotional, unclassical, free brushwork, but generally used to depict a recognizable subject (as distinguished from Abstract Expressionism, which generally abjures the representational). See **styles and schools in the arts.**

Expressionism (literature). A movement that flourished mainly in Germany, roughly from 1910 to 1925. It emphasized inner reaction to experience rather than objective description of it. See **styles and schools in the arts.**

Expressionism (music). Music of the 1910's and 1920's, mainly in Germany and Austria, that was highly subjective and introspective and increasingly dissonant. See **styles and schools in the arts.**

Expressway, expressway. Capitalize in names: *Long Island Expressway.* But: *the expressway.*

extra-. extra-artistic, extracurricular, extra-fine, extrajudicial, extraordinary, extrasensory, extraterritorial.

Exxon Corporation, formerly the Standard Oil Company (New Jersey). While Exxon has dropped the use of the Esso trademark in the United States, it is still used overseas.

eyewitness. But in general *witness* is preferred.

F

F.A.A. for the Federal Aviation Administration.

facade. No accent.

facility. This overused term should be replaced whenever possible by a more specific substitute: *office, base* (military), *installation, pier, building,* etc.

fact-finding (adj.).

fade-. fadeaway (n.), fade-out (n.).

Fahrenheit. This is the temperature scale commonly used in the United States. In it, the freezing point of water is 32 degrees and the boiling point 212 degrees. In general, the scale is not specified in giving the temperature in ordinary contexts. (See **temperature.**) In the special cases that require mention of the scale, use the style *86 degrees Fahrenheit* or (usually in tables) *48°F* (no period after the *F*). Also see **Kelvin** and **centigrade, Celsius.**

Fair Lawn (N.J.).

fairness and impartiality should be the hallmark of all news articles and news analyses that appear in The Times. Obviously, accuracy is a chief element of fairness and impartiality. But accuracy is easily subverted. For instance, a number of facts, each accurate, can be juxtaposed and presented in a tendentious, unfair manner. Even simple, seemingly innocent words can be employed with the same resulting partiality. And even background information can be manipulated (most easily by its mere use or omission) to the detriment of fairness.

But avoiding pitfalls like those is not enough. It is of paramount importance that people or organizations accused, criticized or otherwise cast in a bad light have an opportunity to speak in their own defense. Thus it is imperative that the reporter make every effort to reach the accused or criticized person or persons, or organization, and supply the opportunity to reply. If it is not possible to do so, the article should say that the effort was made and explain why it did not succeed.

Special caution must be exercised when sources of news are anonymous. Except in extraordinary circumstances, such sources should not be permitted to use their anonymity as a base from which to launch attacks against other persons or against institutions. The rare exceptions may be made only after close and careful consultation between the reporter and the responsible editor.

See **corrections** and **sources of news.**

fall (autumn).

fallout (n.).

false titles. Do not make titles out of mere descriptions, as in *harpsichordist Joan Manley.* See **titles.**

Fannie Mae for the Federal National Mortgage Association. Its bonds are known as Fannie Maes.

fantasy (music). In titles in which the word appears without quotation marks, use the English spelling: *Schubert's Fantasy* [not *Fantasia*] *in C for Violin and Piano (Op. 159).*

F.A.O. for the Food and Agriculture Organization. Not *Agricultural.*

far-. faraway, farfetched, far-flung, far-off, far-out (but avoid in its slang contexts), far-reaching, farseeing, farsighted (all adj.).

Far East. It comprises Australia, Burma, Cambodia, China, Hong Kong, Indonesia, Japan, Laos, Malaysia, New Zealand, North Korea, the Philippines, Singapore, South Korea, Taiwan, Thailand and Vietnam.

farm(-). farm club (sports), farmhand, farmhouse, farm team, farmyard.

Far North.

Farrell Lines.

farther, further. Use *farther* for distance, *further* in the sense of additional or continued.

Far West (of the United States).

Fascism. Capitalize in historical references to the Italian Fascist movement and party.

Fascist(s). Capitalize as a noun designating members of the historical Fascist movement or party in Italy. Capitalize *Fascist* as an adjective in a similar sense. But: *The*

Senator said his rival was a fascist (or *had fascist tendencies*). See **neo-Fascism, neo-Fascist.**

Fatah. See **Al Fatah.**

Father (clerical title) may be used in second references to Roman Catholic priests and to some Episcopal clergymen: *the Rev. John P. Manley, Father Manley.*

Father's Day.

faultfinder.

Fauvism. An artistic term coined in 1905 to describe the exuberant, bright-colored paintings of Matisse and others. Often used, lowercased, when describing any painting style employing splashy bright color. See **styles and schools in the arts.**

faux pas.

F.B.I. for the Federal Bureau of Investigation.

F.C.C. for the Federal Communications Commission.

F.D.I.C. for the Federal Deposit Insurance Corporation.

F.E.A. for the Federal Energy Administration.

feast days are listed separately and alphabetically.

featherweight (n., adj.).

Feb. for February before numerals: *Feb. 12.*

Federal (architecture). A somewhat less austere style than Greek Revival, but essentially similar, with more ornament and thin, graceful columns. City Hall in New York is in the Federal style, as are some early Greenwich Village houses. See **styles and schools in the arts.**

Federal (governmental). Capitalize when part of a name or when used as an adjective synonymous with United States: *Federal Reserve Board, Federal Bureau of Investigation, Federal courts, Federal trocps, Federal agents.* The word can often be replaced with *national* to achieve consistent lowercasing in expressions like *city, state and Federal.*

Federal Bankruptcy Act. Chapters of the act should be set in Roman numerals (*Chapter XI,* etc.).

Federal Building.

Federal courts. See **courts.**

Federal Hall National Memorial. This building in New York City, at Wall and Nassau Streets, is the former Subtreasury Building—a fact that should usually be mentioned in stories concerning it.

Federal Home Loan Bank Board, the bank board, the board.

Federal Reserve Board. In subsequent references, *the Federal Reserve, the Reserve, the board, the Fed* (a form best restricted to the financial pages). Also, *the Federal Reserve System, the Federal Reserve Bank of New York* (or *Boston,* etc.), *the system, the bank.*

fellow (academic). *He is the John P. Manley Fellow. He is a fellow of the university.* Capitalize the formal title of a fellowship: *the John P. Manley Fellowship in History.*

fellow (adj.). Do not hyphenate: *fellow American, fellow citizen, fellow worker,* etc.

female (n. and adj.). In general, avoid the nouns *female* and *females* in referring to girls or women. But as an adjective, *female* does not have the disparaging ring that the noun often has. See **male** and **women.**

ferryboat.

ferule (ruler), **ferrule** (metal cap).

fete.

fewer, less. Use *fewer* in reference to a number of individual persons or things: *Fewer than 100 members voted for the proposal.* If the number is one, write *one vote fewer,* not *one fewer votes* or *one fewer vote.* Use *less* in reference to quantity: *Most shoppers are buying less sugar this year.* Also use *less* when, although a number is specified, it suggests rather a quantity or sum: *The police recovered less than $1,500.*

F.H.A. for the Federal Housing Administration.

fiancé, fiancée.

Fiberglas (trademark), **fiberglass.** Also: *glass fiber,* but *fiberglass* is better for the generic use.

Field Marshal Viscount Montgomery of Alamein, Viscount Montgomery, Lord Montgomery, Field Marshal Montgomery. It is never *Marshal* Montgomery.

FIFO for the first-in, first-out system of inventory accounting. Also, *LIFO* for last in, first out.

fifth column.

figures. See **numbers** and **numbers, round.**

Fijian(s). The people of Fiji.

filet mignon. But: *fillet of sole.*

Filipino(s). The people of the Philippines. The adjective is *Filipino* or *Philippine.*

Filipino names. Do not use accent marks, even in the Spanish-appearing names.

films. Quote their titles; capitalize principal words.

filmstrip.

Finn(s). The people of Finland. The adjective is *Finnish*.

fire (v.). In the sense of to dismiss or discharge from a position, this American colloquialism should be used only in informal or feature contexts, and then only if the dismissal is of a summary nature.

fire(-). firearms, firebomb (n. and v.), firebomber, firebombing, firebug, fire escape, fire extinguisher, firefighter, firehouse, fireproof, firetrap.

Fire Department, the department.

firm (n.) is a partnership, and thus not synonymous with *corporation*. See **company and corporation names.**

first(-). first aid (n.); first-aid (adj.); first base; first baseman; first-class (adj.); first come, first served; first floor (n.); first-floor (adj.); first grader; firsthand (adj., adv.); at first hand; first-rate (adj.).

First Lady. Capitalize when used in reference to the wife of a President of the United States or of a foreign country where the term is used, or the wife of the governor of a state. It is *Joan Manley, the First Lady,* never *First Lady Joan Manley.*

First Lieut. John P. (or Joan) Manley, Lieutenant Manley, the lieutenant.

first names, omitting of. Do not use the first name after the title in first references to the current President of the United States, the Vice President, the Governor of New York State, the Mayor of New York City and the Governor of New Jersey.

First names are to be used in first references to all other high-ranking officials in the United States—national, state or city—and to all such officials of foreign governments, as well as to the Secretary General of the United Nations.

First Sgt. John P. (or Joan) Manley, Sergeant Manley, the sergeant.

First Vatican Council. An assembly of the bishops of the Roman Catholic Church that was held in 1869-70. In second references, use *Vatican I.* Follow the same style for the Second Vatican Council, held in 1962-65. It is *Vatican II.*

Fishers Island.

fit. *Fitted* is the preferred past tense and past participle.

Five Years Meeting of Friends (Quakers).

fjord, not *fiord.*

Fla. for Florida after cities and towns.

flag-. flagpole, flagstaff. Also: flagship. But: American-flag ship.

Flagship Cruises.

flat-coated retriever.

flaunt, flout. To flaunt is to make an ostentatious or defiant display; to flout is to show contempt for.

fleet. Capitalize only when part of a title: *Atlantic Fleet, British Grand Fleet.* Also: *Sixth Fleet.*

Fleet Adm. John P. Manley (in the United States Navy), Fleet Admiral Manley, the admiral. See **Admiral of the Fleet,** which is a British rank.

fleur(s)-de-lis.

flier (an airman, a crack train or a widely distributed leaflet).

Flight Lieut. John P. Manley (British), Flight Lieutenant Manley, the flight lieutenant.

floor leader. Do not use as a capitalized title preceding a name. Make it *Representative John P. Manley, the Democratic floor leader,* or *the floor leader, John P. Manley,* or something similar.

Florida East Coast Railway.

Floridian(s).

flounder, founder. To flounder is to stumble or flail awkwardly; to founder is to sink or collapse.

flout. See **flaunt, flout.**

Floyd Bennett Field.

Flushing Meadows, not *Meadow.* Also: Flushing Meadows-Corona Park.

Flying Tiger Line, a subsidiary of Tiger International Inc.

f.o.b. for free on board.

focused.

-fold. With this suffix, spell out any numeral that can be written as a single and unhyphenated word: *twofold, threefold, twentyfold, hundredfold, thousandfold, millionfold.* When the numeral cannot be so written as a word, use figures followed by a hyphen: *22-fold, 106-fold, 200-fold, 3,000-fold.* Any numeral above nine may be used in a headline: *10-fold, 100-fold,* etc. Also: *manifold, manyfold.*

folk(-). folk dance (n.), folk-dance (adj.), folklore, folk music, folk-rock (music), folk singer, folk song.

follow-. follow-through (n.), follow-up (n. and adj.).

Food and Agriculture Organization (F.A.O.), not *Agricultural.*

fool-. foolhardy, foolproof, foolscap.

foot(-). foothill, footloose, footman,

footpad, footpath, foot-pound, footprint, foot race, footstep, footwear, footwork.

football. Points and scores are given in figures: *He scored 9 points in the second quarter. Columbia won, 13 to 6* (or *13-6*). Yards are also given in figures: *He gained 3 yards. He passed 21 yards, to the 8-yard line.* Spell out numbers of touchdowns and downs below 10. *He scored two touchdowns, making a total of 13 for the season. It was a first down.*

Do not capitalize the *all* in *all-America* [no *n*] *player, all-America team, all-East tackle,* etc. But: *He was an all-American at Yale.*

Avoid *fracas, fray, grid, gridder, win* (as a noun), *pigskin* and similar worn-out terms.

forbear (avoid, shun), **forebear** (ancestor).

forbid. Use preposition *to.* But after *prohibit,* use *from.*

fore-. forebear (ancestor), forefather, forefront, foreknowledge, foremast, forestall, foretaste, foretopmast, foretopsail, forewarn.

Foreign Legion, the legion.

Foreign Minister (or Secretary) John P. Manley, the Foreign Minister or Foreign Secretary, the Minister or the Secretary. But: *a foreign minister, foreign secretaries* (for capitalized plural exceptions, see **titles**).

Foreign Ministry. Capitalize in specific references. In subsequent references, *the ministry.*

Foreign Service. Capitalize when referring to the career diplomatic service of the United States; otherwise lowercase: *She was formerly general director of the Foreign*

Service. He was in the British foreign service.

foreign words. See **accent marks.**

foreman, foremen. Use for both men and women. Do not use *forelady* or *forewoman* or *foreperson.* See **women.**

forgo (to refrain from).

former. In news stories *former*, as in *former President*, is generally preferred to *ex-*, but *ex-* is almost always used in headlines.

Formica (trademark).

formulas, not *formulae.*

forswear.

fort. Spell out and capitalize in ordinary reading matter when part of a name: *Fort Hamilton.* The abbreviation *(Ft.)* may be used with the name in headlines and in agate and other special matter. Also see **datelines, integrity of.**

Fort-Archambault, a city in Chad, has been renamed Sarh.

Fort Du Pont (in Delaware).

Fort-Lamy, the capital of Chad, has been renamed Ndjamena.

fortnight. In American news writing, the expression *two weeks* is preferred.

forward, not *forwards.*

founder, flounder. To founder is to sink or collapse; to flounder is to stumble or flail awkwardly.

Fourth Estate. Capitalize when the reference is to the public press.

Fourth of July.

fowl (sing. and pl.).

foxhound.

F.P.C. for the Federal Power Commission.

fractions. When a fraction appears by itself in ordinary matter, it should be rendered in these spelling styles: *one-half inch* (not *½ inch*), *one-half an inch, half an inch, two-tenths, one-twentieth, one twenty-first, one-thirtieth, one thirty-second, 21 thirty-seconds, one-hundredth, two-hundredths, two one-hundredths, 20 one-hundredths, twenty-hundredths, 21-hundredths, one-103d, twenty-five 103ds, nine-thousandths, nine one-thousandths, nine-1,009ths, 63 one-thousandths.*

Note that in these examples the numerator and the denominator are connected by a hyphen when neither of them contains a hyphen: *one-twentieth.* But it is *one twenty-third* when one of those elements does contain a hyphen. Note also that numerals are used to render fractions like *103d*, which would be too cumbersome if spelled out. Finally, note that the first element in *twenty-five 103ds* is spelled out to avoid a confusing pileup of numerals.

Use numerals wherever the fraction appears with a full number in ages, pairs of dimensions, etc.: *3½-year-old, 3½ by 2½* (or *3.5 by 2.5*). In other cases, follow the rule for spelling out below 10: *He reigned for six and a half* [smoother in this case than *one-half*] *years. His reign lasted 31½ years.* See **decimals** and **numbers.**

frame-up (n.).

Franco-. Avoid, in adjectival references to France. Use *French-American, French-German,* etc.

François.

francophone. The word is French, meaning French-speaking. In general, use the English version instead.

francs and centimes. Spell out when the figures are given: *5 francs, 15 million francs, 15 centimes.* See **numbers, round.**

Frankfurt (Germany).

Franklin D. Roosevelt Drive, not *East River Drive.* In headlines: *F.D.R. Drive.*

fraternal societies. Capitalize their names: *Knights of Columbus, Masons, Odd Fellows,* etc. Also capitalize the titles of their officers: *Grand Ruler, Exalted Ruler, Sachem,* etc.

Frau, Fräulein. See **Mr., Mrs. and Miss.**

Fraunces Tavern.

freakish (adj.), not *freak.*

free(-). freebooter, free fall, free-form (adj.), free hand (n.), freehand (adj.), freehanded (adj.), freelance (n., v., adj.), freelancer, freeload (v.), freeloader, freeloading (n. and adj.), free port, free-spoken, freestanding, freestyle (swimming; n. and adj.), freethinker, freethinking (n. and adj.), free throw (basketball), free trade, freeway, freewheel (v.), freewheeler, freewheeling (n. and adj.), free will (n.), freewill (adj.).

free world. Use only in quoted matter or in special contexts where it is clear that we are aware of the editorial nature of the phrase. Usually a specific geographic or political description should be substituted for accuracy.

French, Frenchman(men) and **Frenchwoman(women).**

French bulldog.

French Canadian(s). Without a hyphen. But: *Italian-American(s), Japanese-American(s),* etc.

french cuff.

french door.

french-fried potatoes, french fries.

French Line (Compagnie Générale Transatlantique).

French Somaliland is now the Territory of Afars and Issas (which see).

frère.

freshman (class and member of that class).

Friends, Society of. See **Quakers.**

Friends General Conference. See **Quakers.**

Friends United Meeting. See **Quakers.**

frightened. Use preposition *at* or *by.*

Frigidaire (trademark).

Frisbee (trademark).

F.T.C. for the Federal Trade Commission.

Führer.

Fujiyama or **Mount Fuji,** not *Mount Fujiyama.*

fulfill.

fullback.

full time (n. and adv.), **full-time** (adj.).

fund (v.), **funded, funding.** As a verb, *fund* is useful in a number of special financial contexts; it means, for example, to set aside capital to earn interest. But in general contexts *(The state funded the research),* it is bureaucratic jargon; make it *financed* or *paid for.*

fundamentalist. As a religious designation, this word should be used with care because it can have a pejorative connotation suggesting a closed mentality rather than a theological position. An appropriate alternative in references to conservative Protestants is often *evangelical.*

funeral director may be used interchangeably with *undertaker.* Do not use *mortician.*

furor.

further. See **farther, further.**

fused participles. They should be defused. For example: *The police tried to prevent him jumping* should be changed to *prevent him from jumping* or *prevent his jumping.*

fusillade.

G

Ga. for Georgia after cities and towns.

Gabonese (sing. and pl.). The people of Gabon.

gaiety, gaily.

gale. Use only if the wind meets the National Weather Service's specifications for a gale—38 to 55 miles an hour. See **hurricanes** and **storm.**

gallon. A unit of volume equal to four quarts. A United States standard gallon is roughly 3.8 liters (231 cubic inches). A British imperial gallon is roughly 4.5 liters (277.42 cubic inches). See **ounce** and **pint** and **quart.**

Gambia, not *the Gambia* and not *The Gambia.* The capital is Banjul, formerly Bathurst.

Gambian(s). The people of Gambia.

gamma rays. Like X-rays, gamma rays lie at the shortwave end of the electromagnetic spectrum. Strictly speaking, they differ from X-rays (which see) only in being generated by atomic nuclei rather than by high-energy electrons.

gamut. You can run a *gamut* (a scale of notes or any complete range or extent) or a *gantlet* (a flogging ordeal) literally or figuratively.

gamy.

gangway.

gantlet is a flogging ordeal; *gauntlet* is a glove.

garçon.

garnish, garnishee. Both are correctly used as verbs in the sense of legal attachment of property or wages to satisfy a debt. But *garnishee* is more commonly used (despite objections by lawyers), perhaps because the principal meaning of *garnish* is to adorn or decorate, usually food, with improvement often implied. As a noun, *garnishee* is the object of a legal *garnishment.*

gas. When used to mean gasoline, quote it only if the context does not make clear that gasoline is meant. In headlines, *filling station* will often be useful.

gasification, gasify. But: *liquefaction, liquefy.*

GATT for the General Agreement on Tariffs and Trade.

Gatwick Airport (at Crawley, near London).

gauge.

gauntlet is a glove; *gantlet* is a flogging ordeal.

gay. Do not use as a synonym for *homosexual* unless it appears in the formal, capitalized name of an organization or in quoted matter.

83

gazetteers. Do not quote their titles; capitalize principal words. See **geographic names.**

Gdansk, not *Danzig.* The Polish names rather than the German are used in similar cases, except in historical references.

Gdynia America Line.

G.E. for the General Electric Company.

gefilte fish.

gelatin, not *gelatine.*

Gen. John P. Manley, General Manley, the general.

General Assembly (United Nations), the Assembly.

General Electric Company (G.E.).

Generalissimo John P. Manley, General Manley, the generalissimo or the general.

General Motors Corporation (G.M.).

General of the Army John P. Manley, General Manley, the general.

General Staff. The French General Staff, the General Staff, a general staff. Capitalize only when the reference is to the headquarters organization at the top of a country's armed forces or army. The general staff of a subordinate command, such as a brigade, a division, a corps or a field army, is lowercased.

General Telephone and Electronics Corporation (G.T.E.).

Genevan(s). The people of Geneva, Switzerland, and its namesakes.

genoa (sail), **genoa jib.**

gentleman should not be used as a synonym for *man* in most instances, just as *lady* should usually not be used for *woman.*

genus and species. A biological species is a group of individuals capable of interbreeding and producing fertile offspring. The name of a species is always preceded by the name of the genus, or larger category, of which it is a subdivision. Only the genus name is capitalized: Homo sapiens.

In second references, names may in some contexts be abbreviated: E. coli for Escherichia coli. If a subspecies name is used, it must be accompanied by genus and species names: Homo sapiens neanderthalensis.

The more comprehensive taxonomic classifications of plants and animals are, in ascending order, family, order, class, phylum and kingdom. Capitalize the names of all such classifications except kingdom: the phylum Protozoa. But nouns and adjectives derived from such classifications are not capitalized: protozoan (n. and adj.).

geographic names. For easy reference, some place names are listed separately and alphabetically. In general, with the major exceptions noted in the next three paragraphs, the authority for the spelling of geographic names is the Columbia Lippincott Gazetteer of the World.

Though the gazetteer spells out *Saint* and *Sainte,* they should usually be abbreviated *St.* and *Ste.* when they occur in place names.

Place names in Laos, Thailand and Vietnam are to be spelled according to the current Official Standard Names Gazetteers of the United States Board on Geographic Names, but with the accent marks omitted. Where the board's gazetteers recognize a "conventional form" of a name, in addition to the form in the local language, use the "conventional form." For example: Saigon, not Sai Gon; Vientiane, not Viangchan; Plain of Jars, not Thong Haihin; Red River, not Song Hong.

Place-name spellings in Cambodia follow the Official Standard Names Gazetteer of the United States Board on Geographic Names, edition of August 1963. The board's second edition for Cambodia, published in 1971, may be used as a geographic reference but does not govern the spelling of place names.

Georgian(s).

Georgian (architecture). A more precise name for what is generally called colonial: a simple, straightforward style, usually of brick. The term technically refers to the era that began with the reign of King George I; it should be modified in a reference to a recent Georgian building, like the Harvard Club in New York. See **styles and schools in the arts.**

German(s), East German(s), West German(s) for citizens of the two countries. Often *German(s)* alone will suffice.

Germany. Use by itself only when there can be no misunderstanding. Use *East Germany* and *West Germany* after cities and towns when a locater is required.

Germanys. This, not German*ies*, is the proper plural for Germany. See **plurals of proper names.**

getaway (n.).

Gev (sing. and pl.). A Gev is one billion electron-volts. It derives from the European term *giga-electron-volts* (the prefix *giga-* means one billion). *Gev* replaces the former abbreviation *Bev*. For one million electron-volts the abbreviation is *Mev*.

Ghanaian(s). The people of Ghana.

ghetto(s). Do not overuse in its newer, nonhistorical sense in referring to the areas of cities inhabited by minorities or the poor. That usage has become established, but it is not required, or justified, in every instance. In most cases, *section, district, slum, area, quarter* will suffice, and sometimes a place name alone will have connotations that make it best.

G.I. for general issue, Government issue and soldiers (plural: *G.I.'s;* avoid the plural possessive, *G.I.'s'*). A marine or a Navy man is not a G.I.

gibe (taunt). Do not confuse with *jibe*, which means to accord or (nautically) to shift.

G.I. Bill of Rights. In second references, *the G.I. Bill* or some general description of it. But not *the bill.*

Gibraltar, Strait of.

Gibraltarian(s). The people of Gibraltar.

gigaton, gigatonnage. A gigaton is a unit used to measure the power of nuclear explosions. It is equal to the explosive force of a billion tons of TNT. See **kiloton** and **megaton.**

gilt-edge.

Gimbels. This form (no apostrophe) may be used in references to the New York store. When *Gimbel Brothers* is used, always spell out *Brothers.* The parent company is *Gimbel Brothers Inc.*

Ginnie Mae for the Government National Mortgage Association.

girl. Do not use in references to a woman or a young woman; in that sense, it is usually offensive. Also, do not call a *saleswoman* a *salesgirl.* And *college student* is preferable to *college girl.* See **women.**

girlfriend. Avoid whenever possible. See **boyfriend, girlfriend.**

Girl Scout, a Scout, the Scouts.

give-away (n.).

gladiolus (sing. and pl.).

glamour, glamorous.

Glaswegian(s). The people of Glasgow.

Glens Falls (N.Y.).

G.M. for the General Motors Corporation.

G.N.P. for the gross national product.

goal(-). goalkeeper, goal line, goal mouth, goal post.

gobbledygook.

go-between (n.).

God (Supreme Being). Also capitalize *He, Him, His, Thee, Thou* when the reference is to God, Jesus, the Holy Ghost (or the Holy Spirit) or Allah. But do not capitalize *who, whom,* etc.

god-. godfather, godless, godlike, godmother, godsend, godson, godspeed.

goddamn, goddamned, goddamn it. The expressions are lowercased, but like other profanity they should not be used at all unless there is a compelling reason. See **obscenity, vulgarity, profanity.**

-goer. churchgoer, moviegoer, operagoer, playgoer, theatergoer.

Golan Heights, the heights.

golden retriever.

golf. Spell out the number of holes, tees and strokes below 10: *He took six strokes on the ninth hole* [or *hole 9*]. *He fell behind on the 10th*

hole. But: *He shot a 6.* Also: *72-hole tournament, 2-foot putt, 95 yards, par 4, par-4 hole, two-over-par 6, on the green in 2.* The totals of out and in play are set thus: *36,36-72.* Handicap totals: *83-10-73.*

Competition is held at medal play (lowest score wins) and match play (direct elimination). Some tournaments combine the two, with qualifying medal play preceding match play.

Do not capitalize *open* or *amateur* in names of tournaments, except the United States Open, United States Amateur, British Open and British Amateur.

Birdie, bogey and *par* have attained respectability as verbs.

goodbye, goodbyes.

good day (greeting or farewell).

Good Friday.

good morning (greeting or farewell).

good night (farewell).

good will, ill will. Hyphenate when using as adjectives.

G.O.P. may be used as a synonym for the Republican Party in headlines and direct quotations, but in stories it should be used only to achieve a special (Grand Old Party) effect.

Gospel(s), gospel. Capitalize when referring to one or more of the four books of the Bible so named, or when the word is used in the sense of the Christian message: *He preached the Gospel.* Lowercase in other references: *She is a famous, gospel singer. He swore he was telling the gospel truth.*

got. There seems to be no good reason for using *gotten.*

Gothic, gothic. Capitalize in references to the Goths, the medieval period, the style of architecture and the style of literature, but not in references to printing: *gothic type*. See **Gothic architecture** and **Gothic novel.**

Gothic architecture. The great church style of the pointed arch, the flying buttress and high walls. The term should be used only in reference to architecture of the Middle Ages; St. Patrick's Cathedral and Trinity Church on Wall Street are more properly neo-Gothic. See **styles and schools in the arts.**

Gothic novel. Fiction characterized by horror, fearsome happenings and supernatural occurrences, generally in a gloomy and macabre setting.

Götterdämmerung.

Gov. John P. Manley (of a state), Governor Manley, the Governor. For the Governors of New York and New Jersey, omit first names in first references: *Governor Manley*. Lowercase *a governor* and, usually, *the governors* (for capitalized plural exceptions, see **titles**).

Government, government. Capitalize when referring to a specific national government: *the United States Government, the Pakistani Government*. Also capitalize in a subsequent reference to a specific national government: *The Government cut taxes. The Government's bill differed from the opposition's*. The adjectival form is similarly capitalized: *Government bonds, Government bureaus*. Capitalize the plural if it refers to a small number of national governments specifically identified in the story: *the Chinese and Soviet Governments, the two Governments*. Otherwise: *governments, the NATO govern-*

ments, the European governments, a government, forming a new government.

Lowercase state, provincial and municipal governments: *the city government*, etc. Also lowercase in a general sense: *the principles of government, honesty in government.*

governmental. Lowercase unless it is part of a name.

governmental procedures. When they are a significant element in a news article, they should always be explained to the point of answering the question that naturally arises: What happens now? This is especially true in respect to the steps that must be taken before legislation becomes law. It is also important to report just what is expected in the next stage of the procedure.

Governor-elect John P. Manley, Governor-elect Manley, the Governor-elect (of a state). But in cap-and-lowercase headlines, capitalize: *Gov.-Elect Manley.*

Governor(s) General. Capitalized, unabbreviated and unhyphenated in specific references to the British sovereign's representatives in Canada and elsewhere.

Governors Island.

Gov. Thomas E. Dewey Thruway (formerly the New York State Thruway). In subsequent references: *the Thruway*. The road is operated by the New York State Thruway Authority.

grader. Do not hyphenate *first grader, sixth grader, 10th grader*, etc., in references to members of a specified school grade. But: *third-grade pupil.*

graduate (v.). A person may either *graduate from* or *be graduated* *from*. But revoke the diploma if he writes like this: *John graduated high school. They graduated college in the same year.*

graffiti (pl.), **graffito** (sing.). Graffiti are simply letters, words, slogans, drawings or the like inscribed (most often crudely) on a wall or other surface in public view. The words are not synonyms for works of art.

gram. The basic metric unit of weight, it is roughly the weight of one cubic centimeter of distilled water. It is equal to about one twenty-eighth of an ounce. See **metric system.**

Grand Central Terminal.

grande dame.

grandmaster (chess).

grandmother. Use this description only when appropriate and when, if the subject were a man, *grandfather* would be used. See **women.**

Grand Rabbi. See **Chief Rabbi.**

grandstand.

grave accent. See **accent marks.**

gray. But: *greyhound.*

great-. great-grandchild, great-granddaughter, great-grandfather, great-grandmother, great-grandson.

Great Atlantic and Pacific Tea Company (A.&P.).

Great Britain should be shortened to *Britain* in ordinary news copy.

Great Dane.

Great Lakes, the lakes.

Greek Catholic Church. A Roman Catholic church of the Eastern Rite (which see).

Greek Line.

Greek Orthodox Archdiocese of North and South America.

Greek Orthodox Church. It is the established church of Greece and, like the Russian Orthodox Church, is one of the autonomous Eastern Orthodox churches. See **Eastern Orthodoxy** and **Metropolitan** and **Patriarch.**

Greek Revival (architecture). Classical in spirit, yet simple and austere, with an entrance portico often the only ornament. Most of the early town houses in Greenwich Village are Greek Revival. See **styles and schools in the arts.**

Green Revolution, without quotation marks, in references to the gains brought about by high-yield rice and similar agricultural advances.

Greenwich mean time (G.M.T.).

Greenwich Village. In second references, *the Village.* Do not quote *Village,* except when it stands alone in headlines, and then only if the unquoted word would cause confusion.

greyhound.

grippe.

Group Capt. John P. Manley (British), Group Captain Manley, the group captain.

Group of 10 (leading industrial nations). Its members are Belgium, Britain, Canada, France, Italy, Japan, the Netherlands, Sweden, the United States and West Germany. Switzerland is a limited member.

grown-up (n. and adj.).

grueling.

gruesome.

G.T.E. for the General Telephone and Electronics Corporation.

Guadalupe (Mexico).

Guadeloupe (West Indies).

Guantánamo, Guantánamo Bay (Cuba). Also, in quoted matter or in feature contexts involving the United States naval base there, *Gitmo.*

guarantee is preferred to *guaranty*, except in proper names.

gubernatorial. Euphonious it is not, but it is the only adjective that really does the job, though on occasion the noun *governorship* may be forced into service as a modifier.

guerrilla.

guest. Do not use as a verb except in quoted matter or in special contexts (jocular, perhaps).

guesthouse. But: *guest room.*

Guiana, British, is now Guyana.

Guiana, Dutch, is now Surinam.

guide(-). guidebook, guide dog, guideline, guidepost, guide rail.

Guinea, formerly French Guinea.

Guinea-Bissau, formerly Portuguese Guinea.

Guinean(s). The people of Guinea (formerly French Guinea). The adjective is *Guinean.* These forms may also be used occasionally for the people of Guinea-Bissau (formerly Portuguese Guinea), but only in a context that makes the meaning unmistakable.

Gulf and Western Industries (G.&W.).

Gulf Coast, gulf coast. Capitalize when referring to the region of the United States lying along the Gulf of Mexico; lowercase when referring to the actual shoreline. Capitalize *Gulf Coast States.*

Gulf Oil Corporation.

Gulf Stream. But: *Gulfstream Park.*

GUM. These are the initials of the Russian words meaning State Department Store. GUM, Moscow's largest department store, is on Red Square.

gun-. gunfire, gunman, gunpowder, gunshot, gun-shy, gunsmith.

Gunnery Sgt. John P. Manley, Sergeant Manley, the sergeant.

guns. See **automatic pistol, bullet, caliber, cartridge** and **revolver.**

Guyana, formerly British Guiana.

Guyanese (sing. and pl.). The people of Guyana.

gypsy.

gypsy cab, gypsy-cab driver. But, standing alone: *cabdriver.*

H

habitué.

Hades. But lowercase *hell.*

Haggadah. The Passover text recited at a seder.

Hague, The.

hair(-), -haired. hairbreadth, haircut, hairdo, hairdresser, hairdressing, hair shirt, hairtrigger. Also: brown-haired, fair-haired, longhaired, red-haired, etc. See redheaded.

Haitian(s). The people of Haiti.

half(-). half-afraid, half-and-half (the drink), halfback, half brother, half dollar, half-done, half-dozen (adj.), half-full, half gainer (diving), halfhearted, half-holiday, half-hour (n. and adj.), half-hourly (adj., adv.), half-jokingly, half-moon, half nelson (wrestling), half note (music), half pay, halfpenny, half sister, half time (n., except sports), halftime (n., sports), halftone, halftrack (n.), halfway.

half-mast, half-staff. As a sign of mourning, flags on ships and at naval installations ashore are flown at *half-mast;* flags elsewhere ashore are flown at *half-staff.*

hall-. hallmark, hallway.

Halloween.

halo, halos.

Hamburger(s). The people of the German city.

hammer throw.

hand-, -hand. handbag, handball, handbill, handbook, handful(s), handmade, handout (n.), handshake, handspring. Also: beforehand, left-hand (adj.), longhand (writing), right-hand (adj.), shorthand.

handyman (odd-jobs man).

hangar (shed).

hanged, hung. A person is hanged; a picture is hung.

hanger(s)-on.

hangover (n.).

Hanukkah (Feast of Lights).

Hapag-Lloyd A.G. was formed in July 1970, through a merger of North German Lloyd and the Hamburg-American Line.

Hapsburg, not *Habsburg.*

hara-kiri.

harass.

hard(-). hard-bitten, hard-boiled, hard-earned, hard hat (the headgear and, in slang, its wearer), hardhearted, hard-line (adj.), hard-liner, hardwood.

harebrained.

Harry S. Truman (with a period after the initial, even though the initial does not stand for a name).

Harts Island.

harum-scarum.

Harvard Graduate School of Business Administration. That is the full name, but *Harvard Business School* may be used in a lead to avoid a cumbersome sentence. The full title, if needed, can be worked in later. In subsequent references, *the business school* suffices. The term *B School* should be used only in quoted matter.

Hasid (n. sing.), **Hasidim** (pl.), **Hasidic** (adj.). Also, *Hasidism* in references to the beliefs of the Jewish sect of mystics of which a Hasid is a member.

hatrack.

Hawaii. Do not abbreviate after cities and towns, even in datelines.

Hawaiian(s).

hay(-). hay fever, hayfield, haymaker, hayrick, haystack.

H-bomb. It may be used in stories as well as headlines, but in stories *hydrogen bomb* is preferred unless the context seems to call for *H-bomb*. In cap-and-lowercase headlines, the *b* is capitalized: *H-Bomb.*

He, Him, His, Thee, Thou. Capitalize when the reference is to God, Jesus, the Holy Ghost (or the Holy Spirit) or Allah. But do not capitalize *who, whom,* etc.

head(-). headdress, headhunter, headman, headmaster (which see), headmistress, head on (adv.), head-on (adj.), headroom, headstart, headstrong, headway, headwind.

headline capitalization. See **capitalization.**

headmaster. Except in quoted matter, lowercase and use after the name: *John P. Manley, headmaster; the headmaster.*

headquarters (military). First Army Headquarters, the headquarters. Although it is often used as a singular noun, the plural is more common and preferable.

heart-, -hearted. heartbreak, heartbroken, heartfelt. Also: halfhearted, lionhearted, softhearted.

heart condition. Do not use unless the condition is described. Every heart has some kind of condition. Say *heart ailment, disease, injury,* etc.

heat(-). heatproof, heatstroke, heat wave.

Heathrow Airport (London).

heaven. Lowercase except in this sense: *I thank Heaven.*

heavyweight (n. and adj., boxing).

hectare. Equal to 10,000 square meters or 2.47 acres. Unless there is a special reason to use hectare figures, only acres should be used in news stories.

Heights, the. Capitalize in second references to Brooklyn Heights or Washington Heights. In headlines: *Brooklyn Hts., Washington Hts.*

heliport.

hell. As the nether-place name, it is lowercase, but *Hades* is uppercase. As profanity and slang, *hell* is also lowercase. It is also best avoided as common and tiresome. See **obscenity, vulgarity, profanity.**

helmeted. Avoid the overworked expressions *helmeted police, helmeted troops,* etc. On the rare occasions when it is truly necessary to specify that police officers or troops wore helmets, say *policemen wearing helmets*, etc.

help (v.). Avoid the *help but* construction: *He cannot help but wonder.* Make it *cannot help wondering.*

helter-skelter.

Hemisphere. Capitalize in references to divisions of the earth: *Northern Hemisphere*, etc. But: *the hemisphere.*

Hepplewhite (furniture).

her. Do not use this pronoun in references to countries, except in special contexts. Use *it* or *its* instead. But use *her* and *she* for ships. See **pronouns for countries** and **pronouns for ships.**

Herakleion, not *Candia*, for the city and province in Crete.

herculean.

here-. hereabout, hereafter, herein, hereinafter, hereto.

heretofore is stilted and should normally be replaced by *until now.* On the rare occasions when *heretofore* is appropriate—perhaps for a formal effect—it should not be confused with *theretofore*, which means *until then.*

Her Majesty and similar designations are to be used only in quoted matter or in some special contexts.

Herr. See **Mr., Mrs. and Miss.**

hertz (sing. and pl.) means cycle(s) per second, a term it is replacing in scientific usage. Until *hertz* is firmly established, it should be followed by a parenthetical explanation: *16,500 hertz (cycles per second).*

H.E.W. for the Department of Health, Education and Welfare.

Hialeah Race Course. But it is *a racecourse.*

Hias may be used, without the article, in second references to the United Hias Service.

hide-. hide-and-seek (n.), hideaway (n.), hidebound, hide-out (n.).

high(-). highball (drink), highbrow (n. and adj.), high frequency (n.), high-frequency (adj.), high-grade (adj.), highhanded, high-level (adj.), highlight (n. and v.), high-power (adj.), highroad, highway, highwayman.

high commission. In diplomatic relations between any two member countries of the Commonwealth (which see), high commissions take the place of embassies. Lowercase *high commission* when standing alone. But: *the Nigerian High Commission.*

High Commissioner. In diplomatic relations between any two members of the Commonwealth (which see), high commissioners take the place of ambassadors. Capitalize *High Commissioner John P.* [or *Joan*] *Manley; John P. Manley, High Commissioner to Nigeria; High Commissioner Manley; the High Commissioner; Mr.* [or *Mrs.* or *Miss*] *Manley.* But: *a high commissioner, the high commissioners* (for capitalized plural exceptions, see **titles**).

High Holy Days (Jewish): Rosh ha-Shanah and Yom Kippur.

high mass. It is sung, not said, or it is celebrated. See **mass.**

Highway, highway. Capitalize in names: *West Side Highway.* But: *the highway.* See **Interstate System** for designations of Interstate routes.

hijack (v.) means to steal or otherwise illegally seize a conveyance (land, air or sea) or its contents while in transit. The word, which originally meant to rob bootleggers or rumrunners, did not die with Prohibition. Use *hijacking* for the noun.

hike. Do not use as a synonym for increase, either noun or verb.

hill-. hillbilly, hillside, hilltop.

Hindi (language), **Hindu** (religion).

hippie(s).

hippopotamus, hippopotamuses.

His Holiness (the Pope). Use only in quoted matter.

His Majesty and similar designations are to be used only in quoted matter or in some special contexts.

Hispaniola (island comprising the Dominican Republic and Haiti).

hit-. hit-and-miss, hit-and-run, hit-run (in headlines).

hitchhike (v.), **hitchhiker.**

hitherto is stilted and should normally be replaced by *until now.*

Hobson's choice means that one must accept what is offered or receive nothing at all; there is really no choice.

hockey. Scores are given in figures: *The Rangers won, 3 to 0* (or *3-0*). Numbers of goals below 10 and of periods are spelled out: *He scored three goals in the second period.* But: *The score at the end of the second period was 3 to 1.*

hocus-pocus.

hodgepodge.

Ho-Ho-Kus (N.J.).

-holder. boxholder, householder, jobholder, leaseholder, officeholder, potholder, shareholder, stockholder. But: preferred-stock holder.

holdup (n. and adj.). The *holdup* man *holds up* the victim of the *holdup.*

hole-in-one (n. and adj.).

holidays are listed separately and alphabetically.

Holland America Cruises.

holy communion. A Christian sacrament that is celebrated by a minister, a priest or a bishop. The elements of bread and wine are consecrated by the celebrant and then distributed or administered to the congregation.

Holy Father (the Pope). Use only in quoted matter.

Holy See. The Roman see of the Roman Catholic Church.

Holy Week (the week before Easter).

home(-). homemade, homemaker, homeowner, home plate, home rule, home run, homespun, homestretch, hometown, homework.

Home Lines.

Homo sapiens. See **genus and species.**

homosexuality. See **gay** and **lesbian, lesbianism.**

Hon., the, for the Honorable. Use as *Rev.* (which see) is used, but only in quoted matter.

Hong Kong.

Honolulan(s). The people of Honolulu.

Hoosac Tunnel (Massachusetts).

Hoosick Falls (New York State).

Hoosier(s) may be used for Indianian(s) in some informal contexts only.

hopefully means in a hopeful manner, and its use should be confined to that meaning: *They sought hopefully for the solution so desperately needed.* Do not use *hopefully* in this sense: *Hopefully, they will find the solution so desperately needed.* The intended meaning in such a case is *they hope to find, it is hoped* (parenthetical) or *it is hoped that* or some equivalent phrase, and one of them should be used. The foregoing, it is hoped, will clear up this troublesome matter and enable us to move on hopefully to solutions of other problems.

horror-struck.

hors de combat.

hors d'oeuvre(s).

horse(-). horsecar, horse chestnut, horseflesh, horsefly, horsehair, horsehide, horseman, horse opera, horseplay, horseplayer, horsepower, horse race, horse racing, horseradish, horse sense, horseshoe, horse trade (n.), horse-trade (v.), horse trader, horse trading, horsewoman.

horse races. Capitalize *Kentucky Derby, Belmont Stakes, One Thousand Guineas, Suburban Handicap,* etc.

horse racing. Use figures for times of races: *2:39.* The fraction is used rather than the decimal: *1:12 4/5.* Spell out lengths under 10 unless they contain a fraction: *three lengths, 3½ lengths, 12 lengths.*

The first time prices are mentioned in a story, the type of bet should be specified. *He paid $4.60 for $2 to win. He returned $18.40,*

$9.60 and $5.40 for $2 across the board. Exact odds should be used. If the odds are 35 cents to the dollar, the horse is 7 to 20 (or 7-20) rather than 1 to 3. If the payoff is $4.10 for $2, the odds are 21 to 20, not even money. Exception: If the price is comparatively high, the odds may be rounded out. Thus a horse paying $38.20 for $2 may be listed as 18 to 1 rather than 181-10.

Thoroughbred horses run in stakes (sing. and pl.), harness horses in a stake (sing.) or stakes (pl.).

Harness races are trotted or paced, not run. The words *break* and *broke* should be used with care in harness stories. *He broke from the No. 4 post* could mean either that the horse started from that post or that he broke his stride.

If the horse's name is used in the story, the horse is referred to as *he* or *she*, not *it.* Gelded horses are referred to as *he.* Roman, not Arabic, numerals, are used in horses' names: *Icare IV, Shannon II,* etc.

host. Do not use as a verb except in quoted matter or in special contexts (jocular, perhaps).

hot-blooded.

hot dog, hot-dog stand.

hotels. Capitalize their names: *Waldorf-Astoria Hotel.* Generally, but not always, *Hotel* follows the name.

hot line for a direct communications system such as the one between Washington and Moscow.

hour(-). hourglass, hour hand, hourlong.

hours. See **time.**

house(-). house arrest, houseboat, housebroken, housecoat, housedress, household, housekeeper, houseman, housemother, house organ, house party, housetop, housewares, housewarming, housewife (which see), housework.

House of Commons, the Commons.

House of Lords, the Lords.

House of Representatives (United States), the House.

houses and estates. Do not quote their names: Blair House, The Elms.

housewife. Avoid this word whenever other, more precise characterizations are available. Care should also be taken to avoid suggesting that only housewives do the spending for a household. Men are consumers and shoppers, too, and many couples shop jointly. See **women.**

H.U.D. for the Department of Housing and Urban Development.

-hundreds (of years). In almost all contexts, use the numerals (*1900's,* for example) rather than the words *(nineteen-hundreds).* See **years, decades, centuries.**

hurly-burly.

hurricanes. Do not personalize in using the feminine names (*Alice, Betsy,* etc.) assigned to them. *Hurricane Alice struck the city* is all right, but *Alice behaved capriciously* is not. Such a name should be used sparingly—if possible, only once. Do not call a storm a hurricane unless it meets the National Weather Service's specifications. One is winds near the center of the storm that reach or surpass 74 miles an hour. See **gale** and **storm.**

hymns. Quote their titles; capitalize principal words.

hyphen. Many compounds are formed with the hyphen as a con-nector, but as such words become established the hyphen is often dropped in favor of the solid form. (Compounds are listed separately and alphabetically.)

The hyphen is used in constructions like these: *three-mile hike, 30-car train.* It is also used to avoid confusion in words like *re-form* (meaning to form again).

Hyphens should not be used in constructions like the following if the meaning is clear without them: *sales tax bill, foreign aid plan.* But: *pay-as-you-go plan.* The hyphen is not needed in these forms: *navy blue skirt, dark green paint.*

In many compounds, the hyphen should be used to avoid ambiguity or absurdity: *small-business man,* not *small businessman* (note separation of solid compound; see **compound words**); *unfair-practices charge,* not *unfair practices charge.*

The usefulness of the hyphen in forming compounds that serve as adjectives before nouns is demonstrated in the entries **ill-** and **well-**. An example: *He wore a well-tailored gray suit.* But the hyphen is omitted when the words follow the noun they modify: *The suit was well tailored.*

Do not use the hyphen to connect an adverb ending in *ly* with a participle in such phrases as *newly married couple, elegantly furnished house.* But adjectives ending in *ly* are another matter: *a gravelly-voiced, grizzly-maned statesman of the old school.*

Hyphens are not used in titles like these: *commander in chief, director general, editor in chief, secretary general.* (See separate listings.) Do use the hyphen in titles like *secretary-treasurer.*

The suspensive hyphen is a useful device: *On successive days there were three-, five- and nine-inch snowfalls.* But because of the typographical hazard, copy containing suspensive hyphens should be carefully marked and proofs carefully checked.

Street numbers in Queens take the hyphen: 107-71 111th Street.

Use the hyphen in such expressions as *Italian-American, Japanese-American.* But: *French Canadian.*

I

I. for Island in proper names. The abbreviation may be used in headlines (*Easter I.*), but not in stories. It will appear most frequently on maps. The plural is *Is.: Canary Is.*

I- for Interstate in highway numbers: *I-95.* See **Interstate System.**

Iberia Air Lines of Spain. For first references *an Iberia airliner,* etc., will suffice.

I.B.M. for the International Business Machines Corporation.

ICBM('s) for intercontinental ballistic missile(s).

I.C.C. for the Interstate Commerce Commission.

ice(-). iceberg, iceboat, icebound, icebreaker, icecap, ice cream, ice floe, iceman, ice pack, ice water.

ice age.

Icelander(s). The people of Iceland.

Icelandic Airlines.

IC4A for Intercollegiate Association of Amateur Athletes of America. The abbreviation may be used in first references, but the full name should appear somewhere in major stories.

Idaho. Do not abbreviate after cities and towns.

Idahoan(s).

idée fixe.

identical. Use preposition *with* or *to.*

I.L.A. for the International Longshoremen's Association.

I.L.G.W.U. for the International Ladies Garment Workers Union. Also: *the garment workers* or *the garment workers' union.*

Ill. for Illinois after cities and towns.

ill(-). ill-advised, ill-defined, ill-fated, ill-gotten, ill-humored, ill-mannered, ill-natured, ill-omened, ill-tempered, ill-timed, ill-treated.
  Such forms are hyphenated only when they serve as adjectives before nouns: *It was an ill-timed plan.* The hyphen is not used when the words follow the nouns they modify: *The plan was ill timed.*

Illinois Central Gulf Railroad, a subsidiary of Illinois Central Industries.

Illinoisan(s).

ill will, good will. Hyphenate when using as adjectives.

I.L.O. for the International Labor Organization (which see).

imam. See **Arab names and titles.**

I.M.F. for the International Monetary Fund. Also: *the monetary fund, the fund.*

immigrate, emigrate. *Immigrate* (with preposition *to* or *into*) refers to arriving in a country. *Emigrate* (with *from*) refers to leaving a country.

impanel.

impasse.

implement (v.), **implementation.** There are less tiresome ways of saying these things.

imply, infer. The Bible says that sowers are also reapers. But an exception must be made for those who sow by implying and those who reap by inferring. The current tendency to make *infer* synonymous with *imply* would destroy an essential distinction. Let us continue to use *imply* when a speaker or writer implants allusions or suggestions, and to use *infer* when a listener or reader harvests from indirect or direct statements a crop of his own conclusions. Blessings may ensue.

impostor.

Impressionism (art). Both a style and a movement in painting, initiated by Monet in the 1860's, in which touches of pure, unmixed color are employed to convey a fresh, optical accuracy in the observation of nature. See **styles and schools in the arts.**

Impressionism (music). A movement, mainly French, that developed in the late 19th and early 20th centuries in opposition to Romanticism. Atmosphere and color were emphasized over formal structure. Debussy and Delius were among its main exponents. See **styles and schools in the arts.**

"in," meaning in vogue or faddish, should carry quotation marks only when it precedes the noun it modifies: *Bell-bottom pants were*

the *"in" thing to wear in the early 1920's. Bell-bottoms are in again.* But *out,* in the sense of outmoded or passé, almost never precedes the noun: *The Nehru jacket is definitely out.*

in-. inbound, indoor, infield, infighting, in-law, inpatient (n. and adj.).

in, into. These words are often misused, especially in headlines. You jump *into* the swimming pool. You swim *in* it.

inasmuch as.

Inauguration Day.

Inc. is often superfluous in company and corporation names (which see). When it is used, omit surrounding commas *(Time Inc.)*. Equivalent abbreviations such as *Ltd.* are similarly treated.

include is usually used to introduce a number of names or items that do not constitute a complete listing: *His softball team includes two Ph.D.'s. The cost of the trip included $100 for food and lodging.* See **comprise.**

incommunicado.

Incres Line.

IND for the Independent Subway System, a division of the Metropolitan Transportation Authority. Also: *the A train* (or *line*), *the F train.*

Ind. for Indiana after cities and towns.

indexes, not *indices.*

Indianian(s). Also *Hoosier(s),* but use that only in some informal contexts.

Indians, American. In news stories about American Indians, ordinarily innocent words like *wampum, warpath, powwow, tepee, brave,* *squaw,* etc., can in certain contexts be disparaging and offensive. So, obviously, can *firewater, heap big* and the like. Avoid such contexts and such words when any disparagement is even remotely suggested. See **native(s).**

indispensable.

Indochina. Former French Indochina comprised the now independent states of Cambodia, Laos and Vietnam.

Indonesian names. Many Indonesians, like Suharto, have only one name. First references to people with titles present no problems: *President Suharto* or, before he was President, *Gen. Suharto.* But if he had no title, it would be *Mr. Suharto* in all references.

Generally, the consonant combination *dj* should be changed to *j* (as in the place name Jakarta, not *Djakarta*) and the vowel combination *oe* should be changed to *u* (Suharto, not *Soeharto*).

Industrial Revolution. The one that began in England in the 18th century.

infer. Do not use interchangeably with *imply.* See **imply, infer.**

infrared.

ingénue.

inimitable.

initials in names. Although full first names with middle initials (if any) are preferred in ordinary copy, two or more initials may be used if that is the preference of a person mentioned in the news: *J. P. Manley,* with periods followed by spaces. In American usage, a single initial *(J. Manley)* is not usually appropriate, but that style may be used in a casualty list or other spe-

cial matter. Also, in a pen name or a pre-eminent stage name: *B. Traven.* See **personal names and nicknames.**

innocent and **not guilty.** Legally, there is a difference in respect to a defendant's plea; *pleaded not guilty* is the proper form.

innocuous.

innuendo.

inoculate.

inquire.

insane asylum. It has an ugly ring, and should be avoided except in direct quotations and certain historical contexts. *Mental hospital* is preferred.

inserts in copy. Writers and editors should bear in mind the need for a smooth transition into and out of an insert. This may mean, in some instances, that a one-paragraph insert will turn into a three-paragraph insert when the necessary repair work has been done on the preceding and following paragraphs.

insignia is both singular and plural. An alternative singular is *insigne,* and an alternative plural is *insignias.*

insofar as.

insomuch as.

Inspector John P. Manley (police), Inspector Manley, the inspector.

install, installment.

instill, instilling.

Institute for Advanced Study at Princeton, N.J. *Study* is singular, and the institute is not part of Princeton University.

insure, not *ensure.*

101

Intelsat for the International Telecommunications Satellite Organization.

inter-. interaction, interallied, inter-American, intercollegiate, interfaith, international, interracial, interstate.

Intercollegiate Association of Amateur Athletes of America. The abbreviation *IC4A* may be used in first references, but the full name should appear in major stories.

Inter-Continental Hotels.

intern (n. and v.).

International Brotherhood of Teamsters may be used in first references instead of the full name, the International Brotherhood of Teamsters, Chauffeurs, Warehousemen and Helpers. Also: *the teamsters, the teamsters' union.*

International Business Machines Corporation (I.B.M.).

International Court of Justice (at The Hague), the World Court, the Court.

international date line.

International Labor Organization (I.L.O.). The membership of this United Nations body consists of labor delegates, management delegates and governmental delegates.

International Ladies Garment Workers Union. In subsequent references: *the garment workers' union, the garment workers.* In headlines, *I.L.G.W.U.* is acceptable, but *Garment Union* will often be as handy and more attractive.

International Monetary Fund (I.M.F.). Also: *the monetary fund, the fund.*

International style (architecture). The austere 20th-century style of steel and glass, as in the Seagram Building and countless other examples in New York. See **styles and schools in the arts.**

International Telecommunications Satellite Organization (Intelsat).

International Telephone and Telegraph Corporation (I.T.T.).

International Trade Commission, formerly the United States Tariff Commission.

interrogation point. See **question mark.**

Interstate System (of highways) should be used instead of the full name, the National System of Interstate and Defense Highways. In subsequent references: *the Interstate, the Interstate proposal.* A highway may be referred to as *Interstate 95, Route 95* or *Route I-95.* In headlines: *Rte. 95, I-95, Rte. I-95.*

intra-. intra-atomic, intramural, intrastate, intrauterine.

Intracoastal Waterway.

invitation (adj., sports), not *invitational.*

i.o.u.

Iowa. Do not abbreviate after cities and towns.

Iowan(s).

I.Q. for intelligence quotient.

Iran (formerly Persia), **Iranian(s).** The language is Persian.

Iraqi(s). The people of Iraq. The adjective is *Iraqi.*

IRBM('s) for intermediate-range ballistic missile(s).

Ireland, not *Eire.*

iris, irises.

Irish International Airlines. The preferred name is Aer Lingus (which see).

Irish setter.

Irish terrier.

Irish water spaniel.

Irish wolfhound.

ironclad.

Iron Curtain. Use only in quoted matter or in certain contexts where it is clear that the writer is aware of the editorial nature of the phrase.

irreparable.

I.R.S. for the Internal Revenue Service.

IRT for Interborough Rapid Transit, a division of the Metropolitan Transportation Authority.

Is. for Islands in proper names. The abbreviation may be used in headlines *(Canary Is.)* and will appear most frequently on maps. The singular is *I. (Easter I.).*

I.S. for Intermediate School in almost all subsequent references: *I.S. 109.* Follow the same style as for Public School (which see).

Islam. It can mean not only the Moslem religion but also Moslems generally and the areas of the world where their religion is predominant. The deity of Islam is Allah, and Mohammed is its founder and prophet. The adjective is *Islamic.*

Island, the, for Long Island, in subsequent references.

Israeli(s). The people of Israel. The adjective is *Israeli.*

issue, edition(s). Do not use interchangeably. See **edition(s), issue.**

Istanbul (formerly Constantinople).

it. Use this pronoun, rather than *she,* in references to countries, except in special contexts. Use *she* and *her* for ships. See **pronouns for countries** and **pronouns for ships.**

Italianate (architecture). The style of most 19th-century brownstones in New York, it is characterized by rounded window tops, often with elaborate cornices above them and atop the building itself. **See styles and schools in the arts.**

Italian Line.

italic. Lowercase, as is *roman,* in references to typefaces.

italicizing. In news stories, italics should in general not be used for emphasis or to indicate that a word or phrase is foreign. In the second case, quotation marks will almost always suffice if some special treatment is indeed required. Exceptions may be made in both cases in special instances—in a feature story, perhaps—but the exceptions should be rare.

Italo-. Avoid, in adjectival references to Italy. Use *Italian-French, Italian-Soviet,* etc.

it's (the contraction, meaning *it is*), **its** (the possessive, meaning *of it*).

I.T.T. (without an ampersand) for the International Telephone and Telegraph Corporation.

IUD for intrauterine device (contraceptive).

Ivoirian(s). The people of the Ivory Coast.

Ivy League. It comprises Brown, Columbia, Cornell, Dartmouth, Harvard, the University of Pennsylvania (not Pennsylvania State), Princeton and Yale.

Izmir, not *Smyrna,* except in historical references.

J

jack-in-the-box(es),
jack-in-the-pulpit(s),
jack(s)-of-all-trades,
jack-o'-lantern(s).

jailer.

Jan. for January before numerals: *Jan. 10.*

Jane's All the World's Aircraft, Jane's Fighting Ships, Jane's Weapon Systems. No quotation marks.

Jap. Do not use as a synonym for Japanese.

Japan Air Lines (J.A.L.).

Japanese spaniel.

jargon, in its most common sense, means distinctive words or phrases used in a particular profession, trade, science, occupation or other pursuit. Such language really amounts to specialized clichés: *party* for *person* (law), *aide-mémoire* (diplomacy), *launch* for *launching* (space science), *vigorish* (gambling), *infrastructure* (several fields), *dichotomy* (several other fields), *media* (communications), *hat trick* (sports), *hit* (crime), *overkill* (warfare), *input* (computer technology), *complex* (psychiatry), *corporate image* (business), *peer group* (sociology). Like clichés, jargon should be used with extreme care or in many cases

avoided entirely. After all, jargon also means gibberish. See **clichés.**

Java man (anthropological).

jaywalker.

J. C. Penney Company.

J.D. for Doctor of Law(s). This is the equivalent of the LL.B. (Bachelor of Laws) degree, which it is largely replacing. It is different from the J.S.D. (or S.J.D.) degree. See **J.S.D.**

jeep, Jeep. Lowercase when referring to the military vehicle; capitalize when referring to the civilian vehicle so trademarked.

Jehovah's Witnesses.

Jell-O (trademark).

Jersey is permitted in headlines to mean New Jersey. But after the name of a city or a town, use *N.J.*

Jerseyan(s) or **New Jerseyan(s).**

Jersey Cityite(s). The people of Jersey City.

Jersey Shore, but *Jersey coast.*

Jesus. Since this is a historical name and is correct in all cases, it is the preferred form. But in direct or indirect quotations and in matter directly concerning the Christian religion, *Christ* is also proper. Capitalize *He, Him* and *His* when the reference is to Jesus, God or the Holy Ghost (or Holy Spirit). But lowercase *who, whom,* etc.

jet, jetliner. The first may be used as adjective or noun in writing about any pure-jet plane (no propellers). The second may be used for an airliner that is a pure jet. See **turboprop.**

jetport.

Jewess. Do not use. See **women.**

j.g. for junior grade: Lieut. (j.g.) John P. Manley, Lieutenant Manley, the lieutenant.

J.H.S. for Junior High School in almost all subsequent references: *J.H.S. 113.* Follow the same style as for Public School (which see).

jib (sail).

jibe. It has two meanings. One is to accord; the other, which is nautical, is to shift. Do not use in the sense of taunt; use *gibe* for that.

John F. Kennedy International Airport is the official name, but Kennedy International Airport should be used in almost all first references. For second-reference and headline style, see **Kennedy International Airport.**

Joint Chiefs of Staff, the Joint Chiefs, the Chiefs. Also see **Chairman of the Joint Chiefs of Staff.**

Jordanian(s). The people of Jordan.

J. P. Morgan & Company, the parent company of the Morgan Guaranty Trust Company.

Jr. for Junior in names. It is not preceded by a comma: *John P. Manley Jr.* (or *Sr.*). Also: *John P. Manley 2d.* And in bylines:

By JOHN P. MANLEY Jr.

In a listing, if family names are printed before given names, the expression *Jr.* (or *Sr.*, or *3d*, etc.) comes last: *MANLEY, John P. Jr.,* not *MANLEY Jr., John P.*

J.S.D. for Doctor of Juristic (or Juridical) Science. Also S.J.D. for Doctor of Juridical Science. See **J.D.**

Judge John P. Manley or Judge Joan Manley, Judge Manley, the judge. Do not use Mr., Mrs. or Miss in second references. *Judge* (not *Justice,* which see) is the proper title for the following courts:

All Federal courts except the Supreme Court.

Connecticut, New Jersey and most other state courts outside New York State.

The New York State Courts of Appeals and Claims.

The Criminal, Civil and Family Courts in New York City.

judicial branch (of the United States Government). Also: *executive branch, legislative branch.*

Juilliard School.

jukebox.

July. Do not abbreviate.

jumbo jet. The Boeing 747 and similar airliners.

June. Do not abbreviate.

junior (class and member of that class). Also see **Jr.**

junkie(s). The term should not be used for narcotic addicts or users unless it appears in quoted matter or in special contexts in which it is clear that we are not imposing a cruel judgment of our own.

jury room.

Justice John P. Manley or Justice Joan Manley, Justice Manley, the justice (or: the judge). But it is *the Justice* or *the Associate Justice* in the case of a member of the Supreme Court of the United States. Do not use *Mr., Mrs.* or *Miss* in second references. And do not use *Mr. Justice* except in quoted matter or special feature contexts. *Justice* (not *Judge*, which see) is the proper title for the New York State Supreme Court and for the Appellate Division of that court. Also see **Chief Justice.**

K

Kaddish, the Jewish prayer for the dead, is recited in Aramaic, not Hebrew.

kaffeeklatsch, not *coffee klatch.*

Kan. for Kansas after cities and towns.

Kansan(s).

Kansas Cityan(s). The people of the cities in Kansas and Missouri.

Kansas City Southern Railway, a subsidiary of Kansas City Southern Industries.

karat. This is a measure of the fineness of gold. Pure gold is 24 karats, and one karat is equal to one twenty-fourth part of pure gold. Thus an object made of 18-karat gold contains 18 parts pure gold and 6 parts alloy. See **carat** (a unit of weight for gemstones).

Kashmir, Vale of.

Kearny (N.J.), not *Kearney.*

keen-. keen-edged, keen-sighted, keen-witted.

-keeper. barkeeper, bookkeeper, gatekeeper, goalkeeper, groundskeeper, hotelkeeper, housekeeper, innkeeper, peacekeeper, scorekeeper, shopkeeper, storekeeper, timekeeper, wicketkeeper. But: tollgate keeper.

keeshond, keeshonds.

Kelvin. A temperature scale widely used in science to record very low and very high temperatures. The freezing point of water is at 273.16 degrees Kelvin, and the boiling point at 373.16 degrees Kelvin. Zero is the total absence of heat (absolute zero) and is equal to minus 273.16 degrees centigrade. See **temperature** and **Fahrenheit** and **centigrade, Celsius.**

Kennedy International Airport should be used in almost all first references instead of the official name, John F. Kennedy International Airport. The single word *Kennedy* will suffice for most second references in stories and for headlines that provide a proper context. The airport, formerly known as Idlewild, is in Idlewild, Queens.

Kentuckian(s).

Kenyan(s). The people of Kenya.

Kerry blue terrier.

ketch. A two-masted vessel with the mizzen (the small mast aft) stepped forward of the rudderpost or waterline. See **yawl.**

ketchup, not *catchup* or *catsup.*

key(-). keyboard, keynote, key ring, keystone.

K.G.B., the Soviet Government's intelligence and internal-security agency. Its initials stand for the Russian words meaning Committee for State Security.

Khartoum (the Sudan).

Khmer(s). The people of the dominant ethnic group in Cambodia. The Cambodian language may also be called Khmer.

kibbutz (sing.), **kibbutzim** (pl.). Also: *kibbutznik(s)* in references to a member of a kibbutz, which is an Israeli collective settlement.

kickoff (n.).

kidnap (v. only), **kidnapped, kidnapping, kidnapper.**

kill (n.). One meaning of this noun is stream. Thus it is redundant, for example, to write *the Schuylkill River*. It is *the Schuylkill*.

Kill van Kull, the strait between Staten Island and Bayonne, N.J.

kilogram. One thousand grams, or roughly 2.2 pounds. See **metric system**.

kilometer. A unit of length equal to 1,000 meters or approximately 3,281 feet. It is roughly equal to 0.6 of a mile or five-eighths of a mile. See **metric system**.

kiloton, kilotonnage. A kiloton is a unit used to measure the power of nuclear explosions. It is equal to the explosive force of one thousand tons of TNT. See **gigaton** and **megaton**.

kilowatt-hours.

kimono, kimonos.

kin is a collective word; one person is a *kinsman* or a *kinswoman*.

kind, kinds. It is *that kind* and *those kinds*.

kind of. It is wrong to write, *I like that kind of an apple*. Omit the *an*.

King Henry VIII, the King, Henry VIII, and sometimes Henry. Capitalize *His Majesty* and *His Royal Highness*, but use only in quoted matter.

King Charles spaniel.

King James Version (of the Bible).

Kinshasa, formerly Leopoldville, capital of Zaire, formerly the Democratic Republic of the Congo.

Klansman(men) for members of the Ku Klux Klan (which see).

Kleenex (trademark).

KLM Royal Dutch Airlines. For first references *a KLM airliner*, etc., will suffice.

knee-. kneecap, knee-deep, knee-high, kneepad.

knight (British rank). See **Sir**.

knockdown (n.), **knockout** (n.).

knot. A knot is, among other things, a unit of speed equal to one nautical mile (1.15 statute miles, 6,076 feet or 1,852 meters) per hour. It is thus redundant to use *per hour* after *knots*, as in *10 knots per hour*.

know-how. A trite expression that should be avoided whenever possible in favor of *skill* or some other straightforward synonym.

Kodak (trademark).

kopeck(s).

Koran. The sacred book of Islam. Moslems believe that its text comprises the words of Allah dictated to the Prophet Mohammed through the Angel Gabriel.

Korean(s). The people of the two Koreas. In many contexts, it will be necessary to use *South Korean(s)* or *North Korean(s)*.

Korean names. The Chinese practice of putting family name first is followed in most Korean names: *President Kim Il Sung, President Kim; President Park Chung Hee, President Park.* But in a departure from Chinese practice, the given names *(Il Sung, Chung Hee)* are not hyphenated. In the past, some Koreans, like Syngman Rhee, westernized their names. Rhee was the family name. This practice seems to be disappearing.

Korean War. The 1950-53 conflict. But in texts or quoted matter, *the Korean conflict* is acceptable.

krona, kronor (sing. and pl., Swedish money).

krone, kroner (sing. and pl., Danish and Norwegian money).

Ku Klux Klan, the Klan or the K.K.K. A local unit of this secret society is called a Klan or a klavern, and members are Klansmen(man) or Klanswomen(woman).

Kuomintang (Chinese Nationalist). It is the Kuomintang, not the Kuomintang Party. *Tang* means party.

Kuwaiti(s). The people of Kuwait.

Ky. for Kentucky after cities and towns.

111

L

La. for Louisiana after cities and towns.

labeled.

"La Bohème."

Labor Party, not *Labour*, even if British.

Labrador. Do not use in datelines; use Newfoundland, of which Labrador is a part.

Labrador retriever.

Ladies' Home Journal, The.

Ladies' Professional Golf Association (L.P.G.A.).

lady should not be used as a synonym for *woman* in most instances, just as *gentleman* should usually not be used for *man*. The title *Lady* (see next entry) and the term *First Lady* are different matters. See **women.**

Lady. This title is applied to the wives of British knights, baronets, barons, viscounts, earls and marquesses. It is also applied to women below the rank of duchess who are peeresses in their own right: *the Countess of Cromartie, Lady Cromartie.* When applied to any one of those ranks, the title is never followed by a given name: *Lady Jellicoe,* not *Lady Patricia Jellicoe.*

The title is followed by a given name when it is applied to the daughters of earls, marquesses and dukes: *Lady Mary Grosvenor, Lady Mary.* But never *Lady Grosvenor.* The title is followed by the husband's given name when applied to the wives of the younger sons of marquesses and dukes: *Lady Malcolm Douglas-Hamilton.* In second references, it is *Lady Malcolm,* never *Lady Douglas-Hamilton.*

If a peeress in her own right or a peer's daughter marries, her title does not apply to her husband; if she outranks him she keeps her title: *the Countess of Cromartie and her husband, Lieut. Col. Edward Walter Blunt-Mackenzie.* Another example: *Lady Pamela Berry and her husband, Michael Berry.*

The form *Nancy Viscountess Astor* or *Anne Lady Orr Lewis* is used for widows and divorced women. In second references it is *Lady Astor* and *Lady Orr Lewis,* but never *Lady Nancy Astor* or *Lady Anne Orr Lewis.*

To distinguish between persons of the same name, use the form *Lady (Elizabeth) Jones;* or *Lady Jones, the former Elizabeth Smith;* or *Lady Jones, wife of Sir John Jones;* but never *Lady Elizabeth Jones,* except for the daughters of earls, marquesses and dukes.

113

La Guardia Airport.

laissez-faire.

Laker Airways.

lamb's-wool (adj.).

lamppost.

Lance Cpl. John P. Manley, Corporal Manley, the corporal.

land-. landfall, landfill, landholder, landlocked, landmark, landowner, land-poor, landslide.

Land-Rover. The hyphen is standard equipment.

languor.

Lao, Laotian. The people of Laos are Laotians; the adjective is *Laotian*. But *Lao* (noun or adjective) may be used in contexts requiring specific description of the country's dominant ethnic and linguistic group, especially when contrasted with other ethnic and linguistic groups in Laos.

Laotian names. Because of differences in their ethnic backgrounds, Laotians' names assume a variety of forms. In news copy, for the sake of consistency and certainty, use the names in full on all references: *Maj. Gen. Vang Pao; General Vang Pao.* In headlines, however, if it is known without doubt that part of the name is a surname, or is used alone by Laotians, that part may stand alone: Prince Souvanna Phouma may be referred to as Souvanna.

larceny. See **burglary, larceny, robbery, theft.**

lasso, lassos.

Lastex (trademark). But: *latex,* a substance used in making elastic materials.

late (in the sense of dead). In gen-

eral, use *the late* only in reference to a person who has recently died. It is not needed, for example, in *the late Lyndon B. Johnson.* Avoid a redundancy like this: *She is the widow of the late John R. Doe.* And do not fall into this error: *Only the late Senator opposed the bill.* He was not then deceased.

Latin America, Latin American (person and adj.).

latitude and longitude. Use these forms: *49 degrees north latitude, 24 degrees west longitude, 10 degrees 30 minutes south latitude.* Also: *prime meridian, Greenwich meridian, 17th parallel.*

Latter-day Saints. See **Mormon Church.**

laughingstock.

launch, launching. In rocketry contexts, *launch* should be used only as a verb: *They will launch the missile at 9 A.M. The launching* [never *launch*] *is scheduled for 9 A.M.* As an adjective, use *launching: launching pad,* not *launch pad.* In references to programs, candidacies, etc. (but not military campaigns), *launch* is trite and should be avoided.

Laurel Race Course. But it is *a racecourse.*

law-. law-abiding, lawbreaker, lawmaker, lawsuit.

lawman is fine in western movies, but *law officer* or *law-enforcement officer* or the precise title is better in print.

laws. See **acts, amendments, bills and laws.**

lay-. layman, layoff (n.), layout (n.), layup (sports).

lay, lie. *Lay* means in general to place, to put, to deposit; it requires a direct object. *Lie* means in general to be in a reclining position, to be situated; it thus does not take an object. Some examples of correct use follow:

LAY: *He always lays his hat on the hall table. He laid his hat on the table. At this time, I imagine, he is laying his hat on the table. He had already laid his hat on the table.*

LIE: *Massachusetts lies to the north and New York to the west. He lay quietly, waiting for her return. The demonstrators spent the next three hours lying in the street. Having lain there for three hours, they decided it was futile to remain.*

But consider the hen: She not only *lays eggs;* she also just *lays* (no object stated; eggs understood)—if, that is, she is a *laying* hen.

Lazard Frères & Company (investment bankers). The French firm is Lazard Frères et Compagnie.

lazybones.

lazy susan.

leads, unfamiliar names in. Readers are not likely to struggle past a lead like this: *Tupamaros guerrillas kidnapped Héctor Gutiérrez Ruiz, President of the Chamber of Deputies, tonight, Senator Alembert Vaz said.* This is much better: *A Uruguayan senator said tonight that leftist guerrillas had kidnapped the President of the Chamber of Deputies.*

leak. See **sources of news.**

lean-to.

leatherneck. Use for a marine only in quoted matter or in a feature context requiring colorful effect.

leave alone (to leave in solitude); **let alone** (to refrain from disturbing).

leave-taking.

lectern, podium. One stands *behind* a lectern and *on* a podium.

left(-). left field, left fielder, left guard, left-hand (adj.), left-handed, left-hander, leftover (n.).

left, leftist, left wing. Do not capitalize *left* unless the political divisions in a country are formally designated as *the Left, the Right,* etc., or the word appears in a party name. Do not capitalize *leftist* unless the reference is to such a division or party, or to a member of it. Do not capitalize *left wing* or *left-wing* (adj.) unless the reference is to such a political party or movement. But capitalize terms like *New Left.*

Left Bank (Paris).

legation. Lowercase when standing alone. But: *the Israeli Legation, the United States Legation.*

legionnaire.

legislative bodies. Capitalize *Congress, Senate, House of Representatives* (or just *House), Parliament, Legislature, Assembly,* etc., in any specific reference to a legislative body that is formally so named. *Parliament,* uppercased, should usually be used in place of equivalent foreign terms such as *Knesset* (Israel), *Diet* (Japan) and *Cortes* (Spain). Capitalize a plural form if it refers to a small number of legislative bodies

115

specifically identified in the story: *the Danish and Swedish Parliaments, the two Parliaments.* Otherwise: *parliaments, a parliament.*

legislative branch (of the United States Government). Also: *executive branch, judicial branch.*

Legislature(s), legislature(s). Capitalize when the reference is to one body officially so designated, or to a small number of legislatures specifically identified in the article: *the State Legislature, the Legislature, the California Legislature, the Connecticut and Rhode Island Legislatures, the two Legislatures.* But: *many legislatures, several state legislatures,* etc. Also: *legislator(s), state legislator(s), California legislator(s).*

Lehigh Valley Railroad.

Leif Ericson (the explorer).

Leiv Eiriksson Square (Brooklyn).

Lent, Lenten.

lesbian, lesbianism. Lowercase in references to homosexual women except in names of organizations.

lèse-majesté.

Lesotho. Its people are Basotho (sing. and pl.). The adjective is *Basotho.*

less, fewer. The terms are not interchangeable. See **fewer, less.**

letter(-). letter carrier, letterhead, letterman (sports), letter-perfect, letterpress.

letters that appear in the body of a news story should be set in 8½-point, indented, without quotation marks. Letters printed as texts should be similarly treated, but a letter that appears within the body of an indented text should be quoted or set double indent. Letters may contain the date, salutation and complimentary close and should follow this style, with the signature in caps and small caps:

Feb. 12, 1974
Dear Mr. President:
When I accepted my appointment to your Cabinet two years ago, etc.
It has been an honor to serve, and I am grateful.
Sincerely yours,
JOHN P. MANLEY

Letters to the editors of The Times, when appearing in sections that use a salutation, should begin *To the Editor* (in regular caps and lowercase) rather than, for example, *To the Sports Editor* or *To the Real Estate Editor.* Omit the complimentary close *(Yours very truly).* The signature is caps and small caps, flush right within the indention if any. Set datelines below the signature, also at the right, as in the following example. Should the dateline make more than one line, divide it so that the year remains on the same line as the month and the day:

JOHN P. MANLEY
Stamford, Conn., Oct. 9, 1974

Omit *City* in New York datelines. Omit *New York* after *Brooklyn.* Long Island datelines should read *Hempstead, L.I.* Staten Island datelines should read *St. George, S.I.*

Run up signatures to the last line of the letter whenever there is room for two ems between, unless otherwise ordered:

losses.   JOHN P. MANLEY
Columbus, Ohio, Oct. 10, 1974

letup (n.).

level-headed.

Levi's (trademark).

L.I. for Long Island in headlines and after the names of cities and towns. Never *Long I.*

liaison.

liberal. Do not capitalize as noun or adjective unless the reference is to a political party or movement so named or to a member of such a group.

liberal-minded.

Liberal Party.

Liberty Island, formerly Bedloes Island (until 1956).

libretto (sing.), **librettos** (pl.).

Liechtensteiner(s). The people of Liechtenstein.

Liège (Belgium).

Lieut. (military or police). Lieut. John P. (or Joan) Manley, Lieutenant Manley, the lieutenant. Also (military): Lieut. (j.g.) John P. Manley.

Lieut. Col. John P. Manley, Colonel Manley, the colonel.

Lieut. Comdr. John P. Manley, Commander Manley, the commander.

Lieut. Gen. John P. Manley, General Manley, the general.

Lieut. Gov. Joan Manley (of a state), Lieutenant Governor Manley, the Lieutenant Governor.

life(-). lifeblood, lifeboat, life cycle, life force, lifeguard, life jacket, lifelike, lifeline, lifelong, life preserver, life raft, lifesaver, lifesaving, life-size, life span, life style (which see), lifetime, life vest, lifework.

Life Guards (a unit of the British cavalry).

life style. Do not overuse; there are other ways of saying it.

LIFO for the last-in, first-out system of inventory accounting. Also, *FIFO* for first in, first out.

light-, -light. lighthearted, lighthouse, lightship, lightweight (n., chiefly sports), light-year. Also: firelight, flashlight, gaslight, highlight, lamplight, limelight, searchlight, sidelight, sunlight.

lighted, not *lit.*

light heavyweight (sports).

light-year. A unit of length equal to the distance that light travels in one year at the rate of 186,000 miles per second. That distance is approximately 5,878 billion miles.

likable.

like-, -like. like-minded, like-natured, likewise. Also: businesslike, lifelike, shell-like.

like, as. The day may come when *like* will be fully accepted as a conjunction. But meanwhile do not so use it *(He runs like a fish swims—with no apparent effort)* except when it introduces a noun not followed by a verb *(He deals cards like a riverboat gambler).*

In the following examples, *like* and *as* are correctly used: *Tom, like his father, is a fierce competitor. This gingersnap tastes good, as a cookie should. The piano sounded as if it had been properly tuned. She treated him like a slave. He treated her as a loyal subject treats a monarch. You can easily build one, as I did. You can build one exactly like the one I built.*

Lilco for the Long Island Lighting Company.

lily of the valley.

Limburger (cheese).

linage (number of lines), **lineage** (descent).

Lincoln Center for the Performing Arts, Lincoln Center, the center. *Lincoln Center* will usually suffice in first references.

Lincoln's Birthday (holiday).

line-, -line. linebacker and lineman (football players), linesman (sports official), lineup (n.). Also: airline, balkline, breadline, coastline, deadline, shoreline, sideline, skyline, streamline, waistline.

Linotype (trademark).

liquefaction, liquefy. But: *gasification, gasify.*

lira, lire (sing. and pl., Italian money).

L.I.R.R. and *the Long Island* for subsequent references to the Long Island Rail Road.

lists of names. When names in lists are followed by descriptive matter, they should be set hanging indent, with each name a separate entry, to make them easier to read. See **casualty lists.**

liter. This unit in the metric system is equal to the volume occupied by one kilogram of water under standard conditions; it is roughly equal to one cubic decimeter, 1.06 United States liquid quarts or 0.91 dry quart. See **metric system.**

literally. It is often used when *figuratively* is meant: *The Communist leaders in China are literally walking a tightrope.* And when used correctly, it is usually superfluous.

Litt.D. or **D.Litt.** for Doctor of Literature.

littérateur.

Liverpudlian(s). The people of Liverpool.

living room (n.), **living-room** (adj.).

LL.B. for Bachelor of Laws. Also see **J.D.**

LL.D. for Doctor of Laws.

Lloyd's (insurance), **Lloyds** (bankers).

Lloyd's Register (shipping).

loan. Avoid as a verb; use *lend.* And *lent,* rather than *loaned.*

loath (unwilling), **loathe** (to hate).

localities and regions. Capitalize the names of specific localities and regions: *City of London* (financial district), *Left Bank, East Side, Middle West, Corn Belt.* Such designations are listed separately and alphabetically.

lock-. lockjaw, lockout (n.), locksmith, lockstep, lockup (n.).

Lod (Israel), formerly Lydda.

logrolling.

long(-), -long. longboat, long-drawn-out (adj.), longhair (colloq.), longhaired, longhand, longhorn (cattle), long jump (n., sports; formerly broad jump), long-jump (v., sports), long-range (adj.), longshoreman, long shot, longstanding, long-suffering, longtime (adj.), longwave (n. and adj.). Also: daylong, hourlong, monthlong, weeklong, yearlong.

Long Island, the Island. In headlines and after names of cities and towns: *L.I.* Never *Long I.*

Long Island Lighting Company (Lilco).

Long Island Rail Road, the Long

Island, the L.I.R.R. It is operated by the Metropolitan Transportation Authority.

longitude. See **latitude and longitude.**

longshoreman. A longshoreman is a waterfront laborer. A stevedore, in waterfront usage, is an employer.

long ton. See **ton.**

lookout (n.).

Loop, the (Chicago).

Lord. This British title is borne by barons, viscounts, earls and marquesses. Use it in first references to barons *(Lord Manley)*, and in second references to the others. When applied to any of the four ranks, the title is never followed by a given name. It is followed by a given name when applied to the younger sons of marquesses and dukes: *Lord Charles Cavendish, Lord Charles*, but never *Lord Cavendish.*

Lord & Taylor.

Los Angeles residents are called Angelenos.

Lotos Club.

Louisianian(s).

Louisville & Nashville Railroad, the L.&N.; a subsidiary of Seaboard Coast Line Industries.

lowbrow.

Lower California (Mexico).

lowercase. It is one word—noun, verb and adjective—with this exception: *the lower case* for the case in which type is kept.

Lower East Side (of Manhattan).

low frequency (n.), **low-frequency** (adj.).

low mass. It is said or celebrated, not sung. See **mass.**

L.P.G.A. for the Ladies' Professional Golf Association.

LSI (landing ship infantry), **LST** (landing ship tank).

Luang Prabang (Laos).

Lufthansa German Airlines. For first references *a Lufthansa airliner*, etc., will suffice.

Lunar New Year.

lunchroom.

Lurex (trademark), metallic yarn.

luster.

Lutheran Church in America.

Lutheran Church-Missouri Synod.

Luxembourg (country, Paris gardens and museum).

Luxembourger(s). The people of Luxembourg.

Lykes Brothers Steamship Company. For first references *a Lykes Brothers freighter*, etc., will suffice.

Lyndon B. Johnson Space Center, formerly the Manned Spacecraft Center, at Houston. Also see **Cape Canaveral.**

Lyons (France).

M

M. (for Monsieur). See **Mr., Mrs. and Miss.**

M.A. for Master of Arts. Also: *a master's degree.*

M.A.C. for the Municipal Assistance Corporation (in New York). Avoid its nickname, Big Mac, except in quoted matter.

Mac-, Mc-. When *Mac* or *Mc* occurs in a name in a headline that is set all caps, an apostrophe is used instead of the *ac* or the *c*: *M'ARTHUR, M'CLELLAN,* etc. The *ac* and *c* are used if the setting is caps and small caps or caps and lowercase. Alphabetize names starting with *Mac* or *Mc* by the second letter: *Mabley, MacAdam, Maynard, McNeil.*

Macdougal Street, Macdougal Alley (Greenwich Village); **McDougal Street** (Brooklyn).

Mace. See **Chemical Mace.**

Mach 1, Mach 2, etc., for the speed of sound, twice the speed of sound, etc.

machine gun (n.), **machine-gun** (adj. and v.). Also: *submachine gun.*

Mackenzie (Mountains, River and District, all in the Northwest Territories).

Macy's. This is the style for all the stores of R. H. Macy & Company.

mad-. madcap, madhouse, madman.

Madagascar, not *Malagasy Republic,* except in quoted matter or special formal contexts. The country is never called simply *Malagasy,* but the people are *Malagasy* (sing. and pl.) and the adjective is *Malagasy.*

madam, not *madame,* for the keeper of a bordello.

Madison, Dolley, the wife of James.

madras (fabric).

magazines. Do not quote their names. If an article is the first word in the name of an English-language or foreign-language magazine, capitalize it: The New Yorker, L'Express, Le Point, Der Spiegel. But: Stern, Fortune. Append the word *magazine,* lowercased, if it is needed for clarity or euphony: Time magazine, New York magazine. Quote titles of magazine articles and capitalize principal words.

Magistrate Joan Manley, the magistrate.

Magna Carta does not require the article: *He cited Magna Carta.*

magnitude (stellar). The brightest stars are roughly of first magnitude, whereas those of sixth magnitude are barely visible to the naked eye. With some telescopes, stars of the 20th magnitude or above can be photographed. A star of a given magnitude is 2.512 times brighter than one of the next higher numerical designation.

mah-jongg.

Maine Central Railroad.

Mainer(s). The people of Maine. Also: *State of Mainer(s).*

maître d'hôtel. Do not use *maître d'* except in direct quotation and in jocular contexts.

Maj. John P. Manley, Major Manley, the major.

Maj. Gen. John P. Manley, General Manley, the general.

Majorca. Use it, not *Mallorca* (and not *Spain*), in datelines: PALMA, Majorca, March 7—.

major-domo, major-domos.

majority leader. Do not use as a capitalized title preceding a name. Make it *Senator John P. Manley, the majority leader,* or *the majority leader, John P. Manley,* or something similar.

make-. make-believe, makeshift, makeup (n. and adj.).

(-)maker. bookmaker, dressmaker, homemaker, peacemaker, sailmaker, shoemaker, troublemaker. But some other combinations, not so well established, should not be solidified or hyphenated: auto maker, carpet maker, decision maker, film maker, policy maker.

Malagasy (sing. and pl.). The people of Madagascar. The adjective is *Malagasy.* Ordinarily, do not refer to the country as the Malagasy Republic.

Malay, Malayan, Malaysian. *Malay* (n. or adj.) refers to a member of an ethnic group, Polynesian in background, found on the Malay Peninsula. *Malayan* (n. or adj.) refers to any inhabitant of that peninsula or of Malaya, the territory centering on the peninsula, which became part of Malaysia in 1962. *Malaysian* (n. or adj.) refers to any inhabitant of Malaysia.

male (n.), **female** (n.). In general, avoid both nouns in references to boys and men, and to girls and women. But the adjectives *male* and *female* present no problems. See **female** and **women.**

Malian(s). The people of Mali.

Mallorca (Spain). Do not use; make it *Majorca* instead. In datelines: PALMA, Majorca, May 7—.

Maltese (sing. and pl.). The people of Malta.

mandatary (n.), **mandatory** (adj.).

maneuver.

maneuvers (military). Special designations of forces for purposes of a maneuver are set thus: *Blue fleet, Red army.*

manhattan (cocktail).

Manitoba. Do not abbreviate after cities and towns, even in datelines.

Manitoban(s). The people of Manitoba.

mannequin. A woman who models clothes or a model of the human body used in making or displaying clothes.

man-of-war, men-of-war (warships).

manpower.

mantel (shelf), **mantle** (cloak).

Manufacturers Hanover Corporation, parent company of the Manufacturers Hanover Trust Company.

many-. manyfold, many-hued, many-sided.

Mao Tse-tung. In second references: *Chairman Mao* or *Mr. Mao.*

Marble Collegiate Reformed Church.

March. Do not abbreviate.

Marchioness of Manleyford, the; Lady Manleyford, the Marchioness. Use the non-English equivalents *Marquise* and *Marchesa* where appropriate.

Mardi Gras.

Mariana Islands, not *Marianas Islands.* But: *the Marianas.*

marijuana.

Marine Corps, Marine(s), marine(s). Capitalize *Marine(s)* as a synonym for the United States Marine Corps: *He enlisted in the Marines. A Marine landing. The Marines have landed. (Marine Corps,* not *Marines,* is the preferred second reference in most instances.) But: *three marines, a company of marines.* Also: *the corps.* As a guide to capitalization, the following test applies: If the word *soldier* or *soldiers* would fit logically in place of *marine* or *marines,* the *m* should be lowercased. If *Army, Navy* or *Air Force* can be substituted logically for *Marine* or *Marines,* the *M* should be uppercased.

Marine Corps ranks are listed separately and alphabetically, in full or by abbreviations. Also see **enlisted men's ranks.**

Marine Midland Banks Inc., the parent company of the Marine Midland Bank.

Maronite Church. A Roman Catholic church of the Eastern Rite (which see).

Marquess of Manleyford, the; Lord Manleyford, the Marquess. Use the non-English equivalents *Marquis* and *Marchese* where appropriate. But: *Marquis of Queensberry rules.*

Marseilles (France).

marshal (n. and v.). Also: *marshaled, marshaling.*

Marshall Plan.

Marshal of the Royal Air Force Viscount Portal of Hungerford, Viscount Portal, Lord Portal. This rank cannot properly be shortened. Holders of the rank usually have other titles by which they can be called. *R.A.F. Marshal* is not correct.

martini (cocktail).

MARV('s) for maneuverable reentry vehicle(s).

Marylander(s).

Mason-Dixon line. This short form is preferred to *Mason and Dixon's line.*

mass (religious). Lowercase *mass, high mass, low mass, requiem mass,* etc. High mass is sung, low mass is said. Masses are not *held* and do not *take place;* they may be offered, celebrated, said or sung.

Mass. for Massachusetts after cities and towns.

Massachusettsan(s). The more easily pronounced *Bay Stater(s)* is also acceptable.

mass number. The number of protons and neutrons in a nucleus. It is used to designate isotopes. For example, the carbon 14 nucleus contains six protons and eight neutrons. Mass number differs only slightly from atomic mass (which see).

masterful (overpowering), **masterly** (skillful).

Master Gunnery Sgt. John P. Manley, Sergeant Manley, the sergeant.

master's degree. But: *Master of Arts* or *Science*, etc. Also: *M.A., M.S.,* etc. See **academic degrees and titles.**

Master Sgt. John P. Manley, Master Sergeant (or just Sergeant) Manley, the master sergeant or the sergeant. Also: Chief (or Senior) Master Sgt. John P. Manley, Sergeant Manley.

mastiff.

Matamoras (Tex.), **Matamoros** (Mexico).

Matawan (N.J.), **Mattawan** (Mich.), **Matewan** (W.Va.), **Matteawan** (N.Y.).

matériel.

Matson Navigation Company. For first references *a Matson liner*, etc., will suffice.

matter-of-fact (adj.), **matter-of-course** (adj.).

matzoh(s).

Mauritian(s), the people of Mauritius.

May. Do not abbreviate.

Mayor John P. Manley (or Joan Manley), Mayor Manley, the Mayor, Mr. (or Mrs. or Miss) Manley. Also: Mayor John P. Manley of Detroit. In referring to the current Mayor of New York, omit the first name, even on first reference. Capitalize the plural when it refers to a small number of current mayors who are specifically identified in the article: *the Mayors of Chicago and St. Louis; the two Mayors had met before.* But: *a conference of American mayors; a gathering of 50 mayors; three former mayors.* Also: *a mayor.*

mayoral (adj.), **mayoralty** (n.).

Mays department stores in the New York area are operated by J. W. Mays Inc. In second references: *Mays.* They should not be confused with the stores of the *May Department Stores Company,* a St. Louis-based national retail chain that does not have a New York outlet.

McDonald's, not *MacDonald's,* for the hamburger-shop chain operated by the McDonald's Corporation.

McDonnell Douglas Corporation.

Md. for Maryland after cities and towns.

M.D. for Doctor of Medicine.

Me. for Maine after cities and towns.

Meadow Brook (L.I.), **Meadowbrook** (Philadelphia).

meager.

mean-. mean-souled, meantime, meanwhile. But: mean time (astronomical).

mean, median. In statistics, a *mean* is an average; a *median* is a figure that ranks midway in a list of numbers arranged in ascending or descending order. For example, in a discussion of the varying wages of 51 workers, the mean is the total of their pay divided by 51. The median is a wage that is higher than 25 of the wages and lower than the remaining 25. If the total of items listed is an even number—50, say, instead of 51—the median is the average of the two numbers in the middle of the listing. In other words, if the 25th number in a listing of 50 is 200 and the 26th is 220, the median is 210.

measures. Weights and measures are listed separately and alphabetically. See **metric system.**

Medal of Honor, the medal. Not *Congressional* Medal of Honor.

medals. Capitalize *Medal of Honor, Bronze Star, Purple Heart, Victoria Cross,* etc.

media. Still a plural, despite persistent efforts to turn it into a singular. The singular is, of course, *medium.* See the next entry.

media (in the news sense). Do not use the word alone as a synonym for the press, printed or electronic, except in direct quotation. If absolutely necessary, *news media* may be used. Depending on context, terms like the following are preferred: *press, printed and electronic press, journalism, radio, television, news organizations* and, thank goodness, *newspaper(s).*

median. See **mean, median.**

Medicaid, Medicare. Like *Social Security,* they should be capitalized.

Medical Examiner John P. Manley, Medical Examiner Manley, the Medical Examiner, Dr. Manley. But: *a medical examiner, medical examiners* (for capitalized plural exceptions, see **titles**).

medieval.

megaton, megatonnage. A megaton is a unit used to measure the power of nuclear explosions. It is equal to the explosive force of a million tons of TNT. See **gigaton** and **kiloton.**

melee.

Melkite Church, not *Melchite.* A Roman Catholic church of the Eastern Rite (which see).

memento, mementos.

memorandums, not *memoranda.*

Memorial Day (formerly Decoration Day).

Memphian(s). The people of Memphis, Tenn.

ménage. Also: ménage à trois.

men's wear. But use any variant spellings, such as *menswear,* if they are part of proper names like *Menswear Retailers of America.*

Mercalli scale. A scale of earthquake intensities, expressed in Roman numerals and defined essentially in terms of their damaging effects. An earthquake of intensity I can be felt by only a few people. An earthquake of intensity XII is the most destructive. A system more commonly used is the Richter scale (which see), based on the energy released by the quake.

merchant marine. Lowercase: *United States merchant marine.* Also lowercase titles of merchant marine officers when standing alone.

Mercurochrome (trademark).

merino, merinos.

Merrill Lynch & Company, parent company of Merrill Lynch, Pierce, Fenner & Smith Inc.

Merrimack. It's an ironclad rule in the Navy: The name of the Confederate warship that fought the Monitor in the first battle between ironclads is properly spelled with a *k.*

merry-go-round.

Messrs. may be used to avoid a tiresome repetition of *Mr.* in a listing of three or more: *Messrs. Manley, Brown, Jones and Smith were called on in that order.* See **Mr., Mrs. and Miss.**

Met for Metropolitan Opera. If the art context is unmistakable, *Met* can also be used for the Metropolitan Museum of Art.

meter. When used in the sense of specific measurement, it is the basic unit of length in the metric system. A meter is equal to 39.37 inches or, roughly, 1.1 yards. See **metric system.**

Methodist Church. Avoid in first references when possible. It is now the United Methodist Church.

metric system. The basic units of metric weights and measures are the gram, the meter and the liter. Larger and smaller units are ordered by multiples of 10, defined by prefixes like *kilo-*. Thus, in this decimal system, a kilometer is 1,000 meters. Following are the metric prefixes and their values:

MULTIPLES OF A UNIT

DEKA- denotes 10 units, as in *dekameter.* The form before a vowel is *dek-*, as in *dekare*, which is 10 ares, or 1,000 square meters.

HECTO- denotes 100 units, as in *hectogram.* The form before a vowel is *hect-*, as in *hectare.*

KILO- denotes 1,000 units, as in *kilogram.*

MEGA- denotes one million units, as in *megaton.*

GIGA- denotes one billion units, as in *gigaton.*

TERA- denotes 1,000 billion units (or one trillion), as in *terahertz*, meaning 1,000 billion cycles per second.

FRACTIONS OF A UNIT

DECI- denotes one-tenth, as in *decigram.*

CENTI- denotes one-hundredth, as in *centimeter.*

MILLI- denotes one-thousandth, as in *milliliter* and *millimeter.*

MICRO- denotes one-millionth, as in *microgram.*

NANO- denotes one-billionth, as in *nanogram.*

PICO- denotes one-trillionth, as in *picosecond.*

Many of the more commonly used metric weights and measures are listed separately and alphabetically, as are many of the nonmetric weights and measures used in the English-speaking countries.

Metropolitan (church title). This is a title given in the Eastern Orthodox churches to bishops of the rank just below Patriarch (which see). It is used as the title Bishop would be, and is thus capitalized in all references to a specific individual. See **Eastern Orthodoxy.**

metropolitan district (in sports).

Mev (sing. and pl.). A Mev is one million electron-volts. See **Gev.**

Mexico City, not the official *Mexico, D.F.* (for the Mexican words meaning Federal District). See **City, city.**

M-G-M for Metro-Goldwyn-Mayer Inc.

Mich. for Michigan after cities and towns.

Michigander(s).

mid-. midafternoon, midair, mid-America, mid-Atlantic, midchannel, midcontinent, midday, Mideast (see **Middle East**), midfield, midiron (golf club), midland, midmorning, midocean, midsection, midship, midtown (including Manhattan's), midway, midweek, Midwest (see **Middle West**), midwife. Also: mid-1960, mid-1960's, mid-'60, mid-60's.

Midamerica Commodity Exchange (Chicago).

middle(-). middle age (n.), middle-aged (adj.), middleman, middle-of-the-road (adj.), middleweight.

Middle Ages.

Middle Atlantic States.

Middle East, Mideast. Use Middle East in news stories. Either may be used in headlines. Do not use Near East. The Middle East comprises Cyprus, Egypt, Iran, Iraq, Israel, Jordan, Lebanon, Libya, Saudi Arabia, Southern Yemen, the Sudan, Syria, Yemen and various Arab principalities.

Middle West, Midwest. For uniformity's sake, Middle West is preferred in references in stories to that section of the United States. Either form may be used in headlines.

Middle Western States.

midnight refers to the end of a day, not the start of a new one. See **time.**

Midshipman John P. Manley, Midshipman Manley, the midshipman.

Midwest   Stock   Exchange (Chicago).

MIG('s) for the Soviet aircraft. With a model number: *MIG-21, MIG-21's,* etc.

mile. When *mile* is used without a preceding modifier, it usually refers to the *statute mile,* which is equal to 5,280 feet or about 1,609 meters. A *nautical mile* is equal to about 6,076 feet or 1,852 meters. A *kilometer* (1,000 meters) is equal to about 3,281 feet, roughly 0.6 of a statute mile or about five-eighths of a statute mile. See **metric system** and **knot.**

Military Academy (United States), the Academy, West Point.

military bases. Follow this style for United States Air Force, Army, Marine Corps and Navy bases: *Edwards Air Force Base, the Air Force base, the base* or, in this case, *the air base.* In the case of Navy bases, *Naval* is usually the word in the formal name: *Guam Naval Base, Mayport Naval Station.* In second references, *naval station* or *Navy station* or *naval base* or *Navy base* may be used.

The Air Force uses the designation *Air Force base* for installations only within the United States and its possessions; elsewhere, *air base: Andrews Air Force Base,* in Maryland; *Anderson Air Force Base,* on Guam; *Clark Air Base,* in the Philippines. (For installations that do not have landing facilities, *Air Force station* and *air station* are used similarly.)

For the style for datelines on stories sent from military bases or nearby towns or cities, see **datelines, integrity of.**

military ranks are listed separately and alphabetically, in full or by abbreviations. Also see **enlisted men's ranks.**

Military   Sealift   Command, (M.S.C.).

militate, mitigate. To *militate* (with the preposition *against*) means to have weight or effect against; to *mitigate* means to ease or soften.

militia. Lowercase when standing alone; capitalize when part of a name: *Naval Militia.*

mill-, (-)mill. millowner, millpond, millrace. Also: coffee mill, diploma mill, flour mill, gristmill, paper mill, pepper mill, sawmill, textile mill, windmill.

millennium.

millibar (pressure measurement). One-thousandth of a bar. See **bar.**

millimeter. One-thousandth of a meter, or approximately 0.04 inch. The abbreviation *mm.* should not be used in ordinary writing (when giving calibers of weapons, for example), but it may be used in tabular and other special matter. See **metric system** and **caliber.**

million. See **dollars and cents** and **numbers, round.**

Milwaukeean(s).

-minded. air-minded, high-minded, money-minded, open-minded.

minesweeper.

Minister of Justice John P. Manley; John P. Manley, Minister Without Portfolio; the Minister; a minister; the ministers (for capitalized plural exceptions, see **titles**).

minister (church title). It may be used (always lowercase) in references to most Protestant clergymen. Some Episcopalians prefer *priest.* Most Lutherans and some Baptists prefer *pastor.* The usual style for *minister* is *the Rev. John P. Manley, the minister* or *He had served as minister there for 23 years.* For the Baptists who prefer *pastor,* use it as *minister* was used in the preceding examples. For most Lutherans, who are also *the Rev.* in first references, use *Pastor* before the name in subsequent references: *Pastor Manley.* For an exception, see **pastor.** Also see **rector** and **Rev.** and **Father.**

minisummit. Do not use. See **summit.**

Minn. for Minnesota after cities and towns.

Minnesota Mining and Manufacturing Company. In second references: *the 3M Company.*

Minnesotan(s).

minority leader. Do not use as a capitalized title preceding a name.

Make it *Senator John P. Manley, the minority leader,* or *the minority leader, John P. Manley,* or something similar.

minuscule, not *miniscule.*

miracle rice. Lowercase and omit quotation marks in referring to various high-yield strains of rice. If the context requires some indication that the term is figurative, it may be preceded by *so-called* or *known as.* Also see **Green Revolution.**

MIRV('s) for multiple independently targetable re-entry vehicle(s). Avoid the military jargon usage of the term as a verb, *to MIRV,* meaning to equip a missile with MIRV's.

mishmash.

Miss. See **Mr., Mrs. and Miss.**

Miss. for Mississippi after cities and towns.

missile age.

missiles (military) are listed separately and alphabetically by their abbreviations: ABM('s), ICBM('s), MIRV('s), SAM('s), etc.

mission (diplomatic office). Lowercase when standing alone. But: *the United States Mission, the French Mission.*

Mississippian(s).

Missourian(s).

Missouri-Kansas-Texas Railroad, the Katy; a subsidiary of Katy Industries.

Missouri Pacific Railroad, the Mopac; a subsidiary of the Mississippi River Corporation.

M.I.T. for the Massachusetts Institute of Technology; the institute.

mitigate, militate. To *mitigate* means to ease or soften; to *militate* (with the preposition *against*) means to have weight or effect against.

mix-up (n.).

Mlle. See **Mr., Mrs. and Miss.**

mm. may be used for millimeter, in tabular and other special matter, but not in ordinary writing: *a 105-millimeter gun,* not *105-mm.*

Mme. See **Mr., Mrs. and Miss.**

Mo. for Missouri after cities and towns.

Mobil Oil Corporation. In second references: *Mobil.*

mockingbird.

Moderator (church title). Capitalize when used with name and when standing alone if referring to a specific individual.

modern (architecture). Lowercase, though some scholars maintain that there was a "Modern Age" of architecture that has ended. Since there is increasing talk of an emerging post-modern style, it is often useful to use the word *contemporary* instead of *modern* to avoid confusion. See **styles and schools in the arts.**

Moët & Chandon (the champagne). Informally: *Moët.*

Mogadishu, not *Mogadiscio,* for the capital of Somalia.

Mohammed. That spelling should be used for the founder of the Moslem religion and for people who bear his name unless a person so named makes known a preference for another spelling and can demonstrate that it is well established.

mold.

Molotov cocktail. This slang term for a gasoline bomb is becoming outdated and should be used only in instances where it seems appropriate.

molt.

Monacan(s). The people of Monaco. In quoted matter, *Monegasque(s)* is also acceptable.

money. Except for dollars and cents and pounds and pence, symbols are not to be used in giving sums of money. In such cases, use figures and spell out the monetary unit: *9 francs, 50 pesos, 30,000 lire,* etc.

In printing round sums of dollars in the millions or billions, the style is *$2 million, $1.65 billion.* In cap-and-lowercase headlines, capitalize *Million* and *Billion.* Instead of *$1 trillion,* write *$1,000 billion.* See **dollars and cents, pounds and pence, francs and centimes** and similar listings; also **numbers** and **numbers, round.**

-monger. fishmonger, rumormonger, scandalmonger, warmonger, etc.

mongoose, mongooses.

monkey wrench.

monsignor. Abbreviate only in first references: *Msgr. John P. Manley, Monsignor Manley, the monsignor.*

Mont. for Montana after cities and towns.

Montagnard(s) for the hill people of central Vietnam. The adjective is *Montagnard.*

Montanan(s).

Monterey (Calif.), **Monterrey** (Mexico).

Montgomery Ward & Company, a subsidiary of Marcor Inc. In second references: *Montgomery Ward.*

monthlong.

129

months. Abbreviate January (Jan.), February (Feb.), August (Aug.), September (Sept.), October (Oct.), November (Nov.) and December (Dec.) in datelines and ordinary reading matter when followed by numerals: *Jan. 1, Feb. 16.* Do not abbreviate March, April, May, June and July. See **dates** and **dates, punctuation in,** and **years, decades, centuries.**

Montrealer(s).

moon. For rare instances of capitalization, see **earth, moon, sun.**

moonlight. Do not quote when used to mean working at an additional job. Also: *moonlighter, moonlighting.*

Moore-McCormack Lines.

Moravian Church in America.

Morgan Guaranty Trust Company. The parent company is J. P. Morgan & Company.

Mormon Church. This informal name for the Church of Jesus Christ of Latter-day Saints may be used in first and subsequent references as long as the full title appears at least once in any story that substantially deals with this church.

The church is headed by a president. Other titles are apostle, high priest, seventy,* elder, deacon, teacher and priest. The term *elder* is appropriate in second references to all except deacon, teacher and priest. Thus: *President John P. Manley, Elder Manley, the President of the church. Mr.* and *Dr.* are also appropriate in such references.

The church has stakes, which are the equivalent of dioceses, and a

stake is headed by a stake president. There are also wards, which are local congregations. A ward is headed by a bishop.

It is proper to call members of the church Mormons.

mortician. Do not use in place of *funeral director* or *undertaker.*

Moslem(s). This is the preferred form in references to adherents of Islam. In the names of certain United States organizations, such as the Black Muslims, and in references to their members, *Muslim(s)* may be used. See **Islam.**

mosquito, mosquitoes.

Most Rev., the; Rt. Rev., the. In accordance with the current tendency in the Roman Catholic Church and the Episcopal Church, these terms are omitted in almost all cases before the names of archbishops and bishops. But *the Most Rev.* is used before the name of the Anglican prelate who is the Archbishop of Canterbury and the names of the superiors general of certain Catholic orders. See **Canterbury, Archbishop of; Superior General; Archbishop; Bishop; Rev.; Very Rev.**

mother(-). motherhood, mother(s)-in-law, motherland, mother tongue.

Mother's Day.

motion pictures. In ordinary matter, quote their titles and capitalize principal words.

motor-. motorboat, motorcar, motorcycle, motorman.

Mount. Capitalize in ordinary copy when part of a name: *Mount Vernon.* The abbreviation *(Mt. Vernon)* may be used in headlines and in agate and other special matter.

---

*A seventy is a member of a group of older Mormon men (called a Seventy) who do part-time work in the communities where they live.

mountain standard time (M.S.T.). See **time.**

movements (music). Capitalize the names of movements: *the Scherzo, the Andante,* etc. Lowercase if the movement is referred to by its place in the sequence: *the second movement, the finale.*

movements in the arts. See **styles and schools in the arts.**

M.P. for Member of Parliament or military police.

m.p.h. for miles per hour. Spell out the first time: *The speed limit is 55 miles per hour.* The form *an hour* is also acceptable: *a limit of 45 miles an hour, a 45-mile-an-hour wind.* But *per hour* is preferred in first references if there are subsequent references in which the abbreviation *m.p.h.* is used: *The damage was done by gusts of wind reaching 45 miles per hour. Earlier the wind blew at a steady 45 m.p.h.* In cap-and-lowercase headlines, the abbreviation is always capitalized: *M.P.H.*

Mr., Mrs. and Miss are to be used in news stories not only for citizens of the English-speaking countries but also for citizens of other countries who do not have royal, noble, military, religious or other titles of the kinds that replace the foreign equivalents of *Mr., Mrs.* and *Miss.* The foreign equivalents—*M., Mme., Mlle.; Herr, Frau, Fräulein; Señor, Señora, Señorita; Senhor, Senhora, Senhorita; Signor, Signora, Signorina,* etc.—may be used when desired for special effect, but not in the normal reporting of news. They may also be used in quoted matter if the passage quoted was originally written or spoken in English. But in translating ordinary quoted matter from a foreign language into English, the foreign honorifics should be rendered as *Mr., Mrs.* and *Miss.*

Here are some further guides:

USE OF MR.

In almost every instance, *Mr.* is to be used in second and subsequent references to an adult male who does not have a title of a kind that replaces the ordinary honorific. We do not omit the *Mr.* in subsequent references to a person convicted of crime or having an unsavory reputation. Should the use of *Mr.* in some such cases seem ludicrously out of place, judicious editing and the use of pronouns or terms like *the defendant* or *the suspect* will solve the problem.

Mr. is not needed in subsequent references to people of pre-eminence who are no longer living: Newton, Lincoln, Lenin, Churchill, Picasso, etc. This is also true, especially in the arts and often in science, of some people who are still living—for example, Picasso and Einstein when they were living. The needless *Mr.* most often occurs in reviews. Indeed, in the case of reviews, mere eminence, not pre-eminence, may justify dropping the *Mr.*

Mr. is not used with the names of sports figures in sports-section stories or in stories of sports contests that appear on page 1. But if sports figures appear in general news stories, the *Mr.* should be used. In the obituary of a sports figure, *Mr.* should be used in the passages relating to his birth, his death and any other circumstances not relating to his participation in his sport. It would have been wrong, of course, to write in Babe Ruth's obituary: *Having pointed out the target, Mr. Ruth hit one into the stands.*

Similarly, in columns or articles

dealing with chess or bridge, *Mr.* is not used in passages describing play of a game.

Some youths under the age of 18 should have the *Mr.*, and some should not. There can be no precise rule, but the nature of the story should be controlling. If *Mr.* is omitted, call the subject *Charles* or *Charles Manley*, not *the Manley boy* or *the Manley youth.*

In a listing of three or more last names, *Messrs.* may be used to avoid a tiresome repetition of *Mr.: Messrs. Manley, Brown, Jones and Smith were called on in that order.*

USE OF MRS. AND MISS

In almost all first references to women—married or single, well known or not—given names should be used and the honorifics *Mrs.* and *Miss* should be omitted. *Mrs.* and *Miss* (but not *Ms.*, which see) should be used in subsequent references for women who do not have titles of the kind that replace the ordinary honorifics. Thus:

Golda Meir, former Prime Minister of Israel, is taking her first real vacation in years. Mrs. Meir is spending it. . . .

Jacqueline Onassis bicycled in Central Park unnoticed by photographers. Mrs. Onassis was. . . .

Eleanor Holmes Norton, chairman of the Commission on Human Rights, said yesterday. . . . Mrs. Norton was asked. . . . The chairman was asked. . . .

Chris Evert defeated Billie Jean King. . . . Miss Evert and Mrs. King played. . . .

Ethel Kennedy, the widow of Senator Robert F. Kennedy. . . . (It is, of course, not necessary to use *widow* after all first references in cases like this.)

Jane Doe, daughter of . . . , was married yesterday to. . . .

Joan Manley finds commuting too costly for her budget. Mrs. [or *Miss*] *Manley says. . . .*

Miss is also to be used in subsequent references to women like Marian Anderson, Jessica Tandy, Anne Jackson, Doris Fleischman, Kate Millett and others who are or have been married, but are not known by their married names in their careers. In rare instances, they might be referred to by their married names to achieve some special effect.

In the cases of all married women who figure in the news because of their own activities, the husband's name need not be mentioned unless it is really pertinent to the story or the story raises a question. For example, if the last name is Rockefeller, readers should not have to guess which Rockefeller is the husband.

Sometimes a married woman prefers to use a name that includes her original surname as well as her husband's: Margaret Chase Smith, for instance. When the preference is known, this style should be followed.

In obituaries, a single woman is (for example) *Joan Manley* in both story and headline. If Joan Manley was married and the obituary is being printed because of *her* activities in life, the first reference in the story and the reference in the head should be *Joan Manley.* But if the obituary is being printed for the purpose of recording the death of the wife or widow of John P. Manley, known for *his* activities, then the first reference in the story should be *Joan Manley, the wife* [or *the widow*] *of John P. Manley* . . . and the headline should read *Mrs. John P. Manley.*

If a woman has a title, it is used just as a title is in the case of a man:

Prime Minister Joan Manley, in first references; in subsequent references, *Prime Minister Manley*, *the Prime Minister* or *Mrs.* or *Miss Manley*. Also: *Col. Joan Manley*, *Colonel Manley*, *the colonel*. But not *Mrs.* or *Miss* in subsequent references to the colonel.

The few exceptions to using given names in first references to women would include this example of a case in which the husband's name is a dominant factor:

Mrs. Martin Luther King Sr. was honored today. . . .

But in the case of the senior Mrs. King's daughter-in-law, this form should be followed because of her own prominence:

Coretta Scott King, the widow of Martin Luther King Jr. . . .

As for other exceptions, here are some examples (imagining John P. Manley to be, in the first instance, a world-renowned Baptist evangelist and, in the second, a very famous television personality):

Mrs. John P. Manley announced today that she had converted to Buddhism.

Mrs. John P. Manley died today after a short illness.

But in either of the Manley examples, this form would also suffice:

Joan Manley, wife of the renowned Baptist evangelist John P. Manley, announced today that she. . . .

The *Mrs.* or *Miss* may be dropped in subsequent references to women of pre-eminence who are no longer living: Curie, Flagstad, Bernhardt, Woolf, for example. This is also true of some women still living (Fonteyn, Callas, Nevelson and O'Keeffe, for example), but the use or omission of the honorific may be determined by context: *O'Keeffe ranks with the painters of. . . .* But: *Miss O'Keeffe graciously received. . . .*

Titles used with personal names in place of *Mr.*, *Mrs.* and *Miss* are listed separately and alphabetically. Also see **personal names and nicknames.**

MRV('s) for multiple re-entry vehicle(s). Also see **MIRV('s).**

MS. for manuscript; **MSS.** for the plural.

Ms. As an honorific, use it only in quoted matter, in letters to the editor and, in news articles, in passages discussing the term itself.

M.S. for Master of Science. But: *a master's degree.*

M.S.C. for the Military Sealift Command.

Msgr. John P. Manley, Monsignor Manley, the monsignor.

M.T.A. for the Metropolitan Transportation Authority.

mugging is a lay term rather than a legally defined crime. It may be described as a type of robbery: a theft or an attempted theft involving the use of force against a victim seized by surprise in a public place or a hallway, an elevator, etc. Because the term is imprecise, any mention of mugging should preferably be accompanied by a description of the crime, and of the legal charges. Also see **burglary, larceny, robbery, theft.**

mug shot. This is police jargon and, like most other jargon, should be avoided in ordinary contexts.

multi-. multicolored, multifold, multiform, multilateral.

Muscle Shoals (Ala.).

Muscovite(s). The people of Moscow.

music. Abbreviation, capitalization

and punctuation guides are given in separate and alphabetical listings of various kinds of musical works and terms.

If the commonly used title of a work includes the instrumentation, the instrumentation is capitalized: *Bach's Suite No. 1 for Orchestra, Mozart's Piano Trio in B flat major (K. 254), Beethoven's Serenade for Flute, Violin and Viola (Op. 25)*. If the instrumentation does not commonly appear in the title but is added to it for explanatory purposes, the names of the instruments are not capitalized: *Mozart's Sinfonia Concertante in E flat major* [the common title] *for violin and viola (K. 364)*.

If the title contains a nickname, the nickname is quoted: *Beethoven's "Eroica" Symphony*. If the work has a special full title, all of it is quoted: *"Symphonie Fantastique," "Rhapsody in Blue."* In second references to specific compositions, lowercase *concerto, trio, quartet, symphony, suite,* etc.

Muslim(s). Use *Moslem(s)* instead, except in the names of certain organizations in the United States, such as the Black Muslims, and in references to their members.

mustache, not *moustache.*

mute. Avoid in describing an afflicted person. See **deaf and dumb, deaf-mute.**

My Lai (Vietnam).

N

N.A.A.C.P. for the National Association for the Advancement of Colored People. But it is *NAACP* without points in this official name: the NAACP Legal Defense and Educational Fund Inc.

Nabisco Inc., formerly the National Biscuit Company.

naïve, naïveté.

names of all sorts are listed separately and alphabetically. Also see **abbreviations; acts, amendments, bills and laws; aircraft names; apostrophe; Arabic terms in place names; Arab names and titles; building names; Burmese names; Cambodian names; Chinese names; company and corporation names; Ethiopian names; Filipino names; geographic names; Indonesian names; Jr.; Korean names; Laotian names; Mr., Mrs. and Miss; newspaper names; personal names and nicknames; plurals of proper names; Russian names; Spanish names; Sr.; Thai names; trademarks; Vietnamese names.**

Namibia. See **South-West Africa.**

napoleon (pastry).

Napoleon Bonaparte. But an accent is used in Code Napoléon.

NASA for the National Aeronautics and Space Administration.

NASCAR for the National Association for Stock Car Auto Racing.

N.A.S.D. for the National Association of Securities Dealers.

NASDAQ for the National Association of Securities Dealers Automated Quotations.

nation, national. Lowercase unless part of a formal name or title.

National Airlines.

national anthem(s). Lowercase the expression. Quote the titles and capitalize principal words. See **songs.**

National Baptist Convention of America.

National Baptist Convention, U.S.A., Inc.

National Broadcasting Company. See **NBC.**

National Capitol (the building).

national (or **state** or **county**) **chairman** (of a political party). John P. Manley, Republican national (or state or county) chairman; the national (or state or county) chairman; the chairman.

national (or **state** or **county**) **committee** (of a political party). The Republican National (or State or County) Committee, the national (or state or county) committee, the committee.

National Conference of Catholic Bishops.

national (or **state** or **county**) **convention** (of a political party). The Democratic National (or State or County) Convention, the national (or state or county) convention, the convention.

National Council of the Churches of Christ in the United States of America. The council itself approves a shorter version: the National Council of Churches.

National Geographic Society, publisher of National Geographic. Do not confuse with the American Geographical Society.

National Guard, the Guard. Also: National Guardsman or National Guardsmen, guardsman or guardsmen.

National Institutes of Health.

nationalist. Capitalize only when it is part of the name of a political party or movement or when it refers to a member of a group so named.

Nationalist China for the Chinese Government on Taiwan. In subsequent references, use *Taiwan, Nationalist China* or *the Chinese Nationalists.*

nationality. See **ethnic background of an American in the news** and **natives and residents.**

National Organization for Women (NOW), not *of Women.*

National Security Council, the Council. Do not use abbreviation *N.S.C.* except in quoted matter.

National Weather Service, the Weather Service. Formerly the United States Weather Bureau.

nationwide.

native(s). References to *the natives* are often condescending and offensive, and when they are they should be avoided. An exception is the term *Alaska native(s),* which the Aleuts, Eskimos and Indians of Alaska use with pride in speaking of themselves. Similar exceptions may be made for other areas where the term is used by indigenous groups in a nonpejorative sense. And of course it is acceptable to write *a native of Chicago,* etc. See **Indians, American.**

natives and residents. Terms used to denote natives and residents of many countries, regions, states of the United States, Canadian provinces and cities of the world are listed separately and alphabetically. For example, see **Argentine(s); Liverpudlian(s); Malagasy; Quebecer(s), Québécois.**

Nativity. Capitalize when the reference is to the birth of Jesus.

NATO for the North Atlantic Treaty Organization. Also: *the Atlantic alliance, the alliance.*

Naugahyde (trademark).

nautical mile. See **mile.**

Navajo(s). The Indian(s) and the language.

Naval Academy (United States), the Academy, Annapolis.

Naval Militia (United States), the militia.

naval station. Capitalize only in full names: *Mayport Naval Station, the naval station, the station.* But: *the Navy station.* See **military bases.**

Navy. Capitalize in *United States Navy, British Navy, French Navy,* etc. It is *the Navy* in subsequent references to that of the United States, but lowercase such references to any foreign navy. It is also *Navy* in references to United States Naval Academy sports teams.

navy blue.

Navy ranks are listed separately and alphabetically, in full or by abbreviations. Also see **enlisted men's ranks.**

Nazi, Nazism.

NBC for the National Broadcasting Company. NBC News, NBC Radio and NBC-TV are the full names of NBC divisions. Any of these names, as well as NBC, may be used in first references, depending on context, and NBC alone may of course be used in subsequent references. NBC alone is preferred in some first references, especially when the networks are mentioned together in a lead: *ABC, CBS and NBC will televise President Manley's address to the nation tomorrow night.*

N.C. for North Carolina after cities and towns.

N. Carolina may be used only in headlines—and then only when absolutely necessary—and in tabular and other special matter.

NCR Corporation, formerly the National Cash Register Company.

N.D. for North Dakota after cities and towns.

N. Dakota may be used only in headlines—and then only when absolutely necessary—and in tabular and other special matter.

Ndjamena, the capital of Chad. Formerly Fort-Lamy.

né. See **née.**

near(-). nearby (adj., adv.), near disaster, near escape, near miss, near riot, nearside (adj.), nearsighted.

Near East. Do not use. See **Middle East.**

Neb. for Nebraska after cities and towns.

Nebraskan(s).

Nederland Line (Stoomvaart Maatschappij).

née. Use only with a surname, as in *Joan P. Manley, née Smith.* The masculine form, rarely used, is *né.*

Neediest Cases. Do not use *Hundred* in other than historical references to the annual charitable campaign of The New York Times. In first references, it should be *The New York Times Neediest Cases Fund.* Never refer to it as the *Neediest Fund.* Capitalize *Neediest Cases* when standing alone.

negligee.

Negress. Do not use. See **women.**

Negro (n., adj.), **Negroes.** In general, use *black* rather than *Negro* as noun and adjective, although *Negro* is acceptable in many contexts, both current and historical. The race of a person figuring in the news should be specified only if it is truly pertinent. The same stricture applies to ethnic and religious identifications.

Neiman-Marcus.

nelson (wrestling hold). full nelson, three-quarters nelson, half nelson, quarter nelson.

neo-classical (architecture). Strictly speaking, the term refers to an early revival of Greek or Roman style, not to 20th-century buildings; although it would not be completely erroneous to use it in that context, it is not preferable. See **styles and schools in the arts.**

Neo-Classicism (music). A movement that originated in the first quarter of the 20th century, using Baroque and Classical forms with 20th-century harmonies and rhythms. It remained basically tonal, as opposed to Serialism (which see). Stravinsky and Hindemith were identified with Neo-Classicism during much of their composing careers. See **styles and schools in the arts.**

neo-Fascism, neo-Fascist, for the Italian neo-Fascist party. Its full name is the Italian Social Movement —National Right Wing.

neo-Gothic (architecture). The Gothic revival of the 19th century, when the Gothic style became a major mode of design. There is no firm distinction between what can be called neo-Gothic and what came later, and it may be advisable to refer to 19th-century Gothic buildings with the sort of phrase that would be used with a 20th-century example: *an 1880 church in the Gothic style.* See **styles and schools in the arts.**

Neo-Impressionism (art). A style and movement initiated by Seurat in response to Impressionism; in Neo-Impressionism an attempt is made to systematize the application of color by means of tiny dots of pigment. Also known as Divisionism and Pointillism. See **styles and schools in the arts.**

Nepalese (sing. and pl.).

nerve-racking.

Netherlander(s). The people of the Netherlands; *the Dutch, Dutchmen, Dutchwomen* are also acceptable, but *Hollander(s)* is not. The adjectives are *Netherlands* and *Dutch.*

Netherlands, the (not *Holland*). Do not capitalize *the* in datelines.

Nev. for Nevada after cities and towns.

Nevadan(s).

nevertheless.

new-. newborn, newcomer, newfangled, new-mown.

Newark International Airport.

New Brunswick (Canadian province). Do not abbreviate after cities and towns, even in datelines.

New Brunswicker(s). The people of the Canadian province and of the city in New Jersey.

Newburgh (N.Y.).

Newfoundland. Do not abbreviate after cities and towns, even in datelines.

Newfoundland dog.

Newfoundlander(s). The people of Newfoundland.

New Hampshirite(s).

New Haven line of the Penn Central Railroad (which see). The line was formerly the New York, New Haven & Hartford Railroad.

New Jerseyan(s) or **Jerseyan(s).**

New Left. Also see **left, leftist, left wing.**

New Mexican(s).

New Orleanian(s) or **Orleanian(s).** The people of New Orleans.

news. See **editorial, news** for a distinction to be preserved.

news-. newsdealer, newsletter, newsman, newswoman, newspaperman, newspaperwoman, newsprint, newsroom, newsstand.

New South Wales. Do not abbreviate after cities and towns.

newspaperman, newspaperwoman. Also: *newsman, newswoman.*

newspaper names. Do not quote them. Capitalize the article in the name of an English-language or foreign-language paper: The Detroit Free Press, La Prensa, Al Ahram. Also capitalize the article in second references: The Free Press. It is The Times of London, not The London Times.

The names of newspapers published in foreign languages should not be translated into English: Krasnaya Zvezda, not Red Star; Le Monde, not The World. But Novoye Vremya, a Soviet foreign affairs magazine published in several languages, may be called New Times if reference is made to its English edition.

Following are the names of the major daily newspapers published in New York City:
The Daily News (the Sunday issue is called The Sunday News)
The Journal of Commerce
The Long Island Press
The New York Post
The New York Times
The Staten Island Advance
The Wall Street Journal
In inserting a geographical locater into the name of a newspaper, use parentheses: The Lima (Ohio) News. But: *a Columbus, Ohio, newspaper.*
See **New York Times, The.**

news sources. See **sources of news.**

New Testament.

New World (Western Hemisphere).

New Year's Day, New Year's Eve. Also: *New Year* (the holiday, not the 12-month period), *Chinese New Year, Jewish New Year, Lunar New Year, Vietnamese New Year,* etc.

New York Airways.

New York Board of Rabbis. It represents the three branches of Judaism—Orthodox, Conservative and Reform—in New York City.

New York Botanical Garden, the (in the Bronx), not *Gardens.* Also: the Brooklyn Botanic Garden, not *Botanical.*

New York Central Railroad. Use only in historical references; the line is now part of the Penn Central Railroad (which see).

New York City. But: *the city, the city government.* See **City, city.**

New York Cocoa Exchange.

New York Coffee and Sugar Exchange.

New York Cotton Exchange.

New Yorker(s). The people of the city or the people of the state, but only in contexts where the meaning is clear.

New York Mercantile Exchange.

New York, New Haven & Hartford Railroad. Use only in historical references. See **New Haven line** and **Penn Central Railroad.**

New York School (art). The term describes the Abstract Expressionist painters who emerged in New York as an influential group in the 1940's and 1950's. See **styles and schools in the arts.**

New York State Thruway. It is now the Gov. Thomas E. Dewey

Thruway. In subsequent references: *the Thruway*. It is operated by the New York State Thruway Authority.

New York Stock Exchange, the New York Exchange, the exchange, the Big Board. *N.Y.S.E.* should not be used except in tabular material.

New York, Susquehanna & Western Railroad, the Susquehanna.

New York Times, The. The article is always capitalized in the full names of the newspaper and the company: *The New York Times, The New York Times Company.* In subsequent short-form references, it is *The Times* for the newspaper, but it is *the Times Company* or *the company.* Also see **Neediest Cases.**

Do not capitalize *the* when it immediately precedes *Times* used in the adjectival sense in references like these: *He cited the Times article. He asked the Times reporter to show his credentials. What, he asked, is the Times policy?* The article is capitalized, however, in constructions like these, in which *Times* is a noun: *He cited The Times's article. He asked The Times's reporter to show his credentials. What, he asked, is The Times's policy?* (Note how the possessive is formed: *Times's.)*

In news stories, do not capitalize the titles of officers of the company or editors of the newspaper: *John P. Manley, publisher of The New York Times,* for example. Or, using other titles he holds: *John P. Manley, chairman and president of The New York Times Company.* (In this case, one of these titles would in most contexts be more appropriate than all three.) Also: *editor of the editorial page, managing editor, national editor,* etc.

Lowercasing extends also to *editorial board* and *board of directors.*

Do not use the words *editorial* and *news* interchangeably in references to The Times. Reserve *news* for the news department, its employees and news articles; reserve *editorial* for the department that prepares the editorial page, its employees and an article that appears on the page. Also do not use *edition(s)* and *issue* interchangeably. When referring to all copies of The Times printed on a specific day, the correct term is *issue.* See **edition(s), issue.**

The first page of the daily or Sunday Times may be called the first page, the front page or page 1 (see **page numbers**). The first page of the second part (of the daily, that is) should be called just that, not *second front,* except in certain special contexts in which *second front* will not puzzle readers. Other pages or sections in the daily paper are to be referred to in this manner: *editorial page, Op-Ed page, business/finance section* (or *pages*), *sports section* (or *pages*), *family/style page* (or *pages*), etc.

Some of those styles apply also to the Sunday paper. But the names of the major, separate Sunday sections are to be capitalized as follows:

The New York Times Magazine
The New York Times Book Review
The Week in Review
the Arts and Leisure section
the Travel section
the Business and Finance section
the Real Estate section
the Sports section

In the case of the names that end with the lowercased word *section,* they will usually be preceded by the word *Sunday* and sometimes also followed by the words *of The New York Times* or *of The Times*, or that information will be presented in some other manner.

Then there is the building on West 43d Street. It is *the New York Times Building* or *the Times Building* (with *the* lowercased in both instances). Other Times buildings may be referred to as follows: *The Times's plant at 101 West End Avenue* or *the Times plant at 101 West End Avenue*, or some similar form, such as *the New York Times plant, etc.* (Never *the West Side Plant*.)

The Times's plant in Carlstadt, N.J., or *The New York Times's plant in Carlstadt, N.J.*, or *the Times plant in, etc.* Where relevant, news stories should point out that the plant is a satellite of the main one.

New Zealand. Do not abbreviate after cities and towns, even in datelines.

N.H. for New Hampshire after cities and towns.

nicknames. See **personal names and nicknames.**

Nigerian(s). The people of Nigeria.

Nigerois (sing. and pl.). The people of Niger. The adjective is *Niger*.

night(-). nightcap, nightclothes, nightclub, nightdress, nightfall, nightgown, night life, nightlong, nightmare, night owl, night school, nightstick, nighttime, night watch.

Nine, the, for the member countries of the European Economic Community (which see), but only when the context is unmistakable.

ninepins. Also: *tenpins*.

nineteen-hundreds, 1900's. In almost all contexts, the numerals are the preferred form. See **years, decades, centuries.**

nitrate, nitrite. They are not the same thing.

N.J. for New Jersey after cities and towns. But *N.J.* is omitted from datelines in special New Jersey pages of The Times. In headlines, when the state name appears without the name of a city or a town, use *Jersey*, not *N.J.*

N.L.R.B. for the National Labor Relations Board.

N.M. for New Mexico after cities and towns.

No. for number. Do not use before schools, fire companies, lodges and similar units designated by numerals: *Public School 4* (or *P.S. 4*), *Hook and Ladder 16, Engine 4.* See **streets and avenues.**

Nobel Prize(s) should be capitalized in references to the five prizes established under terms of the will of Alfred Nobel. Also capitalize *Prize* and the category in the names of these prizes:
Nobel Peace Prize
Nobel Prize in Literature
Nobel Prize in Chemistry
Nobel Prize in Physics
Nobel Prize in Physiology or Medicine
The Nobel Memorial Prize in Economic Science is not a Nobel Prize, in the sense that the others are. It was established by the Central Bank of Sweden in 1968 as a memorial to Alfred Nobel, and any subsequent reference should be worded to avoid suggesting that it is one of the prizes established under the will.

nolo contendere means, literally, "I

do not wish to contend," and thus, by extension, no contest. In law, it is a plea in which a defendant in a criminal case, while not admitting guilt, asserts that he will offer no defense against the charge. He is, however, then subject to being judged guilty and to being punished. The effect then is the same as if he had pleaded guilty or had been convicted, but the defendant is not precluded from denying the same charge in any other proceeding.

nol-pros, nol-prossed.

no man's land.

non-. noncombatant, noncommissioned, noncommittal, noncompliance, nonconformist, nonexistent, nonnuclear, nonpareil, nonpartisan, nonplus, nonprofit, nonresident, nonresistant, nonstop, nontitle, nonunion. But: non sequitur.

none. Construe as a plural unless it is desired to emphasize the idea of *not one* or *no one*—and then it is often better to use *not one* or *no one* instead of *none.*

nonetheless.

Norfolk & Western Railway, the N.&W.

North, north. Capitalize in all references to that geographic region of the United States and in subsequent references to a country with *North* in its name, such as North Korea. Also: *Far North.* Lowercase *north* as a point of the compass.

North Atlantic Council (the highest authority of the North Atlantic Treaty Organization), the Council.

North Atlantic Treaty Organization. In subsequent references, it may be *NATO, the Atlantic alliance, the alliance.*

North Carolinian(s).

North Central Airlines.

North Dakotan(s).

Northeast, northeast. Capitalize when referring to that geographic region of the United States; lowercase as a point of the compass.

Northeast Airlines.

Northern, northern. Capitalize when referring to the North (geographic region of the United States). But: *northern Ohio, northern part of South* [or *North*] *Korea, northern half,* etc.

Northerner. Capitalize when used to describe a native or inhabitant of the part of the United States called the North or of a country with *North* in its name, such as North Korea.

Northern Hemisphere, the hemisphere.

North Jersey. This is an exception to the rule that calls for *northern New Jersey, eastern Indiana,* etc. Also: *South Jersey.*

North Pole. But: *the pole, polar.*

North Shore (L.I.). Also: *South Shore.*

North Side. Capitalize when regularly used to designate a section of a city.

North Slope (Alaska).

North Vietnam. Use only in references to the period before the reunification of Vietnam.

North Vietnamese (sing. and pl.) is to be used only in historical contexts.

Northwest, northwest. Capitalize when referring to that geographic region of the United States; lowercase as a point of the compass.

North Western Railway, formerly the Chicago & North Western Railway, a subsidiary of the Chicago and North Western Transportation Company.

Northwest Orient Airlines. In subsequent references, *Northwest* alone suffices.

Northwest Territories (of Canada). Do not abbreviate after cities and towns, even in datelines.

Norwegian America Line.

notes (financial). In the most common financial sense, notes are interest-bearing certificates of governments or corporations that come due in a shorter time than bonds. They normally mature in more than one year but less than eight. See **bonds** and **debentures.**

not guilty and **innocent.** Legally, there is a difference in respect to a defendant's plea; *pleaded not guilty* is the proper form.

not only, but also (and similar constructions). The parallel in such constructions is often destroyed by misplacement of words: *It would not only be unwieldy but also unworkable.* Make it: *It would be not only unwieldy but also unworkable.* Sometimes the *also* after the *but* is omitted, but that omission often impairs the balance of the sentence. Balance may in some cases be achieved by some other word or words, properly placed: *It would be not only unwieldy but unworkable as well.*

notwithstanding.

Nov. for November before numerals: *Nov. 11.*

Nova Scotia. Do not abbreviate after cities and towns, even in datelines.

Nova Scotian(s). The people of Nova Scotia.

Novocain (trademark).

Novosti is a Soviet news-feature syndicate that also functions abroad as an official information agency. The word is Russian for news.

NOW for the National Organization for Women, not *of Women.*

nowadays.

nowise (in no wise).

Nuclear Regulatory Commission (N.R.C.). This commission and the Energy Research and Development Administration replaced the Atomic Energy Commission in 1975.

nucleus (sing.), **nuclei** (pl.).

number of subject and verb. After a *neither-nor* construction, if the subjects are both singular, use a singular verb: *Neither Jack nor Jill was happy.* If the subjects are both plural, use a plural verb: *Neither the Yankees nor the Athletics were hitting.* If one subject is singular and the other plural, use the number of the one after the *nor: Neither the man nor his horses were ever seen again.*

A copulative verb takes the number of the noun preceding it, which is the subject: *What was remarkable was the errors made on both sides.*

When the verb is far removed from the subject, and especially if another noun intervenes, mistakes like this one may occur: *The value of all of Argentina's exports to the United States are given as 183 million pesos.*

Improper identification of subject also causes trouble: *Natalie Gibbs is one of those women who goes in for fantastic dress.* The verb

143

should be *go,* since its subject is *who,* which refers to the plural *women.*

Sums of money are usually construed as singular: *Ten dollars buys less now than five did then.* The thought here is of a sum, not of individual bills or coins. But the plural is used when the idea of individual items is suggested: *Three hundred parcels of food were shipped.*

Total of or *number of* may take either a plural or a singular verb; in general, when the expression is preceded by *a* it is plural: *A total of 102 persons were injured. A number of people were injured.* When the expression is preceded by *the,* it is usually singular: *The total of all department budgets is $187 million. The number of passengers injured was later found to be 12.*

If *couple* conveys the idea of two persons, it should be construed as a plural: *The couple were married.* But: *Each couple was asked to give $10.*

numbers. In general, spell out the first nine cardinal and ordinal numbers in ordinary reading matter: *He walked nine miles. There were eight applicants. He was the sixth. The game ended in the fifth inning.* Use figures for numbers above nine: *The table was set for 10. There were 50 in the audience. He owns 63 horses. The game finally ended in the 15th inning.*

The spelling-out-below-10 rule does not apply to the following:

Ages. See **ages of people and animals.**

Figures in headlines and tabular matter.

Figures in some financial contexts *(The stock advanced 3 points).*

Figures containing decimals *(3.4 inches of snow).* See **decimals.**

Statistics.

Results of voting. See **votes.**

Percentages. See **percent.**

Sums of money. See **money.**

Times of day. See **time.**

Days of month. See **dates.**

Latitude and longitude (which see).

Degrees of temperature. See **temperature.**

Dimensions, measurements, weights and proportion (which see) when they consist of two or more elements.

Numbers that are part of titles *(Chapter V, Article 6).*

Sports points, scores and times. See **sports.**

Mentions of the Twelve Apostles and the Ten Commandments.

Round numbers are rendered both in numerals and in words. In the thousands, it is almost always numerals: *5,000; 2,300.* In the millions, this is the usual form: *four million, 10 million.* The adjectival form: *four-million-year span, 12-million-year span.* In the case of dollar and sterling sums: *$10 million, £25 million.* When a range is given, the word is repeated: *$5 billion to $15 billion;* never *$5 to $15 billion,* except in this adjectival form, with hyphens: *$5-to-15-billion program.* Do not hyphenate the simple adjectival form: *$10 million loan.*

But spelling out is often appropriate: *Fifty to sixty thousand voted. They planned to enlist a million workers. He said his opponent was a hundred percent wrong.* (See the next entry: **numbers, round.**)

The rules for spelling out and for use of figures apply also to adjectival forms: *four-mile hike, 11-mile hike, five-day week, 40-hour week, five-ton truck, 9,000-ton ship, two-million-member union, 10-million-vote margin, 3.5-inch snow.*

In ordinary reading matter, spell out any number that begins a sentence: *Five hundred delegates attended.* In series including both numbers that would ordinarily be spelled out and numbers that would ordinarily be given in figures, make the style conform: *4 submarines, 10 destroyers and 15 carriers; the 9th and 10th centuries.* This does not apply to streets and avenues.

Use *to* between numerals in giving the results of voting and rulings by a court with more than one judge: *a vote of 51 to 3, voted 51 to 3, a 51-to-3 vote, ruled 5 to 4, a 5-to-4 ruling.* But the *to* can be dropped in headlines: *5-4 Vote.*

In headlines, figures may be used for all cardinal and ordinal numbers except, in some cases, *1* and *1st. One Hurt* is preferred to *1 Hurt,* and *First Prize* to *1st Prize.* Likewise *First Aid,* not *1st Aid.* But *1-Cent Tax* (or *1c Tax*), *1 Percent* and similar constructions may be used.

Ordinal numbers are expressed in figures as follows: *2d, 3d, 4th, 11th, 21st, 33d, 124th.*

numbers, round. Round numbers in the thousands are usually expressed in figures: *He ordered 5,000 cases of beer.* But spelling out is sometimes appropriate: *He said he knew a thousand better ways.*

Round numbers in the millions and billions generally follow the rule of spelling out below 10: *three million people, 16 million people.* But: *3.5 million people.* Hyphenate the adjective form: *three-million-year span, 16-million-year span.* The spelling-out rule does not apply in the case of money: *$3 million.* Also: *$13 million, $1.5 billion, £7 billion, 6 million francs, 4.5 million francs.* But spelling out is called for here: *I wish I had a million dollars.* Or: *a million dollars'*

worth *of free publicity.* (Note the apostrophe.)

When one of two round numbers appearing together contains 10 or a higher figure and the other does not, follow this style: *9 million to 10 million people.*

In expressing a range of values, repeat *million* or *billion,* as follows: *60 million to 75 million; $5.5 billion to $8 billion.* Never *$5 to $15 billion,* except in this adjectival form, with hyphens: *$5-to-15-billion program.* But do not hyphenate the simple adjective form: *$10 million loan.*

Following are further examples of the style for round numbers that are not sums of money:

one million tons or *a million tons.*

two and a half million tons.

two million to three million tons (not *two to three million*).

2 million to 11 million tons.

1.5 million tons.

1.75 million tons.

1.5 million to 3 million tons.

300,000 to one million.

555 billion gallons.

In general, do not use *trillion, quadrillion, quintillion,* etc.; they are hard to grasp. Instead, express the number in millions or billions (*billion,* of course, being used in the American sense of 1,000 million). The following table shows how very large numbers may be expressed. In each case, the zeros follow the numeral *1.*

12 zeros—a million million or 1,000 billion (instead of *trillion*).

13 zeros—10,000 billion.

14 zeros—100,000 billion.

15 zeros—a million billion (instead of *quadrillion*).

16 zeros—10 million billion.

17 zeros—100 million billion.

18 zeros—a billion billion (instead of *quintillion*).

numbskull.

Nuncio. See **Papal Nuncio** and **Apostolic Delegate.**

nursemaid.

nurseryman.

N.Y. for New York after cities and towns.

nylon.

O

O, oh. The vocative *O* is always capitalized, whether occurring at the beginning of a sentence or at some intermediate point: *For Thee, O Lord. Oh* is capitalized only when occurring at the beginning of a sentence: *Oh, what a shame! But, oh, how glad we were!* The form *O* is virtually obsolete as far as ordinary usage is concerned and is found principally in quotations from poetry, in classical references and in religious matter.

OAPEC for the Organization of Arab Petroleum Exporting Countries. Also: *OPEC* for the Organization of Petroleum Exporting Countries.

O.A.S. for the Organization of American States.

obbligato.

objet(s) d'art, not *object(s) d'art.*

obscenity, vulgarity, profanity. In 1896, Adolph S. Ochs stated that his intentions in respect to The New York Times included the presentation of the news "in language that is parliamentary in good society." However much society and The Times may have changed since then, Times policy regarding obscenity and offensive vulgarity remains much the same: They should not appear in the paper. As for profanity: It should not appear,

either; but profanity in its milder forms can on some occasions be justified.

A notable exception in the case of obscenity and extreme vulgarity was made in 1974 during The Times's publication of transcripts of White House conversations concerning Watergate. Certain expressions unquestionably objectionable by our standards were printed because of the light they shed on news matters of the utmost importance. Editors judged that it would not suffice, as it would in almost all cases, to say merely that an unspecified obscenity or vulgarity had been used.

The 1974 case thus provides this guide for judging when an obscenity or extreme vulgarity should be used: only when the printing of the objectionable word or words will give the reader an obviously essential insight into matters of great moment—an insight that cannot be otherwise conveyed. Most such instances would almost certainly involve a person of high standing—a President, perhaps, as in the 1974 case—as the user of the offensive word or phrase or as a participant in a conversation in which some other person used it.

The responsibility for keeping objectionable expressions out of the paper begins with the reporter. But if the reporter feels that such an expression is essential, he or she should not simply go ahead and write it into the story; the reporter should consult with the departmental editor. Then the matter should be discussed with higher authority.

A decision not to use an expletive does not always end the matter. Allusions to an expletive can be as offensive as the actual word. In particular, news stories should not give readers the impression that a reporter is saying, in effect: "Look, I want to use this word, but *they* won't let me. This is as close as I can come to it." One way of achieving that undesirable effect is to use a device like this: *g--d---* (instead of *goddamn*). There are more acceptable, more graceful solutions, although they are not always easy to achieve.

Profanity in its milder forms is a lesser problem than obscenity and offensive vulgarity, but still a problem. A *hell* or a *damn* is really not offensive to a great degree. But if the paper is peppered with such words, the news report is cheapened and the cumulative effect is indeed offensive. Thus profanity, mild or strong, should never be used as a matter of course; in fact, it should not be used at all unless there is a compelling reason. To relax our standards in this respect would be to change the character of The Times.

Occident, Occidental. Capitalize when referring to Europe or the Western Hemisphere or to an inhabitant of one of those regions.

Oct. for October before numerals: *Oct. 14.*

octavo, octavos.

octet (music). See **quartet** or **trio.**

odd-, -odd. odd-looking, odd-numbered. Also: 20-odd, 200-odd.

O.E.C.D. for the Organization for Economic Cooperation and Development.

off-, (-)off. off-color (adj., before a noun), offhand, offshoot, offshore, offside. Also: blastoff (n.), blast off (v.) and layoff, playoff, send-off, standoff, stop-off, takeoff (all n.).

Off Broadway, Off Off Broadway. *He is directing an Off Broadway* [or *Off Off Broadway*] *play. A survey showed that Off Broadway* [or *Off Off Broadway*] *was flourishing.* But: *The play was produced off Broadway.* And: *The play was produced off Off Broadway.*

office(-). office boy, office girl, officeholder, officeseeker.

officials. Their titles are listed separately and alphabetically. See **company officers.**

offshore oil. Use instead of *tidelands oil* unless the deposits are in the area between the low-tide and high-tide marks.

Offtrack Betting Corporation, the OTB.

oh. See **O, oh.**

Ohio. Do not abbreviate.

Ohioan(s).

oil(-). oil burner, oilcloth, oilfield, oilman, oilskin, oilstove.

O.K., O.K.'d, O.K.'s. Do not use *okay.*

Okla. for Oklahoma after cities and towns.

Oklahoman(s).

old-. old-fashioned, old-school (adj.), old-timer.

Old City. The walled part of Jerusalem.

Old English sheepdog.

Old Testament.

Old World.

Olympic Airways.

Olympic Games, the Games.

O.M.B. for the Office of Management and Budget.

one-. one-piece (adj.), oneself, one-sided.

one-man, one-vote; one man, one vote. Hyphenate when the phrase is used adjectivally: *the one-man, one-vote rule.* Otherwise, omit the hyphens: *the principle of one man, one vote.*

One Thousand Guineas (horse race).

ongoing. An overworked adjective that should be replaced when possible by one of its many synonyms: *continuing, progressing, under way,* etc.

onlooker.

only. Place it next to the word it modifies: *He ate only a sandwich,* not *He only ate a sandwich.* See **not only, but also.**

onside.

Ontarian(s). The people of Ontario.

Ontario. Do not abbreviate after cities and towns, even in datelines.

Op Art. A movement in abstract painting in which neat, often geometrical forms are embellished with color so intense that it induces an optical illusion of movement. The movement arose in the 1960's. See **styles and schools in the arts.**

OPEC for the Organization of Petroleum Exporting Countries. Also:

OAPEC for the Organization of Arab Petroleum Exporting Countries.

Op-Ed page. The Times's and others'.

open-. open-field (adj.), openhanded, openhearted, openwork.

opera. Capitalize and quote a title: *"Aïda" is an opera by Verdi.* The names of characters in operas should not be quoted: *Aïda, Carmen, Violetta, Mimì,* etc. Also: *opéra bouffe, Opéra-Comique, operagoer.*

OPIC for the Overseas Private Investment Corporation.

opinion polls. Any major news article giving the results of a public-opinion poll should include the name of the poll sponsor, the number and types of people surveyed, the dates of the survey, the procedures used (that is, whether interviews were conducted by mail, by telephone or in person) and the probable margin of error in percentage terms for a sample of the size used in the poll. It is also desirable to describe specifically the questions that were asked and the choices of answers available to the respondents.

Obviously all of this information cannot be included in every polling story. Common sense should prevail. But if there is ever a doubt, the reporter should include as much of the information as possible. The responsible editors can then decide how much should be used.

The terms *opinion poll, poll, survey, opinion sample* and *cross section* should be limited to truly scientific soundings of opinion. They should not be applied to stringer roundups and man-in-the-street stories by reporters. Indeed, in some cases such roundups and stories might well contain warnings that the interviews are not a scientific sampling and that only limited conclusions can be drawn from them.

opposition (political). Do not capitalize, even when referring to a formally designated political faction opposing the party in power in a foreign country: *The Labor opposition divided on the issue. The opposition party failed again.*

opus (music). Abbreviate, capitalize and parenthesize in a title: *Chopin's Rondo in E flat major (Op. 16).* But: *His Opus 16 is moving.*

oral, verbal. Use *oral* to convey the idea of words that are spoken. *Verbal* is less precise; its chief meaning is words used in any manner—spoken, written or printed.

orbit. It may be used as a transitive and intransitive verb: *The United States orbited a weather satellite. The satellite orbited.*

Ore. for Oregon after cities and towns.

oregano.

Oregonian(s).

organdy.

Orient, Oriental. Capitalize when referring to Asia and the East or to an inhabitant of those regions. Also: *an Oriental rug.*

Oriental Orthodoxy. A group of Christian churches, also known as Monophysite churches, that broke from the main body of Christianity after the Council of Chalcedon in 451 in a dispute over the divine and human nature of Jesus. They are the Coptic Church of Egypt, the Syrian Orthodox (Jacobite) churches in Syria and in India, the Ethiopian Orthodox Church, the Syrian Orthodox Church of Antioch and the Armenian churches. Also see **Eastern Orthodoxy** and **Eastern Rite.**

Orient Overseas Line.

Orlon (trademark).

Orly Airport (Paris).

ORT, Women's American. In second references: ORT, without the article. ORT stands for Organization for Rehabilitation Through Training.

Orthodox Church in America. It is a denomination formed by a merger of the Russian Orthodox Greek Catholic Church of America and several other Orthodox churches.

Orthodox Judaism.

OSHA for the Occupational Safety and Health Administration.

OTB for the Offtrack Betting Corporation.

ounce. A United States fluid ounce is equal to 1.04 British imperial fluid ounces or 29.57 milliliters. A British fluid ounce is equal to 0.96 United States fluid ounce or 28.41 milliliters. In the avoirdupois system of weights, an ounce is equal to 437.5 grains; in the troy and apothecary systems, 480 grains.

out-, -out. out-and-out, outboard, outbound, outclimb, outdo, outdoor, outfield, outmaneuver, out-of-doors (adj.), outpatient, outrigger, outrun, outscore, outspoken, outtrade. Also (all n.): fade-out, fallout, hide-out, pullout, walkout.

outer continental shelf. Also: *continental shelf, continental slope.*

Oval Office (in the White House).

over-, -over. overabundant, overalls (outer garments), overexcitable, overexpand, overindulgence, overproduction, overprompt, overreach, overripe, oversensitive. See **overall, over all.** Also (all n.): carry-over, change-over, hangover, holdover, takeover, turnover, walkover.

overall, over all. Use the single-word form as an adjective: *overall policy.* But two words in phrases like these: *Over all, the Democrats made gains. The Senate's political coloration will be little affected over all.*

Overseas National Airways.

overture. Capitalize in a title: *Beethoven's "Egmont" Overture.* But: *a Beethoven overture.* Also capitalize when the overture is referred to the source: *the Overture to* [not *of*] *"La Gazza Ladra," by Rossini.*

oxford (cloth, shoes).

oxford blue. The color, that is; not a man who, let us say, has rowed for his university. He is an *Oxford Blue.*

oxford gray.

Oxonian(s). The people of Oxford in England or students or graduates of Oxford University.

Ozark Air Lines.

P

Pa. for Pennsylvania after cities and towns.

Pacific. The actual shoreline of the Pacific Ocean is the Pacific *coast;* the region of the United States lying along the shoreline is the Pacific *Coast,* the *West Coast* or *the Coast.* Also: *Pacific Coast States, Pacific States, Pacific Northwest, North Pacific, South Pacific.*

Pacific Far East Line.

Pacific standard time. (P.S.T.). See time.

Pacific Stock Exchange.

page numbers. Lowercase, even in references to pages in The New York Times: *page 1, page 32, page 112.* But a page reference that is not part of a sentence (in brackets at the end of a paragraph, for example, or at the end of a bracketed paragraph) is of course capitalized. In special matter, abbreviations may be used: *p. 5, 321 pp., pp. 19, 20 and 21, pp. 19-21.*

paintings. Quote their titles; capitalize principal words.

Pakistani(s). The people of Pakistan.

palate (part of mouth), palette (artist's paint board), pallet (bed; also, portable platform).

Palestine Liberation Organization (P.L.O.). Not *Palestinian.*

pallbearer.

Pan-. It is generally hyphenated: *Pan-African, Pan-American* (in the general sense), *Pan-German, Pan-Slav.* But: *Pan American World Airways, Pan American Union.*

Panamanian(s).

Pan American World Airways, Pan Am.

P & O Lines.

paneled.

panhandle.

panic-stricken.

pants suit.

papal. Lowercase unless part of a name or title.

Papal Nuncio. Bishop (or Archbishop) John P. Manley, the Papal Nuncio; the Nuncio. But: *a papal nuncio, papal nuncios* (for capitalized plural exceptions, see titles). A nuncio is a Roman Catholic diplomat accredited by the Pope to a foreign government with which the Vatican has diplomatic relations. An apostolic delegate is the envoy of the Pope to the church or the hierarchy in a foreign country with which there is no treaty. See Apostolic Delegate.

paper-. paperback, paper-backed, paper-bound, paperhanger, paperweight.

papier-mâché.

Papua New Guinea. No hyphen.

Paraguayan(s).

parallel (latitude). See **latitude and longitude.**

paralleled.

parentheses and brackets. In general, parentheses are used to indicate an interpolation by a writer in his own copy. If an editor makes an ordinary interpolation that the writer of a news story should have made but overlooked, parentheses should also be used: *Cardinal Manley cited the encyclical "Pacem in Terris" ("Peace on Earth"). Or: In 1962, the painting sold for £100 ($280).*

Use parentheses in Q. and A. matter when describing an action not directly a part of the interrogation: *Q. Will you kindly point out the figures. (Handing the witness a list.)*

A nickname interpolated in an actual name should be enclosed in parentheses: *Anthony (Tough Tony) Anastasia.* The parentheses should also be used in making a differentiation such as this in proper names: *the Springfield (Mass.) General Hospital,* indicating that *Mass.* is not part of the name. But use commas in *a Springfield, Mass., hospital.* See **comma** and **newspaper names.**

When a clause in parentheses comes at the end of a sentence and is part of it, put the period outside the parentheses: *The witness did not identify the automobile (a Cadillac, according to earlier testimony).* If the parenthesized matter is independent of the sentence

and requires a period, the period is placed inside the closing mark: *The university was not identified. (It developed later that he was speaking of Harvard.)*

Do not place a comma before a parenthesis mark; if a comma is indicated after the sentence or phrase preceding the parenthesis, the comma should be placed outside the closing parenthesis mark: *The university (Harvard), he said, was not involved.*

Do not use dash and parenthesis together.

Brackets, in general, are used to enclose an interpolation by an editor or, in a datelined story, material from another place. Bracketed matter in a news story should be paragraphed and indented unless it is merely a phrase or a short sentence that may be interpolated without making the original paragraph cumbersome. Bracketed matter should not appear in a story not carrying a dateline; rather, the material should be woven into the story.

When bracketed material in a datelined story includes a reference to a day of the week, the reference should name the day: *Thursday,* for example, rather than *yesterday* or *today.*

In bracketed matter that is more than one paragraph long, place a bracket at the beginning of each paragraph and at the end of the last paragraph only.

In quoted matter, the brackets are used in place of the parentheses to indicate that the person quoted did not make the interpolation. Such an interpolation in a news story thus might be made either by the writer of the story or by the editor: *"Then," he said, "I went to see Manley [Attorney General John P. Manley]."* Bracketing into a quotation should, however, be a last resort. A writer or editor should make every effort to adjust the introductory or surrounding language so that the quotation can stand on its own.

parenthetical attribution. The interpolated phrase of attribution is often misused: *In Laos the State Department announced that two attachés were missing.* The phrase *the State Department announced* is a parenthesis, and does not govern the tense of the verb that follows. It should be set off by punctuation: *In Laos, the State Department announced, two attachés are missing.* Another example: *While the building was being renovated Mr. Brown said that the document had been found in a closet.* It should read: *While the building was being renovated, Mr. Brown said, the document was found in a closet.* Ignorance of a parenthesis may result in ambiguity: *In 1973 the witness testified that he never saw the defendant.* Note the difference commas can make: *In 1973, the witness testified, he never saw the defendant.*

parimutuels (n.), **parimutuel** (adj.).

paris green.

Parisian(s).

Parkway, parkway. Capitalize in names: *Northern State Parkway, Garden State Parkway, Taconic State Parkway.* But: *the parkway.*

Parliament(s), parliament(s). Capitalize in any specific reference to a legislative body that is so named, or to a small number of parliaments specifically identified in the story. See **legislative bodies.**

parliamentarian. Use only in referring to an expert on parliamentary procedure, not in referring to a member of a parliament.

parliamentary.

partially, partly. Ordinarily, use *partly*, not *partially*, to mean in part.

particles. The use of the particles *de, du, di, da, le, la, van, von, ter,* etc., in personal names is discussed under **personal names and nicknames.**

part time (n. and adv.), **part-time** (adj.).

partway.

Party, party. Capitalize in names of political parties: *Republican Party, Democratic Party, Conservative Party, Liberal Party, Labor Party, Communist Party,* etc. But: *the party, the parties.*

party designations for members of Congress and of state legislatures are given as follows: *Senator John P. Manley, Republican of New York; Representative Joan P. Manley, Democrat of Utah; Assemblyman John P. Manley, Democrat of Buffalo.* If a legislator has been elected with the support of two parties: *State Senator Margaret B. Manley, Conservative-Republican of Rochester.* When dealing with a district in the New York metropolitan area, specify the section or county: *Representative John P. Manley, Democrat of Brooklyn* (or *Newark,* or *the South Bronx,* etc.).

pass-. passbook, passkey, password.

passé.

passenger-miles.

passer(s)-by.

Passover.

past master.

pastor. This title for clergymen in charge of local congregations is normally associated with Lutherans and Roman Catholics, but can also be used for Baptists and some other Protestants. For a Lutheran, a first reference to *the Rev. John P. Manley* is normally followed by this subsequent reference: *Pastor Manley*. If a Lutheran clergyman does not have a congregation, but rather occupies a nonparochial position such as seminarian or denominational executive, *Mr.* or *Dr.*, if that is the case, is also appropriate in subsequent references. For other churches, use *pastor* as *minister* or *priest* is used: *the Rev. John P. Manley, pastor of, etc.*, or *He had been their pastor.* See **Father, minister, rector, Rev.**

pâté. Also: pâté de foie gras.

Paterson (N.J.), **Patterson** (N.Y.).

PATH for Port Authority Trans-Hudson, formerly the Hudson & Manhattan Railroad Company (which was nicknamed the Hudson Tubes).

Patriarch. This is a title given in the Eastern Orthodox churches and the Ethiopian Orthodox Church to certain high-ranking bishops: *Patriarch Pimen, head of the Russian Orthodox Church.* In second references: *Patriarch Pimen* or *the Patriarch.* Sometimes an Orthodox prelate, as in this case, is known by a single name. See **Eastern Orthodoxy** and **Metropolitan.**

patrolled, patrolling.

patrolman is not to be used for a policeman in New York City, where the title is *Police Officer.* In cities and towns where *patrolman* is official, the style is: *Patrolman John P. Manley, the patrolman* or *the policeman.* See **Police Officer.**

pawn(-). pawnbroker, pawnshop, pawn ticket.

pay-. pay-as-you-go (n. and adj.), paycheck, payday, paymaster, payoff (n.), payroll.

PBS for the Public Broadcasting Service, a group (not a network) of public television stations organized to buy and distribute programs selected by a vote of its members. In New York, WNET (Channel 13) is a member of PBS.

PBW Stock Exchange, formerly the Philadelphia-Baltimore-Washington Stock Exchange.

pct. Do not use as abbreviation for *percent* in articles, subheads or headlines. See **percent.**

peace-. peacekeeper, peacekeeping, peacelike, peacemaker, peacemaking, peacetime.

peach Melba.

peccadillo, peccadilloes.

peck. One-quarter of a bushel or eight quarts. The United States peck is equal to 8.81 liters; the British imperial peck, 9.09 liters.

peddler.

peer. A peer is a member of one of the five degrees of British nobility —baron, viscount, earl, marquess, duke (which see). A baronet or a knight is not a peer. A peer's son or daughter who bears a courtesy title is not a peer. For example: *the Duke of Marlborough,* a peer; *the Marquess of Blandford,* his son; *the Earl of Sunderland,* his grandson.

To distinguish between peers of the same name, use the full title or territorial designation: *Viscount*

156

Alexander of Hillsborough and *Earl Alexander of Tunis, Viscount Alexander* and *Earl Alexander*. When the names are not in juxtaposition, each may be called *Lord Alexander* in second references.

A special case: Sometimes the title is not used in first references to a peer who is well known in a profession. It is *Lord Snow* or *C. P. Snow*, but never *Lord C. P. Snow* or *Lord Charles Snow*. And never *Mr. Snow* in subsequent references.

If a peer renounces an inherited title, he or she is then known by the family name: *Anthony Wedgwood Benn* (formerly *Viscount Stansgate*), *Mr. Benn*.

Sometimes a Briton is designated a life peer, with the title Baron or Baroness. A life peer sits in the House of Lords, but the title is not inheritable. An example is Baroness Spencer-Churchill, the widow of Sir Winston Churchill.

Peking (not *Peiping*).

Pekingese (dog).

Peking man (anthropological).

penal code.

pence. See **pounds and pence.**

pendant (n.), **pendent** (adj.).

Penn Central Railroad, the Pennsy, a subsidiary of the Penn Central Transportation Company.

Pennsylvania Company, the investment company subsidiary of the Penn Central Transportation Company. In second references: *Pennco.*

Pennsylvanian(s).

Pennsylvania Railroad. Use only in historical references; the line is now part of the Penn Central Railroad (which see).

Pennsylvania Station.

penthouse.

people, persons. In general, use *people* for round numbers and groups (the larger the group, the better *people* sounds), and *persons* for precise or quite small numbers: *One million people were notified. He notified 1,316 persons. He said 30 people had been asked to volunteer. Only two persons showed up. Seventeen persons were injured.* The important thing is to avoid the ridiculous: *As we all know, persons are funny.*

people's democracy, people's republic. The expressions, which seem to imply editorial value judgments, should be avoided in lowercase unless it is clear that the reference is to a country's official characterization of itself. In uppercase they are cumbersome, as in *People's Republic of China.* Use *China* alone.

Pepsico Inc., formerly the Pepsi-Cola Company.

percent, percentage. *Percent* is one word with no point, and a preceding number is expressed in figures (except when the number begins a sentence): *80 percent, 8 percent, one-half of 1 percent.* But: *five percentage points, 12 percentage points.* The symbol % may be used with the figure in headlines and tabular matter: *5% Raise, 93%.* Do not use the abbreviation *pct.* in articles, subheads or headlines. It may be used in tabular and other special matter.

Do not use *percent* when *percentage point* is meant: If an interest rate rises to 11 percent from 10 percent, it is a rise of one percentage point, but it is an increase of 10 percent. Similarly, a decline in rates to 7½ percent from 10 percent is a decline of two and a half percentage points, but it is a decrease of 25 percent. It is, of course, impossible to have a percentage decline greater than 100 percent.

perigee. The lowest altitude of an orbiting space vehicle or other object in relation to the earth. *Perigee* also has the general meaning of the lowest or nearest point. See **apogee.**

period. Various uses of the period are shown throughout in the separate and alphabetical listings. See especially **abbreviations.**

An important thing to remember about the period is that it is used to end a sentence and that the insertion of one can often mean two easy-to-read sentences instead of one cumbersome sentence.

Do not use the period after *percent; 8vo, 12mo;* Roman numerals; serial references such as *(1)* and *(a);* sums of money in dollar denominations (set *$50* unless cents are added: *$50.69*).

permanent representative (at an international organization or conference). Although the expression is widely used officially, it is best avoided in news stories because it is imprecise: "permanent" representatives are often changed or withdrawn. The preferred expressions are *delegate, chief delegate, representative* and *chief representative* (all of which see) but not *Ambassador* (which see).

permissible.

Perón, Peronism, Peronist.

Persia. The former name of Iran. Use only in references to the past.

Persian (not *Iranian*) is the principal language of Iran.

Persian lamb.

-person. Do not use compounds like these: *chairperson, foreperson, newsperson, salesperson.* Also, do not use *Assemblyperson, Congressperson, Councilperson.* See **women.**

personal names and nicknames. In general, do not contract given names or use other nicknames unless the person mentioned is known only by the informal name (*Alex, Ben, Beth, Fred, Sue,* etc.). But there are some news stories (often in the sports pages, but increasingly found elsewhere) in which nicknames are entirely appropriate.

When nicknames are used, do not enclose them in quotation marks: *John (Butch) Manley, Honest John Manley, Jack Manley, Jack the Ripper; John P. Manley, alias James Anderson.* But in letters written to The Times by readers, names and nicknames may in general be printed as received.

The particles *de, du, di, da, le, la, van, von, ter,* etc., appear in many personal names. Although there are many exceptions, they are usually lowercased in foreign names: *Charles de Gaulle.* They are usually capitalized in the names of United States citizens: *Martin Van Buren.* But again there are exceptions: *Francis I. duPont.* An individual's preference is to be respected. (See **du Pont, duPont, Du Pont.**)

A lowercased particle in a name remains in lowercase when it appears in the interior of a sentence without a preceding first name or title, as in *the de Gaulle legend.* But such a particle must be capitalized when it begins a sentence or a headline or a subhead.

Do not use a comma in names that end in *Jr.* or *Sr.* or that include an ordinal number: *John P. Manley Jr., John P. Manley 3d.*

Titles and ranks used with personal names are listed separately and alphabetically. See **Mr., Mrs. and Miss;** also see **initials in names** and, for a list of the various separate and alphabetical entries, **names.**

persona non grata. It is not necessary to translate this diplomatic expression.

personnel.

persuade, convince. Either may be followed by an *of* phrase or a *that* clause, but only *persuade* may be followed by the infinitive *to.* Thus: *They persuaded him to leave.* Never *convinced him to leave.*

Pesach (Feast of Passover).

petit larceny, petty larceny. Use *petit* in direct quotations or in strictly legalistic contexts. Otherwise *petty larceny* is preferred.

Petrodollar and similar coinages like *Eurodollar* or *Eurocurrency* should be used only when their meaning is clear and their appearance unremarkable.

Petty Officer John P. Manley, Mr. (or Petty Officer) Manley, the petty officer.

Pfc. John P. (or Joan) Manley, Private Manley, the private.

P.G.A. for the Professional Golfers' Association.

pharmacopoeia.

phases (numbered). Use Arabic numerals to designate phases of a formal program or course of action, usually governmental: *Phase 1 and Phase 2 of the Administration's economic control program were not popular. Neither were Phases 3 and 4.*

Ph.D. for Doctor of Philosophy.

phenomenon, phenomena.

Philadelphian(s).

Philadelphia Yearly Meeting of the Religious Society of Friends.

Philippine (adj.), **Philippines** (n., always singular). Also see **Filipino(s)** and **Filipino names.**

Philips N.V. This Dutch company's affiliate in the United States is the North American Philips Corporation.

Phillips Petroleum Company.

Phnom Penh.

phony (adj. and n.). There are many fine synonyms for this tiresome colloquialism: *counterfeit, deceiver, dissembler, fake, false, falsified, forged, forgery, fraudulent, impostor, pretender, pretentious, sham, spurious,* etc. Choose the one that best fits the context, and note the improvement. In rare instances, of course, the inelegant *phony* cannot be denied.

Photostat (trademark). But: *photocopy* (n. and v.).

piano, pianos.

pick(-). pick-me-up, pickpocket, pickup (n. and adj.), pick up (v.).

pickets, not *picketers.*

picnic, picnicking.

pièce de résistance.

piecemeal.

Pietà. Without quotation marks. See **sculptures.**

pigeonhole (n. and v.).

pilaf.

pileup.

pilotboat.

pince-nez.

pinch-hitter, pinch-runner.

Ping-Pong (trademark). The general term is *table tennis.*

Pinocchio.

pint. The United States liquid pint is equal to 16 United States fluid ounces, 0.83 British imperial pint or 0.47 liter. The British imperial pint is equal to 20 British fluid ounces, 1.20 United States pints or 0.57 liter. See **quart, gallon** and **ounce.**

pipeline.

pistol. A pistol is a hand weapon. It may be a revolver (which see) or an automatic pistol (which see).

pitchout (n.), **pitch out** (v.), in baseball and football.

Pithecanthropus erectus.

Pittsburg (Kan.), **Pittsburgh** (Pa.).

Place. Spell out and capitalize in ordinary reading matter when part of a name: *Patchin Place.* The abbreviation *(Patchin Pl.)* may be used in headlines if necessary and in agate and other special matter.

place-kick (n., v., adj.), **place-kicker.**

place names. See **geographic names.**

plainclothesman.

Plain of Jars (Laos), not *Plaine des Jarres.*

plaque.

plaster of paris.

Plattsburgh (N.Y.).

play-. playbill, play-by-play (adj.), playgoer, playhouse, playoff (n.), playwright.

plays and revues. In ordinary mat-

ter, quote their titles and capitalize principal words.

plea bargain (n.), **plea-bargain** (v.), **plea bargaining** (n.), **plea-bargaining** (adj.).
   The verb is intransitive only: *The lawyer advised his client to plea-bargain.* But never: *The lawyer plea-bargained the case.*

Plexiglas (trademark).

P.L.O. for the Palestine Liberation Organization.

plow.

ploy. Use with caution; the word often connotes deviousness.

plurals of abbreviations, letters and figures. These plurals are usually formed by adding *'s,* as in *M.D.'s, C.P.A.'s, A B C's, p's and q's, size 8's.* But shortened word forms do not take the apostrophe: *co-ops, vets* (for veterinarians, but not for veterans, except in the name AMVETS).

plurals of combined words and compounds. These are variously formed. The plurals of military titles are for the most part formed by adding *s* to the second word, which is usually the more important element of the compound: *major generals, lieutenant colonels,* etc. But the *s* is added to the first word in *sergeants major, adjutants general* and *inspectors general.* In civilian titles the *s* is added to the first word, usually the more important element: *attorneys general, postmasters general,* etc. The *s* is also added to the more important element in words like *courts-martial* and *rights of way.* When compounds are written as one word, the plurals are formed in the normal way. This guide applies also to such words as *cupfuls, handfuls, table-spoonfuls, breakthroughs.*

plurals of common nouns. Ordinarily the plurals are formed by the addition of *s* or *es: hammers, saws, churches, boxes, gases.* Words ending in *o* preceded by a vowel take the *s: folios, taboos.* Words ending in *o* preceded by a consonant usually take *es: echoes, embargoes, mosquitoes, Negroes* (always capitalized), *potatoes.*

Words ending in *y* preceded by a vowel take the *s* only: *alloys, attorneys, days.* When words end in *y* preceded by a consonant, the *y* is changed to *i* and *es* is added: *armies, ladies, skies.* For exceptions, see **plurals of proper names.**

Some words are the same in the plural as in the singular: *chassis, deer, sheep, swine, fowl,* etc. The collective plural of *fish* is the same as the singular, but *fishes* may be used in the sense of specific kinds: *certain fishes.*

The original plurals of some nouns of foreign derivation are to be used: *data, phenomena,* etc. The plurals of some other nouns of foreign derivation are formed in the English manner: *memorandums, curriculums, formulas,* etc.

plurals of proper names. The plurals of proper names are formed by adding *s* or *es: Cadillacs, Harolds, Joneses, Charleses.* In forming the plurals of proper names ending in *y,* the *y* is not changed to *ie* as it is in some common nouns: *Harrys, Kennedys, Germanys, Kansas Citys.* There are some exceptions, like *Alleghenies, Rockies, Sicilies.*

plus. Do not use as a conjunction: *He was a fine scholar, plus he was a nice fellow. Plus* is properly used as a preposition *(five plus one),* a noun *(His skill at debate was re-*

garded as a big plus) or an adjective *(a plus factor).*

P.M. (time). Capitalize: *10:30 P.M. yesterday.* Avoid this redundancy: *10:30 P.M. last night.* Also: *10 P.M.,* not *10:00 P.M.* See **time.**

pocket(-). pocket book (a small book), pocketbook (a billfold, purse or handbag), pocketknife, pocket veto.

podium, lectern. One stands *on* a podium and *behind* a lectern.

poetess. Use *poet* instead. See **women.**

poetry. In news stories, quote the titles of poems (unless a title appears above a reproduced poem) and capitalize the principal words. Normally, verse that appears in a story is set in 7-point italic and indented, but special circumstances may call for other sizes. When long poems or long excerpts from poems appear separately, roman may in some instances be preferable to italic because roman is easier to read. Do not use quotation marks with poetry that is reproduced in verse style in a news story or separately.

point. See **period.**

Point. Spell out and capitalize in ordinary reading matter when part of a name: *Montauk Point.* The abbreviation *(Montauk Pt.)* may be used in headlines and in agate and other special matter.

point-blank.

pointer (dog).

Pointillism (art). See **Neo-Impressionism.**

points of the compass. Spell out in ordinary reading matter: *north, northeast, north-northeast,* etc. Abbreviations (without periods)

161

may be used in ship news and yachting matter: *N, NE, NNE.* See **latitude and longitude.**

Polaroid (trademark). Also: *the Polaroid Corporation.*

pole vault (n.), **pole-vault** (v.), **pole-vaulter.**

Police Commissioner John P. Manley, the Commissioner.

Police Department, the department.

Police Headquarters, headquarters.

policeman, policewoman. See following entry.

Police Officer John P. Manley or Joan Manley. *Police Officer* is the title to be used for members of the New York City force formerly designated *patrolman* or *policewoman.* In subsequent references: *Officer Manley, the police officer* or *the officer.* In writing about the police in other cities and towns, use their official designations. See **patrolman.**

police ranks are listed separately and alphabetically. The titles are capitalized in first and subsequent references when they precede a name. When a title stands alone, it is uppercased only if it refers to the head of a police force; otherwise it is lowercased.

police stations. Lowercase, even when referring to a specific station: *47th Street station* or *station house.* See **precinct.**

policyholder.

Polish National Catholic Church of America.

politic (v.), **politicking.**

political parties. Capitalize *Party* in names: *Democratic Party,*

Republican Party, Communist Party, Labor Party, etc. Also capitalize designations of members: *Democrats, Republicans, Communists, Laborites.*

polls. See **opinion polls.**

Pomeranian (dog).

Pontiff. Capitalize when referring to a specific pope. But: *a pontiff, pontiffs* (for capitalized plural exceptions, see **titles**).

pontifical. Lowercase unless part of a name or title.

poodle.

Pop Art. A style and movement dating from the 1950's (in England) and the 1960's (in America) in which the visual materials of popular culture are transformed into stylized forms of fine art. In general, capitalize *Pop* in reference to fine art, and lowercase in references to more general aspects of mass culture. See **styles and schools in the arts.**

Pope. Capitalize with a name *(Pope Paul VI)* or when standing alone if a specific individual is referred to. But: *a pope, popes* (for capitalized plural exceptions, see **titles**).

Port-au-Prince (Haiti).

Port Authority of New York and New Jersey, formerly the Port of New York Authority. Also: *the Port Authority, the authority.*

Port Chester (N.Y.).

portland cement.

Port of Spain (Trinidad).

Portuguese (sing. and pl.).

Portuguese Guinea is now Guinea-Bissau.

posh words (like *posh* itself). Unless the aim is to caricature a gushing style, avoid trite terms like *chi-chi, posh, swank, swanky*. A perceptive writer will make the point with revealing detail: *busboys in crimson velvet cummerbunds* or *gold satin bedsheets* or whatever.

possessives are usually formed by the addition of *'s* to a singular noun even if it already ends with *s;* for a plural, the usual form is *s'*. But exceptions are numerous; see **apostrophe.**

post-. post-bellum (adj.), postclassic, post-Columbian, postgraduate, post-mortem, postnuptial, postwar.

post(-)(mail). postbox, postcard (but: postal card), postman, postmark, postmaster, post office, postpaid, post road.

Postal Service, capitalized, may be used in first and subsequent references to the United States Postal Service, which has replaced the Post Office Department.

potpourri.

potter's field.

pound. As a unit of weight in the avoirdupois system, it is equal to 16 ounces or 7,000 grains. In the troy and apothecary systems, it is equal to 12 ounces or 5,760 grains.

poundcake.

pounds and pence. The symbol £ is usually used with figures: *£15,000, £3 million, £74 million, £23.6 billion*. In the simple adjectival form, do not use a hyphen: *£2.5 million lawsuit*. But hyphens must be used in a modifier like this: *a £10-to-11-million increase*. As with dollars, it may sometimes be appropriate to spell out indefinite and round sums and omit the symbol: *half a million pounds* or, in cases of ambiguity, *pounds sterling*. Spell out *penny*

or *pence* when it appears alone in sums: *a halfpenny* (never *a half-pence* or *one-half pence*), *1 penny* (never *1 pence*), *3 pence, 98 pence*. The expression *new penny* or *new pence* may be substituted when necessary to distinguish the present decimal currency from the pre-1971 system. Detailed sums of pounds and pence are set thus: *£8.75, £9.40*. The expressions *cent* and *cents* are not used in the British system. Shillings were discontinued in 1971, as were the old word forms *twopence, sixpence*, etc. See **dollars and cents** and **money** and **numbers, round.**

power(-). powerboat, power brake, power dive (n.), power-dive (v.), powerhouse, power mower, power plant, power play, power station.

Power Authority of the State of New York. But *the State Power Authority* may be used in first references.

P.R. for Puerto Rico after cities and towns.

Prairie States.

pre-. preadolescent, preconvention, predecease, predetermined, pre-empt, pre-emptory, pre-existent, prejudge, prenatal, pre-Roman, preview, prewar.

precinct. Spell out numbers through the ninth, and capitalize: *Fourth Precinct*. But: *43d Precinct*. Also: *the Central Park Precinct*. A police precinct is the territory covered by a command; do not refer to a police station as a precinct.

prefixes and suffixes. Words formed from them and from other combining forms will be found under the separate and alphabetical listings of the prefixes, suffixes and other combining words. Avoid prefix pileups like this one: *non-bipartisan.*

prelude (music). Capitalize in a title: *Chopin's Prelude in C sharp minor.* Also: *the Prelude to the Third Act of "Die Meistersinger."*

Premier. Do not use in references to the first minister of a national government. Use *Prime Minister* or, as in West Germany and Austria, *Chancellor.* Also use *Prime Minister* if the first minister formally has a title like Chairman of the Council of Ministers. *Premier* is used, however, for the heads of some non-sovereign governments, including those of the Canadian provinces, the Australian states, associated states in the Caribbean, etc.: *Premier John P. Manley, Premier Manley, the Premier.* But: *a premier* and, usually, *premiers* (for capitalized plural exceptions, see **titles**). Also see **Prime Minister.**

premiere.

prepositions. The prepositions that may be used after certain words are a matter of idiom. Some of those words that precede the prepositions in such idioms are listed separately and alphabetically, followed by the preposition(s) that may be correctly used after them. See, for example, **forbid** and **prohibit.** The listings should not be taken to mean that such words are invariably followed by prepositions.

Presbyterian Church in the U.S. (Southern). But it is *the United Presbyterian Church in the U.S.A.* (Northern). The words *Northern* and *Southern* are not part of the names, but are usually appended for differentiation.

Presidency, Presidential. Capitalize when the reference is to the office of the President of the United States; otherwise lowercase.

President, president. It is *President Manley* (without first name) in a first reference to the President of the United States. First names are used in first references to presidents of foreign countries. In subsequent references: *President Manley, the President, Mr.* [or *Miss* or *Mrs.*] *Manley.* Capitalize *a President* and *Presidents* in all references to the Presidency of the United States, even general ones; general or plural references to other presidents are usually lowercase *(France will elect a president);* for capitalized plural exceptions, see **titles.**

Lowercase *president* in references to an officer of a company, an association, a club, a university, etc.

President-elect John P. Manley, President-elect Manley, the President-elect (of a national government; otherwise lowercase). In cap-and-lowercase headlines, capitalize *-Elect.*

President pro tem (of the Senate).

press secretary. Always lowercase and always separated from the name by a comma: *John P. Manley, the White House press secretary.*

prevent. Use preposition *from.* Also see **fused participles.**

price fixing (n.), **price-fixing** (adj.).

priest. Do not capitalize when directly following a name or in second references.

prima-facie (adj.).

Primary Day.

Prime Minister John P. Manley, Prime Minister Manley, the Prime Minister. The title *Prime Minister* should always be used instead of *Premier* to designate the first minister of a national government unless that minister has the title *Chancellor,* as in West Germany and Austria. (See **Chancellor.**) *Prime Minister* should also be used if the first minister formally has a title like Chairman of the Council of Ministers. Use *Premier* in quoted matter only, and only if the quoted words were originally spoken or written in English. Also: *a prime minister* (lowercase) and, usually, *the prime ministers* (for capitalized plural exceptions, see **titles**). *Premier* (which see) is the correct title for the heads of some nonsovereign governments, including those of the Canadian provinces.

Prince Charles, the Prince.

Prince Edward Island. Do not abbreviate after cities and towns, even in datelines.

Princes Bay (S.I.).

principal (of a school). Except in quoted matter, lowercase and use after the name: *John P. Manley, principal of, etc.; the principal.*

principal, principle. *Principal* is basically either a noun meaning a chief person or thing, or an adjective meaning first in rank, importance or degree. *Principle* means, basically, a fundamental truth, doctrine or law, or a guiding rule or code of conduct, or method of operation.

prior to is often stilted and should usually be replaced by *before.*

private (military rank). See **Pvt.**

private first class. See **Pfc.**

prizefight.

pro(-). pro-Arab, proclassical, pro-French, pro rata, prorate, prorated, proslavery.

probe (n. and v.). Do not use for *inquiry, investigation* or *investigate.*

Procter & Gamble Company. In second references: *P.&G.*

products and purposes of companies and other organizations appearing significantly in the news. When the names of organizations do not identify products or purposes, the writer is obligated to do so. For example: What does the National Manufacturing Company manufacture? What is the purpose of an organized group of analysts that puts out a report on oil prices, for instance? Who are its clients or sponsors? Does it have any regular connection with the oil industry? Or, what do the Friends of Amity hope to accomplish? And for whom?

Prof. John P. Manley, Professor Manley, the professor. Also: *John P. Manley, professor of history* (or *chairman of the department of history*). But if he holds a special chair: *John P. Manley, the Ebenezer Benton Professor of History.* Also see **emeritus.**

profanity. See **obscenity, vulgarity, profanity.**

Professional Golfers' Association (P.G.A.).

programmed, programmer, programming.

prohibit. Use preposition *from.* And after *forbid,* use *to.*

Prohibition. Capitalize in all references to the period (1920-33) in the United States when alcoholic beverages were outlawed under the 18th Amendment and the Volstead Act. The 18th Amendment may be informally referred to in some contexts as *the Prohibition amendment.*

prone (lying face down), **supine** (face up).

pronouns and missing antecedents. Pronouns require nouns or pronouns as antecedents. An adjective will not serve: *The bitterness of the German resistance indicated their awareness of the danger.* But *the Germans' resistance* gives *their* its needed antecedent.

pronouns for countries. Use the pronoun *it* in references to all countries, except in contexts where it is appropriate to personify by using *she* or *her,* as in this instance: *Verdun stands as a symbol of what France owes her sons.*

pronouns for ships. Use the pronouns *she* and *her* in references to ships and other vessels, even when they have masculine names.

pronunciation key. When a hard-to-pronounce name or term first appears significantly in the news—especially one that is central to a story or a profile—it should be accompanied by a pronunciation key, with uppercasing to denote the stressed syllable: *Sauvagnargues (pronounced so-vahn-YARG); Wyszynski (pronounced vi-SHIN-skee); Cholmondeley (pronounced CHUM-lee).*

proofreader's marks and an example of marked proof will be found at the end of this manual.

propeller.

proper names. Proper names of all sorts are listed separately and alphabetically.

prophecy (n.), **prophesy** (v.).

prosecutor, Prosecutor. When the title is official, as in New Jersey, the capitalization is the same as for *District Attorney* (which see).

protégé (masc.), **protégée** (fem.).

Protestant churches are listed separately and alphabetically.

Protestant Episcopal Church. The preferred name is now *the Episcopal Church,* although *the Protestant Episcopal Church* also remains official and may be used when it seems appropriate.

prototype. The first of its kind. The original model, not a copy.

proved, proven. In general, *proved* is preferred: *The prosecutor had proved the defendant's guilt.* But as an adjective preceding a noun, *proven* is better: *a proven remedy, proven oil reserves.* And the Scottish legal verdict is *not proven.*

provided. Use *provided,* not *providing,* in the sense of *if: He will make the trip, provided he gets a week off.*

proviso, provisos.

provost marshal, provost marshals.

Prudential Lines.

P.S. for Public School in almost all subsequent references: *P.S. 10.* See **Public School.**

pseudo-. Dictionary style is to solidify almost all compounds formed with *pseudo.* But in some cases it is best to avoid awkwardness by using a hyphen between vowels: pseudoclassic, pseudo-intellectual, pseudo-official, pseudoscience, pseudosophisticated.

P.T.A. for the Parent-Teacher Association.

PT boat for motor torpedo boat.

Public Broadcasting Service. See **PBS.**

Public School. In most first references, use *Public School 10* (do not use *No.* before the number). But in certain contexts, *P.S.* may be more appropriate in first references: *good old P.S. 10.* In almost all subsequent references, *P.S. 10* is preferable.

Puerto Rico. Use *P.R.* after the names of cities and towns.

pug (dog).

puli(s) (dog).

Pulitzer Prize(s). Capitalize *Prize(s)* when it appears directly after *Pulitzer.* But the categories in which the prizes are awarded should not be capitalized: *Pulitzer Prize for international reporting, Pulitzer Prize for biography,* etc.

pulsar. An astronomical object emitting highly rhythmic radio pulses. The pulsars are believed to be neutron stars—the collapsed remnants of burned-out stars—spinning at high velocity and beaming radio emissions into space like a rotating beacon.

punctuation is discussed under **colon, comma, dash, ellipsis, exclamation mark, hyphen, parentheses and brackets, period, question mark, quotation marks, semicolon.**

Purim (Feast of Lots).

push button (n.), **push-button** (adj.).

pussyfoot.

putout (n.).

putsch. Lowercase except in referring to a specific uprising that has come to be known by name: *the Beer Hall Putsch.*

Pvt. John P. (or Joan) Manley, Private Manley, the private.

PX for post exchange.

pygmy.

Q

Q. and A. See **testimony.**

Qantas Airways.

QE2 may be used in subsequent references to the ocean liner Queen Elizabeth 2. The queen who sits on the throne is *Queen Elizabeth II.*

Q-Tips (trademark). Also: *cotton swabs.*

Quai d'Orsay.

Quakers. This is a fully acceptable nickname for members of the Society of Friends. Quakers belong to *monthly meetings,* which are the equivalent of local congregations in other churches and, in addition to Sunday worship services, hold monthly business meetings. Members of monthly meetings in a local area are organized into *quarterly meetings;* there are also *yearly meetings,* which are roughly comparable to dioceses in other churches. In references to a specific body, capitalize *Monthly Meeting, Quarterly Meeting, Yearly Meeting,* as in *the Philadelphia Yearly Meeting.*

In the eastern United States, most Quakers attend "unprogrammed" services in which they sit in silence until a worshiper is moved to speak. In the Middle West and elsewhere, Quakers hold "programmed" services, with clergymen, music and other elements of traditional Protestant services. The Friends General Conference and the Friends United Meeting are respectively the principal national organizations of unprogrammed and programmed Quakers.

quark. A hypothetical subatomic particle from which such nuclear particles as protons and neutrons would be formed. Unlike all known particles, it would carry a fractional electric charge. The name was derived by Murray Gell-Mann from the reference by James Joyce in "Finnegans Wake" to "Three quarks for Muster Mark!"

quart. Two pints. The United States liquid quart is equal to 32 United States fluid ounces, 0.83 British imperial quart or 0.95 liter. The British quart is equal to 40 British fluid ounces, 1.20 United States quarts or 1.14 liters. See **pint, gallon** and **ounce.**

quarter(-). quarterback, quarter-deck, quarterfinal, quarterfinalist, quarter horse, quarter-hour (n. and adj.), quartermaster, quarterstretch.

quartet. Capitalize in the title of a musical work: *Brahms's Quartet No. 3 in E flat major (Op. 67), Schubert's "Death and the Maiden" Quartet.* Capitalize in the name of an ensemble: *the Budapest*

169

String Quartet. But: *a new quartet, a quartet of singers.*

quarto, quartos.

quasar. Also known as quasi-stellar radio source. The quasars are widely believed to be the most distant objects observable in the heavens.

quasi(-). A separate word when used with a noun: *quasi comfort, quasi contract, quasi scholar.* Hyphenate when using with an adjective: *quasi-judicial, quasi-stellar.*

Quebec. Do not abbreviate after cities and towns, even in datelines.

Quebecer(s), Québécois. The people of Quebec have two ways of describing themselves. In general, *Quebecer* is preferred in news stories, but *Québécois* (sing. and pl.) may be used in references to the distinctive French Canadian culture of Quebec: *a Québécois novelist,* or, *"Above all,"* the separatist leader said, *"I am proud to be a Québécois."* Also: *Parti Québécois,* an exception to the general rule of translating the names of political parties.

Queen Elizabeth or Queen Elizabeth II. Also, *the Queen* and sometimes *Elizabeth.* Capitalize *Her Majesty* and *Her Royal Highness,* but use only in quoted matter or special feature contexts.

Queen Elizabeth 2 for the ocean liner. *QE2* (solid, no points) may be used in subsequent references in stories, and in headlines if necessary.

Queen Mother, as in *Queen Elizabeth the Queen Mother* (without a comma after *Elizabeth*). In second references: *the Queen Mother* or *the Queen.*

Queensboro Bridge. But: *Triborough Bridge.*

Queens' College (Cambridge), **Queen's College** (Oxford).

Queens-Midtown Tunnel.

question mark. It is used to indicate a direct query: *What are the problems facing the country?* Indirect questions do not require the mark: *They asked if he could attend.* Requests cast in the form of questions also take the period rather than the question mark: *Will you please register at the desk. May I take your coat.* See **quotation marks.**

questionnaire.

queue. In the sense of a waiting line or lining up, the word should usually be replaced in news stories by more usual American synonyms.

quick-. quick-fire (adj.), quicklime, quicksand, quicksilver, quick-witted.

quintet (music). See **quartet** or **trio.**

quotation marks. Quoted matter in stories, spoken or written, is enclosed in double (outside) or single (inside) quotation marks: *"I do not know the meaning you attach to 'workweek,' " he said. "Please tell me."*

In headlines and subheads the single mark is used: *JONES PROTESTS 'UNFAIR' CHARGES.*

The period and the comma should be placed inside the quotation marks, as in the first of the foregoing examples. The colon and the semicolon are placed outside: *He defined "workweek": the average number of hours worked weekly by the men in his factory.* Question marks and exclamation marks may come before or after the quotation marks, depending on the meaning: *The crowd shouted, "Long live the*

King!" Just imagine, he was afraid of "elephants without trunks"! "Who are these 'economic royalists'?" he asked. Have you read "Lord Jim"?

If an expression in a foreign language is quoted, any parenthetical translation should also be quoted: *"Pacem in Terris" ("Peace on Earth").*

In continuous quoted matter that is more than one paragraph long, place a quotation mark at the beginning of each of the paragraphs and at the end of the last paragraph only.

Do not quote Q. and A. matter or dialogue in which each paragraph begins with the speaker's name or designation (such as *the judge* or *the witness*). Do not quote texts or textual excerpts (except, of course, quotations within a text) that are carried in textual form.

In general, the use of slang words should be justified by the context and should not require quotation marks. But the marks should be used with words or phrases employed in an arbitrary or opposite sense, as in *That sad day was the only "happy" one he could recall.*

Other guides for using or not using quotation marks are given throughout in separate and alphabetical listings. For example, see **anthems, dictionaries, magazines, opera, paintings, plays and revues, poetry.**

Also see **quotations.**

quotations. When two persons are quoted in succession, the second quotation should begin a new paragraph, preceded by the identification of the speaker, to make it immediately clear to the reader that the speaker has changed.

If a quotation begins with a sentence fragment, do not go on to quote one or more full sentences. Instead, close the quotation marks at the end of the fragment and introduce the full sentences as a separate, further quotation, preferably beginning a new paragraph, as follows:

The President said the ceremony represented "the beginning of the difficult task of administering clemency."

"Instead of signing these decisions in a routine way," he continued, "I want to underline the commitment of my Administration to an evenhanded policy of clemency."

If a quotation comprises several sentences, the attribution should either precede the quotation or follow the first sentence; if the first sentence is long, the attribution may be interpolated between phrases of it. In other words, a quotation should not go beyond a phrase or a brief sentence before the reader is told who is speaking.

A long quotation, especially one consisting of several sentences, should not hang from a stubby or abrupt introduction, such as *He said,* at the beginning of the paragraph. Instead, the attribution should be expanded and run into the preceding paragraph, or should be moved down to follow the first phrase or sentence of the quotation.

When attribution introduces a quoted sentence fragment or a single quoted sentence, a comma should precede the quotation marks; if the quotation is longer than one sentence, it should be introduced with a colon.

An abrupt interruption in dialogue or Q. and A. matter should be marked by a two-em dash (twice the length of a normal dash):

"Your Honor," she said, "please let me finish my——."

"Overruled!" the judge shot back.

A quotation that trails off inaudibly or indecisively should end with four points: *"I wonder," the philosopher mused. "What if, right at this moment, on another planet. . . ."*

quotations, ellipsis in. See **textual excerpts.**

quote(s) used as a noun instead of *quotation(s)* is colloquial: *He tried to support his flabby thesis with quotes from the great masters of English verse.* But *quotes* for *quotation marks* is somehow easier to accept.

R

Rabbi John P. Manley, Rabbi Manley, the rabbi. Also see **Chief Rabbi.**

Rabbinical Assembly. A Conservative group.

Rabbinical Council of America. An Orthodox group.

race(-). racecourse, racegoer, race horse, race track, raceway. But it is *Race Course* in some proper names.

race of a person in the news. Race should be specified only if it is truly pertinent. The same stricture applies to ethnic and religious identifications.

rack, wrack. *Rack* means to stretch, strain, torture; *wrack* means to wreck, ruin, destroy. Thus, *nerve-racking* describes something that strains or tortures the nerves. As for *wrack*, its work is better done by *wreck, ruin, destroy* or the like.

racquet, not *racket*, for the light bat used in tennis, badminton, squash racquets and similar games.

Radarman John F. Manley, Radarman Manley, the radarman. Also: Radarman 1st Class (or 2d Class, etc.) John P. Manley.

radio. Lowercase *radio station WQXR*, etc. Also see **television programs** and **ABC, BBC, CBC, CBS** and **NBC.**

radio-. radioactive, radioactivity, radiogram, radio-isotope, radioman, radiophone, radiotelephone, radiotelescope.

radio station, foreign. Do not capitalize *radio* in *Moscow radio, Peking radio, Havana radio* and the like. But the form *Radio Moscow* is permitted in quoted matter.

R.A.F. for the Royal Air Force.

railroader, railroad man.

railroads. Principal railroads in the United States and Canada are listed separately and alphabetically. In some cases, their names are followed by abbreviations or nicknames that may be used in subsequent references.

rain-. raincoat, rainfall, rainproof, rain-soaked, rainstorm.

raise. Use instead of *rise* for increase in pay: *He received a $10 raise.* But not this redundancy: *He received a $10 pay raise.*

raison d'être.

Randalls Island.

RAND Corporation.

rape. It is preferred to *criminal attack, criminal assault, sexual attack* and other imprecise terms.

rapid-fire (adj.).

rapprochement. *Warmer relations* or *reconciliation* or some other equivalent is usually better in first references than *rapprochement*, which often seems overelegant. See **détente** (a more useful word).

rate. birth rate, death rate, insurance rate, interest rate, tax rate.

rayon.

RCA Corporation, formerly the Radio Corporation of America. *RCA* in second references.

re-. reappear, reconstruct, recover (regain), re-cover (cover again), re-elect, re-election, re-enter, re-entry, reform (change for the better), re-form (form again), remake, reopen, reunion, re-use (n. and v.).

R.E.A. for the Rural Electrification Administration.

Reading Railroad. It is owned by the Reading Company.

ready. Avoid using as a verb, in headlines or in stories. In a sentence like *City Hall was readied for the inauguration,* it is usually possible to substitute a more natural verb, such as *prepare.*

ready-. ready-made (n. and adj.), ready-to-wear (n. and adj.).

REA Express Inc., formerly the Railway Express Agency.

realtor. This is a designation for a real-estate agent belonging to a board affiliated with the National Association of Real Estate Boards.

Rear Adm. John P. Manley, Admiral Manley, the admiral.

rear guard (n.), **rear-guard** (adj.).

rebut, refute. *Rebut* means to respond to a statement or speaker, taking issue; *refute* means to prove the statement or speaker wrong or false. Unless the intention is to say that one side demolished the other's argument, use *rebut, dispute, deny* or *reject,* not *refute.*

recherché (adj.).

reconnaissance.

Reconstruction. Capitalize in references to the reorganization of the Southern states of the United States after the Civil War. The period of time is usually given as 1867-77.

record(-). record-breaking, record changer, record-holder (person), record player.

record, new. The redundant *new* should not be used in a context like this: *He set a new record in the high jump.* But this is all right: *The new record exceeded the old by two inches.*

Recruit John P. Manley, the recruit.

rector is to be used in referring to an Episcopal clergyman in charge of a parish: *the Rev. John P. Manley, rector of, etc.* See **minister** and **pastor.**

Red. Capitalize as noun or adjective when used as a synonym for Communist. To avoid confusion, especially in headlines, do not use as synonym for a Russian or, in the plural, for the Soviet Union's Government. But *Red nations* (including the Soviet Union) is acceptable, especially in a difficult headline.

Red China. Do not use for China, except in direct quotations or special contexts. See **China.**

redheaded is all right for people having red hair and for redheaded woodpeckers and the like. But for people with hair of other hues, *-haired* is preferred: *brown-haired,* *fair-haired*, etc. And *red-haired* is fine, too.

red shift. A measure of the extent to which characteristic wavelengths of light from a distant astronomical object have been lengthened (shifted toward the red end of the spectrum) by motion of that object away from the earth. The effect is analogous to the lowered pitch of a horn on a receding vehicle. In an expanding universe, the extent of this shift is taken as an indicator of distance.

referable.

reference works. Do not quote the titles of almanacs, dictionaries, encyclopedias and similar reference works. Capitalize principal words.

referendums, not *referenda*.

reform, Reform (political). If the word is part of the official name of a political group and thus capitalized in first references, it should also be capitalized in second references: *the Reform group*. That indicates that the characterization is the group's, not the writer's. If the word is not part of a name and thus cannot be capitalized in all references, the writer must exercise the greatest care to avoid giving the impression that The Times accepts avowals of "reform" as valid. One man's reform may well be another man's retrogression. The problem is especially difficult when the word *reform* is used in headlines, where the context may be limited.

Reform, Reformed (religious). Various Jewish synagogues and Jewish organizations are Reform (not Reformed) groups: for example, the New York Federation of Reform Synagogues. Various Christian churches have *Reformed* in their names.

Reformed Church in America.

refute, rebut. The words are not interchangeable. See **rebut, refute.**

Regents, Board of. It is *the Regents* or *the board* in subsequent references to any state board so named, including New York's, and in all references to the Regents examinations.

regime.

regiment (military). Do not abbreviate: *Fifth Regiment, 13th Regiment,* etc.; *the regiment.* In the United States Army, most regiments have been eliminated, though individual battalions (formerly parts of those regiments) keep their old numbers for symbolic reasons. In such cases, the word *regiment* is omitted: *First Battalion, 21st Infantry.*

regions. Geographic regions are listed separately and alphabetically.

Regular Army (of the United States).

reinforce.

relative. Use *relative*, not *relation*, for a person.

relativity, theories of. Einstein's "special" theory deals with the constancy of the observed speed of light (regardless of motion by the light source or the observer) and defines the convertibility of energy into matter and vice versa. Einstein's "general" theory assumes an equivalence between gravity and acceleration. It accounts for the bending of light and slowing of time by a strong gravity field.

religion. Religious holidays, organizations, titles, etc., are listed separately and alphabetically.

religion of a person in the news. Religion should be specified in a news story only when it is clearly pertinent. The same stricture applies to ethnic and racial identifications of persons figuring in the news. Also see **devout.**

Renaissance. Capitalize when referring to the movement and the period that followed the medieval period. Lowercase in its general meaning: *a renaissance of poetry.*

repertory (not *repertoire*).

replica. Strictly speaking, it means a facsimile, copy or reproduction—dimensions, materials, workmanship and all—by the maker of the original. In this sense, the copy is usually one of a work of art. The word has also come to mean any such close reproduction, not necessarily by the original maker. For anything less than that, however, *replica* should not be used.

Representative John P. Manley, Democrat of Utah; the Representative (if he is a member of Congress or of a state legislature). Do not abbreviate, except in headlines: *Rep. Manley.* In articles about a state that has state representatives, use *State Representative* or *United States Representative* on first reference when necessary for clarity.

representative (at an international organization or conference). Lowercase and use the preposition *at: John P. Manley, representative at the United Nations conference on the law of the sea; Mr. Manley; the delegate.* Also see **delegate.** In news stories, avoid substituting the expression *Ambassador* or *permanent representative* (which see).

representative at large. No hyphens. Capitalize if it is a governmental title: *Representative at Large.*

Representative-elect John P. Manley, Representative-elect Manley, the Representative-elect. In cap-and-lowercase headlines: *Rep.-Elect Manley.*

Republic. Capitalize when used alone if the United States is meant.

Republican national (or **state** or **county**) **chairman.** John P. Manley, Republican national (or state or county) chairman; the national (or state or county) chairman, the chairman.

Republican National (or **State** or **County**) **Committee,** the national (or state or county) committee, the committee.

Republican National (or **State**) **Convention,** the national (or state) convention, the convention.

Republican Party.

requiem mass.

Reserve(s). Capitalize the *Active Reserve, Air Force Reserve, Army Reserve, Enlisted Reserve, Naval Reserve, Organized Reserve Corps, Ready Reserve,* etc. Also: *the Reserve, the Reserves, Reserve officer.* But: *a reservist, the reserves* (meaning men, rather than organizations).

resin.

rest(-). rest cure, rest home, rest house, rest period, restroom, rest stop.

restaurateur, not *restauranteur.*

restructure is overworked. See **structure** (v.).

result of. Use *as a result of* rather than *as the result of.* There may be more than one result.

résumé.

Resurrection. Capitalize when the reference is to Jesus, or to the rising of the dead at the Last Judgment.

retired. Do not abbreviate or capitalize in denoting military status: *Col. John P. Manley, retired.* Abbreviations for the various services, such as *U.S.A., U.S.N., U.S.M.C.,* may be used: *Capt. John P. Manley, U.S.N., retired,* etc. Sometimes, especially if the person is well known, it is not necessary to give the retirement status in the first reference. It may be worked in later, in a more graceful manner: *General Manley, who retired from the Army in 1969, became president of the company two years ago.*

retriever (dog).

Reuters. In stories it is *Reuters,* without an article, or *the Reuters news agency.* Also, in datelines: LONDON, Jan. 10 (Reuters)—etc. Use the credit line in 5-point Regal type above the dateline on page 1 stories and, when needed, on undatelined stories inside the paper:

By Reuters

Rev., the. The Rev. John P. Manley (or the Rev. Joan Manley). For most Protestants the normal second reference is *Mr.* or *Mrs.* or *Miss,* but never *the Rev. Manley.* For Roman Catholics, and some Episcopalians, *Father* is used in subsequent references: *Father Manley.* Lutheran clergymen are normally called *pastor (Pastor Manley)* in subsequent references. (For an exception, see **pastor.** Also see **minister** and **rector.**)

Never use *Rev.* without the preceding *the* except in headlines. And whenever *Rev.* is used, even in headlines, it must be followed by a given name or initials: *Rev. John Manley.*

Rev. Dr., the. The Rev. Dr. John P. Manley, Dr. Manley. Use *Dr.* only if it represents an earned doctorate. See **D.D.,** which is not an earned degree.

reveille (the signal and the assembly) is not capitalized.

Revolutionary War. The American one, that is. Also: *the American Revolution, the Revolution.*

revolver. A revolver is a hand weapon with a revolving chamber that holds the cartridges. It is different from an automatic pistol, which has a magazine that holds the cartridges. Both are properly called pistols.

R.F.D., for Rural Free Delivery, remains in wide use although it has officially been supplanted by *R.R.,* for Rural Route.

rhapsody. Capitalize in a title: *Brahms's Rhapsody in E flat (Op. 119).* Quote if part of a title that is assigned to the work by a composer and goes beyond a mere description of the kind of work: *Gershwin's "Rhapsody in Blue."*

rhinoceros, rhinoceroses.

Rhode Islander(s).

R.I. for Rhode Island after cities and towns.

RIAS for Radio in the American Sector (of Berlin).

Richter scale. A scale of earthquake magnitudes, expressed in Arabic numerals. Broadly speaking, this scale reflects the amount of energy released by the quake. It is based on the amplitude of motion induced by the earthquake in a certain type of seismograph at a distance of 100 kilometers from the epicenter (the point on the surface directly over the point of origin). An increase of one unit in magnitude represents a tenfold increase in ground motion. But the increase in released energy is far greater—roughly thirtyfold for a one-unit increase in magnitude. Earthquakes as weak as magnitude 3 can be felt by those close to the source. A single earthquake can properly be assigned only one magnitude although its intensity as defined at any one locality by the Mercalli scale (which see) is determined by local factors and distance from the source.

Riddle Airlines.

riffraff.

right(-). right-hand (adj.), right-handed, right-hander, right(s) of way.

right, rightist, right wing. Do not capitalize *right* unless the political divisions in a country are formally designated as *the Right, the Left,* etc., or the word appears in a party name. Do not capitalize *rightist* unless the reference is to such a division or party, or to a member of it. Do not capitalize *right wing* or *right-wing* (adj.) unless the reference is to such a division or party.

right(s) of way.

Rikers Island.

Ringling Brothers and Barnum & Bailey Circus. It is operated by Ringling Brothers-Barnum & Bailey Combined Shows Inc.

Rio Grande, not *Rio Grande River.*

rise. Do not use for increase in pay; use *raise* (which see).

riverfront.

Road. Spell out and capitalize in ordinary reading matter when part of a name: *Fordham Road.* The abbreviation *(Fordham Rd.)* may be used in headlines and in agate and other special matter.

roadbed.

robbery. See **burglary, larceny, robbery, theft.**

Robert College (Turkey).

rock, rock-and-roll, rock 'n' roll. The single word *rock,* noun or adjective, will usually suffice in first references (just as *jazz* does in its case). Of the two longer forms, *rock-and-roll* is preferred to *rock 'n' roll,* but the latter may be more suitable in some instances. Also: *folk-rock.*

Rockefeller Center.

Rockefeller University, not *Institute.*

rocket age.

rockets. Use Arabic numerals in rocket designations: *Saturn 5.*

Rockville Centre (L.I.).

role.

roll-call.

Rolls-Royce. The hyphen is standard equipment. When Rolls-Royce Ltd. went bankrupt in 1971 its holdings were divided between two new companies. They are: Rolls-Royce (1971) Ltd., a state-owned company that took over the airplane engine manufacturing interests, and Rolls-Royce Motors Ltd., a publicly owned company that took over the automobile manufacturing interests.

roman, Roman. Do not capitalize when the reference is to typefaces. But capitalize *Roman* (and *Arabic*) *numerals.* See **Roman numerals.**

Roman Catholic Church. In first references, it is *the Roman Catholic Church,* not *the Catholic*

Church. Also: *a Roman Catholic, a Roman Catholic church*. Second reference: *the Catholic Church, a Catholic church, a Catholic*. But use *Roman* in subsequent references also if the context does not make clear what is meant by *Catholic*. Do not capitalize *the church* standing alone.

Romanesque (architecture). The heavier style of arches that preceded the Gothic. As with the other historical styles, in discussion of more recent examples (and there was a great amount of Romanesque church-building in the late 19th century) it is best to modify the label with a date or a clarifying adjective. See **styles and schools in the arts.**

Roman numerals. Here are some examples of these numerals:

I	1	XC	90
II	2	XCIX	99
III	3	C	100
IV	4	CCXXII	222
V	5	CCCXCVIII	398
VI	6	CDXXXV	435
VII	7	D	500
VIII	8	DCXLVIII	648
IX	9	DCC	700
X	10	DCCCLXXII	872
XII	12	CMI	901
XV	15	M	1,000
XX	20	MCCLXXXI	1,281
XXIV	24	MD	1,500
XXX	30	MDLIII	1,553
XXXVII	37	MDCII	1,602
XL	40	MDCCLXXVI	1,776
XLI	41	MDCCCXCI	1,891
L	50	MCMLXXV	1,975
LVI	56	MM	2,000
LX	60	MMMM or M$\overline{\text{V}}$	4,000
LXX	70	$\overline{\text{V}}$	5,000
LXXVII	77	$\overline{\text{C}}$	100,000
LXXX	80	$\overline{\text{M}}$	1,000,000

The system is based on seven letters: I, V, X, L, C, D and M. A re-

peated letter repeats the value. When a letter follows one of greater value, the two values are added. The value of a letter preceding one of greater value is subtracted from that letter's value. When a letter stands between two of greater value, its value is subtracted from that of the last letter and the remainder is added to the value of the first. A bar over a letter increases the value a thousandfold.

Romanticism (music). The dominant force from about 1825 to 1910. It is characterized by a personal and emotional extension and free use of classic forms. Its principal composers included Chopin, Liszt, Schumann, Berlioz and Wagner. *Late Romanticism* and *Post-Romanticism* are often used to describe the last decades of the period and the music of such composers as Mahler and Richard Strauss. See **styles and schools in the arts.**

room(-), (-)room. room clerk, roomful, roommate. Also: bedroom, classroom, reading room, schoolroom, stateroom, stockroom, storeroom, workroom.

room names. Capitalize names of specially designated rooms: *Oak Room, Oval Office, Pump Room*. See **building names.**

Roosevelt Island (in New York City), formerly Welfare Island and, before that, Blackwells Island.

Rosh ha-Shanah (Jewish New Year).

R.O.T.C. for the Reserve Officers Training Corps.

round is used without an apostrophe in expressions like *all-round athlete, round-the-clock negotiations, round-the-world voyage, the year round*. Do not use hyphens in adverbial forms: *He sailed round the world in a tiny sloop.*

round(-). roundabout, round-bottomed, roundhouse, round robin (n.), round-robin (adj.), round trip (n.), round-trip (adj.), roundup (n.).

round numbers. See **numbers, round.**

route. Capitalize in names of roads: *Route 16.* The abbreviation may be used in headlines and special matter: *Rte. 16.* Also: *Route 9W, Rte. 9W.*

rowboat.

Royal Dutch/Shell Group. The major United States affiliate is the Shell Oil Company.

Royal Mail Lines.

Royal Netherlands Steamship Company. For first references *a Royal Netherlands ship,* etc., will suffice.

Royal Rotterdam Lloyd.

Royal Viking Line.

R.R., for Rural Route, has officially supplanted *R.F.D.,* for Rural Free Delivery, which nevertheless remains in common use.

Rte. This abbreviation for *Route* in the names of roads may be used in headlines and special matter, but not in news stories: *Rte. 16, Rte. 9W,* etc.

Rt. Rev., the; Most Rev., the. In accordance with the current tendency in the Episcopal Church and the Roman Catholic Church, omit these terms before the names of bishops and archbishops in almost all cases. But *the Most Rev.* is used before the name of the Anglican prelate who is the Archbishop of Canterbury and the names of the superiors general of certain Roman Catholic orders. See **Canterbury, Archbishop of; Superior General; Archbishop; Bishop; Rev.; Very Rev.**

rubber stamp (n.), **rubber-stamp** (v. and adj.).

ruble.

rugby (football).

Rumania.

Rumanian(s).

run-. runaround (n.), rundown (adj.).

runner(s)-up.

running mate.

Russia. See **Soviet, Soviets, Soviet Union.**

Russian(s). The words *Russian* and *Russians* may be used in general references in stories and headlines to citizens of the Soviet Union as a whole, although the Russians are only one of that country's many nationalities. The words should not be used when the reference is specifically to nationalities other than Russian—Georgians or Ukrainians or Uzbeks, for example. Phrases like *the Soviet people* are preferred in general references.

Russian names. Follow this system of transliteration for Russian names: Where there are English equivalents for letters in Russian use those equivalents. For other letters and symbols use phonetic renderings: *zh,* as in Zhukov; *kh,* as in Kharkov; *ts,* as in Trotsky; *ch,* as in Chernyshevsky; *sh,* as in Shostakovich; *shch,* as in the middle of Khrushchev; *ya,* as in Yalta.

Following is a complete transliteration table:

А а	a	У у	u
Б б	b	Ф ф	f
В в	v	Х х	kh
Г г	g	Ц ц	ts
Д д	d	Ч ч	ch
Е е	e[1]	Ш ш	sh
"	ye[2]	Щ щ	shch
"	yo[3]	ъ	—
Ж ж	zh	ы	y
З з	z	ь	—
И и	i	Э э	e
Й й	i	Ю ю	yu
К к	k	Я я	ya
Л л	l		
М м	m	ADJECTIVAL ENDINGS	
Н н	n	ый	y
О о	o	ий	i
П п	p	ая	aya
Р р	r	яя	yaya
С с	s	ое	oye
Т т	t	ее	eye

[1]Use *e* after consonants.
[2]Use *ye* after vowels and after "soft sign," and in initial position.
[3]Use *yo* in certain special cases (see the following note).

There are two forms of *e* with three sounds: *ye*, as in Yevgeny; *yo*, as in Pyotr; *eh*, as in Edda. In written Russian, *ye* and *yo* look the same; only the pronunciation is different. Where we know the pronunciation is *yo*, we use it. Example: *Semyon* (spelled *Semen* in Russian). If in doubt, use *ye* or *e*.

Surnames that have the *ski* type of ending in Russian are spelled with *y* in English. Example: *Malinovsky*. Polish names take *i*. Example: *Kolinski*. Surnames with the *ov* type of ending are spelled with *v*, not *ff*. Example: *Suvorov*, not *Suvoroff*.

Women's names in Russian and some other languages have feminine endings. We use them if a woman has an independent reputation under such a name. For example, *Viktoriya Brezhnev*, not *Brezhneva*. But it is *Maya Plisetskaya*, not *Plisetsky*, for the ballerina.

Familiar names that have been rendered into English incorrectly should continue to be used in their familiar forms. Examples: *Peter the Great*, not *Pyotr*; *Khrushchev*, not *Khrushchyov*; *Rachmaninoff*, not *Rakhmaninov*. (Another exception: *czar*, not *tsar*.)

Emigré Russians decide how to spell their own names. Example: *Nicholas Kalashnikoff*, not *Nikolai Kalashnikov*.

Some names have been rendered incorrectly because they came into English through other languages. Be careful about taking Russian names from non-Russian sources. Whenever there is time, consult a Russian-speaking editor or reporter.

Russian Orthodox Church. It was once the established church of Russia and is, like the Greek Orthodox Church, one of the autonomous Eastern Orthodox churches. See **Eastern Orthodoxy** and **Metropolitan** and **Patriarch.**

Russian Revolution. Also: *the Bolshevik Revolution, the Revolution. October Revolution,* while correct, is often confusing to readers because subsequent calendar changes have placed its anniversary date in November.

Russian wolfhound.

Russo-. Avoid, in adjectival references to Russia or the Soviet Union. Use *Russian-Chinese, Soviet-American,* etc.

Rwandan(s). The people of Rwanda.

S

Sabena Belgian World Airlines. For first references *a Sabena airliner*, etc., will suffice.

saber (a sword). But: Sabre, Super Sabre and Sabreliner (all aircraft).

SAC for the Strategic Air Command.

sacrilegious.

safe-. safe-conduct (n.), safecracker, safe-deposit (adj.), safeguard (n. and v.), safekeeping.

Sahara means desert. Thus *Sahara Desert* is redundant; it is *the Sahara*. Also: *the sub-Saharan region. Sub-Sahara* is not the name of a place; use only the adjectival form. See Sahel.

Sahel. This geographic term, absorbed into the French language from Arabic, refers to a coastal or border strip and is often used to designate the belt of African countries south of the Sahara. Because the term is imprecise and unfamiliar to many readers, it is best avoided in favor of a more precise one, such as *sub-Saharan region*. If *Sahel* occurs unavoidably in quoted matter, it should be explained gracefully in a phrase preceding or following the quotation. See Sahara and sub-Saharan.

sail-. sailboat, sailcloth, sailfish, sailmaker.

sailboats. For descriptions of the sailboat rigs now commonly used see catboat, sloop, cutter, yawl, ketch, schooner. Also see yacht and yachting.

sailing classes. Capitalize *Star Class, Lightning Class*, etc.

Saint and Sainte. See St. and Ste.

Saint John (New Brunswick), St. Johns (Quebec), St. John's (Newfoundland).

salable.

salesgirl, saleswoman. Use the latter, not the former, which can be disparaging. Do not use *salesperson*. See women.

saloonkeeper.

SALT, for the strategic arms limitation talks, may be used only in quoted matter; otherwise spell out the name of the conference or, better, avoid the pileup of adjectives by paraphrasing: *negotiations on limiting strategic arms*. When the acronym *SALT* appears in a quotation, the surrounding copy should be phrased to make its meaning clear.

Saltaire (L.I.).

Saluki (dog).

Salvadoran(s). The people of El Salvador.

salvo, salvos.

SAM('s) for surface-to-air missile(s). Also: SAM-2, SAM-6, SAM-6's, etc.

Samoyed (dog).

San Antonian(s).

San Diegan(s).

Sands Point (L.I.).

Sanforized (trademark).

San Franciscan(s).

sang-froid.

sanitarium, sanitariums.

Sanmarinese (sing. and pl.). The people of San Marino.

São Paulo (Brazil).

Sarajevo.

Sardinia. Use instead of *Italy* after Sardinian cities and towns when a locater is required. See **datelines.**

Sarh, a city in Chad. Formerly Fort-Archambault.

Saskatchewan. Do not abbreviate after cities and towns, even in datelines.

Saskatchewaner(s).

Satan. Also capitalize *Devil* if Satan is meant. Lowercase *a devil* and *devils.*

satellites. See **earth satellites.**

Saturn Airways.

saturnalian.

Saudi(s) or **Saudi Arabian(s).** The people of Saudi Arabia.

sauté, sautéed, sautéing.

savings and loan associations are not banks. A headline reference to such an association should begin with *Savings* or *Savings-Loan.* The irreducible minimum seems to be *Savings Unit.*

Saviour. This is the spelling when the reference is to Jesus or to God. Use *savior* for other meanings.

S.C. for South Carolina after cities and towns.

scaloppine.

Scandinavian Airlines System, S.A.S.

Scarborough (N.Y.).

S. Carolina may be used only in headlines—and then only when absolutely necessary—and in tabular and other special matter.

scheme. Do not use as a synonym for plan or project; in American usage, *scheme* may connote deviousness.

Schnauzer (dog).

school(-). school board, schoolbook, schoolboy, schoolchildren, schoolgirl, schoolhouse, schoolmaster, schoolroom, school ship, schoolteacher.

School Chancellor John P. Manley (the head of a school system), Chancellor Manley, the Chancellor, Mr. Manley. But: *John P. Manley, the chancellor of Queens College* [or *of New York University, etc.*]; *the chancellor.*

school colors. Capitalize when referring to a school or a school athletic team by its colors or color: *the Blue and White, the Crimson, the Big Red,* etc. Also: *The Crimson strategy paid off.* But: *Columbia's colors are blue and white*

school names. Do not use *No.* before numerical designations of public schools: *Public School 4, P.S. 4; Intermediate School 9, I.S. 9; Junior High School 113, J.H.S. 113.* Capitalize full names: *Lincoln High School, Manley Junior High School.*

schools in the arts. See **styles and schools in the arts.**

schooner. Now usually a two-masted yacht with the taller mast (main mast) stepped aft of the shorter mast (foremast). The rare schooner with more than two masts is designated as a three-masted (or four-, etc.) schooner.

Schuylkill, the. Do not use *River* after *the Schuylkill; kill* means stream.

S.C.I. for the State Commission of Investigation (the one in New York State).

scientific and related terms are listed and defined throughout this manual separately and alphabetically. See, for example, **angles, angstrom, apogee, atomic mass, chemical elements, genus and species, Gev, hertz, light-year, perigee, pulsar** and **relativity, theories of.** Also see **metric system** and **weights and measures.**

scoreboard, scorecard.

scores. See **sports.**

Scot(s), Scotsman(men), Scotswoman(women) for the people of Scotland. The preferred adjective is *Scottish* except in certain instances where *Scotch* is established, as in *Scotch whisky. Scot* and *Scots* are also acceptable as adjectives, but for the sake of consistency are best restricted to quoted matter.

scotch plaid, but *a Scottish tartan.*

Scotch tape (trademark).

Scotch whisky. *Scotch* by itself often suffices in contexts that clearly involve whisky.

scot-free.

Scottish terrier.

screenplay.

Scripture(s), scriptural, scriptural citations. Capitalize the noun in singular and plural when referring to books of the Old and New Testaments. Lowercase the adjective. Give scriptural citations as follows: *II Corinthians 4:3, Mark 9.* Typical citations might read: *He took as his text II Corinthians 4:3. He read from Psalm 4. He quoted Isaiah 12.* But in some contexts a reference to a psalm may be better thus: *the Sixth Psalm, the 23d Psalm.* Lowercase *a psalm.*

sculptress. Use *sculptor* instead. See **women.**

sculpture (v. as well as n.). Do not use *sculpt, sculpted* or *sculpting* in any sense.

sculptures. Quote their titles; capitalize principal words. But generic titles like Pietà are not quoted.

scurrilous.

S.D. for South Dakota after cities and towns.

S. Dakota may be used only in headlines—and then only when absolutely necessary—and in tabular and other special matter.

S.D.R.'s for special drawing rights (financial).

sea(-). seacoast, seafarer, seafood, seagoer, seagoing, seaplane, seaport, seashore, sea wall, seaweed.

Seaboard Coast Line Railroad, a subsidiary of Seaboard Coast Line Industries.

Seaboard World Airlines.

Sealyham terrier.

Seaman John P. Manley (of the Navy), Seaman Manley, the seaman. Also: Seaman 1st Class (or 2d Class, etc.) John P. Manley.

Sears, Roebuck & Company. In second references: *Sears, Roebuck* or *Sears.*

seasons. Do not capitalize *spring, summer, autumn, fall, winter.*

SEATO for the Southeast Asia Treaty Organization.

S.E.C. for the Securities and Exchange Commission.

second(-). second base, second baseman, second best (n.), second-best (adj.), second-class (adj.), second-degree (adj.), second grader, secondhand (adj. and adv.), second nature, second-rate (adj. and adv.), second sight, second thought, second wind.

Second Lieut. John P. Manley, Lieutenant Manley, the lieutenant.

Second Vatican Council. An assembly of the bishops of the Roman Catholic Church (1962-65). In second references, use *Vatican II.* Follow the same style for the First Vatican Council (1869-70). It is *Vatican I.*

Secretary, secretary. Secretary of Labor John P. Manley (or Foreign Secretary, etc.), Secretary Manley, the Secretary. But: *a secretary, the secretaries* (for capitalized plural exceptions, see **titles**). Also: *John P. Manley, secretary of the company* (or *club,* etc.); *the secretary.*

Secretary General (of the United Nations, for example) John P. Manley, the Secretary General. No hyphen in this or similar titles, like *director general.*

secretary-treasurer. Hyphenate such two-title compounds.

Securities Exchange Act. It is not the Securities and Exchange Act, al-

though the commission is the Securities and Exchange Commission.

Security Council (United Nations), the Council.

securityholder.

seder. A Passover feast in the home of Jews, at which the Haggadah is recited.

self-. self-abasing, self-adulation, self-conscious (also: un-self-conscious), self-governing, self-government, selfhood, self-made, selfness, self-respect, selfsame, self-service.

semi-. semiannual, semidarkness, semifinal(s), semifinalist, semi-invalid, semiofficial, semisweet, semiyearly.

semiannual, semiyearly. Twice a year, or biannual; every two years is *biennial.* To aid comprehension, avoid the prefix form when possible and use *twice a year.*

semicolon. The semicolon is used principally as a mark of division in sentences containing statements that are closely related but require a separation more emphatic than a comma: *Peace is indivisible; if any European country is menaced, all are menaced. The contestants were ready; the timekeeper was not. The assignment was difficult; still, he carried it out.*

The semicolon is also used in a series of three or more things that includes defining matter: *Those present were Thomas A. Jones, a banker; Harriet G. Smith, a lawyer; Harold I. Abbot, a tax consultant, and John Trenton, a principal stockholder.* (Note the comma before the *and.*)

If a semicolon and a closing quotation mark or a closing parenthesis appear together in a sentence, the semicolon should follow the other mark: *He said it was "bills, bills, bills"; she said he was stingy.*

In headlines, the semicolon is used only in tops or crosslines. Do not use this mark in banks; the dash is used instead.

semimonthly means twice a month. Every two months is *bimonthly.* To aid comprehension, avoid the prefix form when possible and use *twice a month* or, for bimonthly, *every two months.*

Seminola Park, Seminole Racing Park.

semiweekly means twice a week. Every two weeks is *biweekly* (which can also mean twice a week, but not in this book). To aid comprehension, avoid the prefix form when possible and use *twice a week.*

Senate. Capitalize all specific references, domestic and foreign.

Senator John P. Manley, Republican of Arizona; the Senator. Also: *a senator; the senators* (for capitalized plural exceptions, see **titles**). Do not abbreviate, even in headlines. In referring to a state that has state senators, use *State Senator* or *United States Senator* on first reference when necessary for clarity.

Senator-elect John P. Manley, the Senator-elect. In cap-and-lowercase headlines: *Senator-Elect.*

senatorial.

send-off (n.).

Senegalese (sing. and pl.).

Senhor, Senhora, Senhorita. See **Mr., Mrs. and Miss.**

senior (class and member of that class). Also see **Sr.**

senior citizen(s). Avoid the term whenever possible.

Señor, Señora, Señorita. See **Mr., Mrs. and Miss.**

separate.

Sept. for September before numerals: *Sept. 17.*

septet (music). See **quartet** or **trio.**

sepulcher. Do not use the *re* ending: *Church of the Holy Sepulcher.*

sequence of tenses. In newspaper writing, the governing verb is generally in the past tense. For precision's sake, the tenses of other verbs in a sentence must be properly related to it. The following examples are offered as a guide:

He said he was sick. He was sick at the time he said so.

He pointed out that the earth is round. The *is* is right because the earth is always round.

He said he had been sick. He was sick at some time before the saying.

He said he was sick on July 4. Here a *had* is not needed to put the sickness back in time before the saying; *July 4* does that.

Mr. Jones is a sick man, Dr. Manley said, and cannot work. This means that Jones was sick when the doctor so reported. The *said* is not the governing verb, but merely a parenthetical interpolation and thus *is* and *cannot* are correct. They would change to *was* and *could not* if the sentence read *Dr. Manley said that Mr. Jones, etc.*

Mr. Jones was a sick man, Dr. Manley said, and could not work. Here the meaning is that Jones was sick at some time in the past before the doctor spoke.

serenade. Capitalize in a title: *Beethoven's Serenade for Flute, Violin and Viola (Op. 25).* But: *a Mozart serenade.*

sergeant. See **Sgt.**

sergeant-at-arms.

sergeant first class. See **Sgt.**

sergeant(s) major. See **Sgt. Maj.**

Serialism (music). A composing technique that originated in the first quarter of the 20th century. At first identified as "the 12-tone system," it was developed by Arnold Schoenberg and refined by Anton Webern and Alban Berg. A serial composition is built on a specific sequence, or "row," of tones, not necessarily including all 12 tones of the chromatic scale; the sequence controls the shape and development of the work. See **styles and schools in the arts.**

Sermon on the Mount.

serve, service. As verbs meaning to provide a service, they are not interchangeable. People are *served*, individually or in groups (a club, a town, a nation). Inanimate objects or systems that are maintained, inspected, supplied, repaired, etc., are *serviced*. A newspaper *serves* its readers; mechanics *service* the presses. A company or an institution is *served* by its employees or its supporters. And a horse at stud *services* a mare.

serviceable.

serviceman, servicewoman.

set(-). setback (n.), set piece (n.), set-piece (adj.), set-to (n.), setup (n.).

setter (dog).

Seventh-day Adventists.

Sèvres.

sewage (waste matter), **sewerage** (a drainage system).

ex distinctions. In referring to

women, avoid words or phrases that seem to imply that The Times views men as the norm and women as the exception, or descriptions that would be irrelevant if the subject were male. For a detailed discussion of terminology, and of ways to avoid giving offense, see **women.**

sextet (music). See **quartet** or **trio.**

Seychellois (sing. and pl.). The people of the Seychelles.

Sgt. (military and police). Sgt. John P. (or Joan) Manley, Sergeant Manley, the sergeant. Also (military): Sgt. 1st Class (or 2d Class, etc.) John P. Manley.

Sgt. Maj. John P. Manley, Sergeant Major (or just Sergeant) Manley, the sergeant major or the sergeant. Also: sergeants major.

Shabuoth (Feast of Weeks).

Shakespearean.

shake-up (n.).

shantung (cloth).

SHAPE for Supreme Headquarters Allied Powers (Europe).

shape-up (n.).

Shariah, the legal code of Islam. It is roughly comparable to the Talmudic tradition in Judaism.

she. Do not use *she* and *her* in references to countries, except in special contexts. Use *it* instead. But use *she* and *her* for ships. See **pronouns for countries** and **pronouns for ships.**

sheepdog.

sheik, sheikdom. See **Arab names and titles.**

shell shock (n.), **shellshocked** (adj.).

Shepheard's Hotel (Cairo).

Sheriff John P. Manley, Sheriff Manley, the sheriff.

Sherman Antitrust Act, the antitrust act.

Shetland (wool and pony).

ship-. shipboard, shipbuilder, shipmate, shipowner, shipshape, shipyard.

ship lines are listed separately and alphabetically.

shippers. They are not carriers. They are the individuals or companies whose goods are moved by carriers. The carriers include shipowners, whose vessels move cargoes.

ships. Do not quote their names. Use the pronouns *she* and *her* in references to ships and other vessels even when they have masculine names. Do not confuse measurements of weight with measurements of freight capacity· see **tonnage.**

shish kebab.

shop(-), (-)shop. shopkeeper, shoplifter, shop steward, shopworn. Also: barbershop, bookshop, machine shop, pawnshop, repair shop, sweatshop, toyshop.

short(-). short circuit (n.), short-circuit (v.), short cut (n.), shorthand, shortsighted, shortstop, shortwave (n. and adj.).

short ton. See **ton.**

shot-put, shot-putter, shot-putting.

show-. showboat, showdown, showman, show-off (n.), showroom.

shut-. shutdown (n.), shut-in (n.), shutout (n.).

S.I. for Staten Island in headlines

and after the names of communities. Never *Staten I.*

S.I.A. for the Securities Industry Association.

Sicily. Use instead of *Italy* after Sicilian cities and towns when a locater is required. See **datelines.**

sick(-). sickbed, sick call, sick leave, sick list, sickroom.

side(-). side arm (weapon), sidearm (style of pitching), sideboard, sideline, sidesaddle, sidestep, sidestroke, sideswipe, sidewalk, sidewise.

Sierra Nevada, not *Sierra Nevada Mountains.*

sightsee, sightseeing, sightseer.

Signal Corps (United States), the corps.

signaled.

signatory, signer. Except in quoted matter or special formal contexts, use the simpler word, *signer,* to describe a country that has subscribed to a treaty or other agreement.

signature, signing. Use *signing* for the act or ceremony of endorsing a treaty or a document: *the signing of the cease-fire agreement.* Reserve *signature* for the actual name written at the end of a document.

signatures should be set in caps and small caps: JOHN P. MANLEY. See **letters.**

Signor, Signora, Signorina. See **Mr., Mrs. and Miss.**

Simhath Torah (Rejoicing in the Law).

simon-pure.

Sinai, not *the Sinai.* But: *the Sinai Desert, the Sinai Peninsula.*

Singaporean(s).

Sinhalese. The language of Sri Lanka (which see).

Sino-. Avoid in adjectival references to China. Use *Chinese-American, Chinese-Russian,* etc. But: *Sinologist.*

SIPC for the Securities Investor Protection Corporation. It is treated as an acronym, pronounced SIP-ick.

Sir John Manley, Sir John. In headlines: *Manley.* The title, unfailingly followed by a given name, is borne by British baronets and knights, who are not peers. When relevant, it should be specified whether Sir John is a knight or a baronet.

sitdown, sit-in, sit-up (all n.).

Six Nations. The Iroquois Confederacy.

Sixth Avenue (Manhattan). See **Avenue of the Americas.**

sizable.

sizes. Express in numerals: *size 8 dress, size 44 long, 11½B shoes, 16½ collar.*

skeet shooting (n.). But: *trapshooting.*

skeptical.

ski, skied, skier, skiing, ski jumping.

skillful.

skin-dive (v.), **skin diving** (n.).

Skye terrier.

slang and colloquialisms. Use only in appropriate contexts. Do not, for example, say in an ordinary political story that a candidate is a *shoo-in* or that he accused his opponent of having been *smashed* (unless, of course, the words appear in quoted matter). Also avoid the faddish— *grooving* and *rapping*, for instance —in unsuitable contexts. But when

slang or a colloquialism is used, do not self-consciously enclose it in quotation marks.

sloop. A single-masted yacht that usually has one headsail (most often the jib). The mast is quite far forward. The distinction between sloop and cutter (which see) has almost disappeared.

slowdown (n.).

smallpox.

SmithKline Corporation, formerly Smith, Kline & French Laboratories.

Smithsonian Institution.

smokescreen.

Smokey Bear, not *Smokey the Bear.*

smolder.

smooth fox terrier.

Smyrna. Use *Izmir* instead, except in historical references.

snapshot.

sneak thief.

snow-. snowball, snow-blind, snowbound, snowfall, snowflake, snowmobile, snowplow, snowstorm.

so-called (adj.), **so called** (adv.).

Socialism, socialism. Capitalize if the reference is to a political party or movement that professes socialism. Lowercase in a general sense: *He told Congress that the plan smacked of socialism.*

Socialist. Capitalize as noun or adjective only if the reference is to a political party or movement that professes socialism, or to its members.

Social Security. When the Federal system of benefits is meant, it should be capitalized, as should *Medicare* and *Medicaid.*

Social Security Act.

Society of Friends. See **Quakers.**

Soho (London), **SoHo** (Manhattan; the name is derived from *South of Houston* Street).

solo, solos.

Somali (sing. and pl.). The people of Somalia.

somber.

some-. somebody, someday (adv.), someone, sometimes (adv.).

sonata. Capitalize in a title: *Beethoven's "Moonlight" Sonata, Beethoven's Sonata in E flat, "Les Adieux."*

songs. Quote the titles of songs, popular or classical, including national anthems. If the title is in English, all the principal words are capitalized: *"Get Me to the Church on Time."* If the song is in French, Spanish or Italian, the first word is generally capitalized: *"Nuit d'étoiles," "Il bacio."* If the song is in German, the first word and every noun are capitalized: *"An den Frühling."*

sonic barrier. See **sound barrier.**

sophomore (class and member of that class).

S O S (distress signal). Use thin spaces between the letters, and no points.

Sotheby Parke Bernet.

sound barrier. In general, avoid the term *breaking the sound* [or *sonic*] *barrier.* There is no such barrier, although it was once believed that the speed of sound was a barrier that airplanes could not surpass.

The barrier was the design of the planes.

soundtrack, soundtruck.

source documents. Stories report ing the findings of commission: study groups and the like shoul, when the findings appear signif cant, give information as to the availability of the source document or documents. This information should include the title of the document, the name of the agency or group producing it, the address at which it is available, the number of pages and the price or the fact that the document is free.

sources of news. The best news source—best for a newspaper and best for its readers—is the source that is identified by name. But it is also true that a newspaper, to give its readers information vital to them, must sometimes obtain it from sources not in a position to identify themselves.

The decision to permit anonymity of a source must first of all be justified by the conviction of reporter and editor not only that there is no other way to obtain the information, but also that the information is both factual and important.

When it is established that anonymity of the source cannot be avoided, the nature of the source must be specified as closely as possible. The bald and meaningless *sources said* will not do, and *reliable sources* is not much better. *United States diplomat* is better than *Western diplomat*, which is better than *diplomat.* And better still is *a United States diplomat who took part in the meeting.*

The description of an anonymous source should never be misleading. Do not, for instance, say *State Department sources* when a single person was the source. Also, in observing rules of the game that government officials impose, try to avoid ludicrous evasions of identity of a source such as *a senior official aboard Secretary Manley's plane.* Something like *reporters traveling with Secretary Manley on his plane were told* may actually take the reader closer to the source.

The term *news leak* or just *leak* often crops up in connection with anonymous sources. Basically, a leak is a disclosure of confidential information by a source who chooses to remain anonymous. Some leaks are unsolicited; others are induced by diligent reporters. Some serve a worthy general purpose; others may serve a selfish purpose of the source. Such motives should be specified in a news article as fully as possible.

Because readers understand that information is sometimes leaked by the source to promote his own interests, the word *leak* should not be used indiscriminately. Such use is unfair to reporters who dig out the news on their own, often by cultivating special sources of news, and who do not merely wait for information to be dropped into their laps.

See **corrections** and **fairness and impartiality**.

South, south. Capitalize in all references to that geographic region of the United States and in subsequent references to a country with *South* in its name, such as South Korea. Lowercase *south* as a point of the compass.

Southampton (L.I.).

South Asia comprises Afghanistan, Bangladesh, India, the Maldives, Nepal, Pakistan and Sri Lanka.

South Carolinian(s).

South Dakotan(s).

Southeast, southeast. Capitalize when referring to that geographic region of the United States; lowercase as a point of the compass.

Southeast Asia comprises Burma, Cambodia, Indonesia, Laos, Malyasia, The Philippines, Singapore, Thailand and Vietnam.

Southern, southern. Capitalize when used in reference to the South (geographic region) of the United States. But: *southern Utah, southern Italy, southern part of North [or South] Korea, southern half,* etc.

Southern Baptist Convention.

Southerner. Capitalize when used to describe a native or inhabitant of the part of the United States called the South or of a country with *South* in its name, such as South Korea.

Southern Hemisphere, the hemisphere.

Southern Pacific Railroad. It is owned by the Southern Pacific Company.

Southern Railway.

Southern Tier (New York State).

South Jersey. An exception to the rule that calls for lowercase in *southern New Jersey, southern Ohio, southern France,* etc. Also: *North Jersey.*

South Pole. But: *the pole, polar.*

South Shore (L.I.). Also: *North Shore.*

South Side. Capitalize when regularly used to designate a section of a city.

South Vietnam. Use only in references to the period before the re-unification of Vietnam.

South Vietnamese (sing. and pl.) is to be used only in historical contexts.

Southwest, southwest. Capitalize when referring to that geographic region of the United States; lowercase as a point of the compass.

South-West Africa. The disputed territory in southern Africa. It is called Namibia by the United Nations, which declared South Africa's mandate revoked in 1966. South Africa has not recognized the revocation and retains effective control. In that situation, the style remains *South-West Africa.*

Soviet, Soviets, Soviet Union. In headlines, *Soviet* (without the article *the*) and *Soviet Union,* as well as *Russia* and *U.S.S.R.,* may be used as nouns meaning the country or its government. Do not use *the Soviet.* And do not use *Soviets,* in headlines or stories, as a synonym for the Soviet Union or its people. The noun *soviet* means a council. *Russians* may be used in general references to the people in stories and headlines, and *Soviet* may be used as an adjective in this sense: *the Soviet people, Soviet officials, Soviet writers,* etc. See **Russian(s).**

space(-), spacecraft, space flight, spaceman, space platform, spaceport, spaceship, space station, spacesuit, space walk.

space age.

space vehicles. Do not quote their names; use Arabic numerals in designations: *Apollo 11, Gemini 4, Sputnik 5, Skylab 2.*

spaniel.

Spanish-American War.

Spanish Civil War, the civil war.

Spanish Line.

Spanish names usually include the mother's family name, which comes after the father's family name. Thus, in a second reference to José Molina Valente, it is usually *Molina,* not *Valente.* But some people use both the father's and the mother's family names in second references. Names often include *y* (for *and*): José Molina y Valente. A married woman may use her maiden name in the middle position: Isabel Martínez de Perón, the widow of Juan Perón.

SPAR for Coast Guard Women's Reserve, but *a Spar* for a member.

Speaker of the Assembly, Speaker of the House. Always capitalized, unlike *majority leader, minority leader, whip,* etc., because it might otherwise not be recognized as a title. Also: *the Speaker.*

spearfishing.

Specialist 4 (or 5, 6, etc.) John P. Manley, Specialist Manley, the specialist. Never *Specialist 5th Class,* etc., and note that with specialist grades, unlike most others, the higher the numeral the higher the rank.

species. See **genus and species.**

specter.

Speech From the Throne. In Britain and Canada.

speeches and lectures. Quote their full titles and capitalize principal words.

speed(-). speedboat, speed demon, speed trap, speedup (n.), speedway.

spelling. The dictionaries to be used as authorities for spelling are Webster's New World Dictionary of the American Language (Collins-World), in the first instance, and Webster's Third New International Dictionary of the English Language (Merriam), for words not to be found in the New World Dictionary.

The chief authority for the spelling of geographic names is the Columbia Lippincott Gazetteer of the World. Exceptions to the style of this gazetteer include *St.* and *Ste.*, which should usually not be spelled out in place names. The exceptions also include place names in some countries in Southeast Asia that are to be spelled in the style of the Official Standard Names Gazetteers of the United States Board on Geographic Names, but with accent marks omitted. (See **geographic names** for details.)

Many troublesome words, especially compounds, are listed separately and alphabetically. Spellings given in the manual are the ones to use in cases of conflicts with the dictionaries or the gazetteers.

spell out, in the sense of explaining or detailing, is overworked and should be replaced whenever possible with synonyms like *detail, enumerate, explain, list, specify.* Above all, avoid the redundant *spell out in detail.* But *spell out* is fine in the sense of actually rendering letter by letter. And so is *spell.*

spilled, not *spilt.*

spinster. Like *old maid, spinster* has connotations that are best avoided. Find other ways to say that a woman is unmarried, if that fact is really pertinent. See **women.**

split infinitive. It should generally be avoided, but can sometimes be justified. For instance: *He was*

obliged to more than double the price. But *to clearly show* should not have been split. A compound verb, however, should usually be separated when it is used with an adverb. See **adverb placement.**

split-up (n.).

spokesman, spokesmen. Use for both men and women. Do not use *spokeswoman* or *spokesperson.* See **women.**

sports. Scores and points are given in figures: *The Yankees won, 6 to 1* (or *6-1*). *He scored 8 points in the first half. He shot a 4.* Numbers of runs, touchdowns, baskets, goals, strokes, etc., are spelled out below 10: *They had four hits and three runs in the eighth inning. In the 12th inning, they got their 11th hit, for a total of 10 runs. He took three more strokes.*

Times of sports events are expressed in figures: *3:01, 2:55½, 0:53.* When a time in seconds is given for the first time, it is set thus: *59.3 seconds.* In a subsequent reference, it is *0:59.3.* Also: *1 minute 3.2 seconds, 1:03.2.*

The names of sports events, stadiums, bowl games, etc., are capitalized but not quoted: *Kentucky Derby, Yankee Stadium, Rose Bowl Game, World Series,* etc.

Sports titles should precede a proper name only when the position is appointive or elective: *Coach Jack Manley, Manager Ralph Houk, Trainer Hirsch Jacobs.* But not *Outfielder Hank Aaron* or *Jockey Eddie Arcaro.*

See **automobile racing and rallies, baseball, basketball, boxing, cricket, football, hockey, horse racing, swimming, tennis, track and field, yachting.**

sports(-), sports car, sports editor, sportsman, sports page,

194

sportswear, sportswoman, sportswriter.

sportscast, sportscaster. Do not use except in quoted matter.

spring, springtime.

springer spaniel.

sputnik. Lowercase except in designations like *Sputnik 5*, in which Arabic numerals are to be used.

Spuyten Duyvil.

squad (police). Lowercase *sex crime squad; safe, loft and truck squad,* etc.

Squadron Leader John P. Manley (British), Squadron Leader Manley, the squadron leader.

Square. Spell out and capitalize in ordinary reading matter when part of a name: *Washington Square.* The abbreviation *(Washington Sq.)* may be used in headlines and in agate and other special matter.

squash racquets, squash tennis. The two are similar, but not the same. Thus *squash* alone cannot be used in first references.

Sr. for Senior in names. Do not use a comma: *John P. Manley Sr.* (or *Jr.*). And in bylines:

By **JOHN P. MANLEY Sr.**

In a listing, if family names are printed before given names, the expression *Sr.* (or *Jr.* or *3d,* etc.) comes last: *MANLEY, John P. Sr.,* not *MANLEY Sr., John P.*

Sri Lanka, formerly Ceylon. The people are still called Ceylonese (n. and adj.), but *Sri Lanka* may also be used as an adjective. The language is Sinhalese.

SS. for Saints, as in the names of some churches: *the Church of SS. Peter and Paul.*

S.S. for steamship. Except in date-lines (which see), the preferred style is to omit the abbreviation before a vessel's name and to write instead *the liner United States.*

SST for supersonic transport (airplane).

St. for Street. The abbreviation should be used only in headlines and special matter.

stable-. stableboy, stablehand, stableman, stablemate.

stadiums, not *stadia.* Capitalize the names of stadiums, playing fields and indoor sports arenas: *Shea Stadium, Yankee Stadium, the Yale Bowl, Franklin Field, Madison Square Garden (the Garden).*

staffer(s). Do not use for *staff member(s)* or *member(s) of the staff.*

Staff Sgt. John P. Manley, Staff Sergeant (or just Sergeant) Manley, the staff sergeant or the sergeant.

stagehand.

staid (sedate).

stalactite (hangs from a cave roof like an icicle), **stalagmite** (rises from cave floor).

stanch (v.). Use *stanch* in the sense of stopping the flow of a liquid—blood, for instance—and in similar contexts. Use *staunch* (adj.) in the sense of steadfast or resolute.

stand-. standby (n., adj.), stand-in (n.), standoff (n.), standout (n., adj.), standpatter.

Standard & Poor's Corporation. In second references: *Standard & Poor's, S.&P.*

standard-bearer.

Standard Oil Company (Indiana). In second references: *Indiana Standard* or *Standard of Indiana. Amoco* is a trademark of the company.

Standard Oil Company (Ohio). In second references: *Sohio.*

Standard Oil Company of California. In second references: *Socal.*

St. Andrew's (Westchester), **St. Andrews** (Scotland).

St. (for Saint) **and Ste.** (for Sainte). They are almost always abbreviated in place names (an exception to the style followed in the Columbia Lippincott Gazetteer). Except for place names, and occasionally the name of a building or a church, *St.* is generally used before the name of any saint, whether male or female: *St. Agnes, St. George.* The abbreviation for the plural is *SS.*, as in *SS. Peter and Paul.*

"Star-Spangled Banner, The." The titles of anthems, like those of other songs, should be quoted. See **songs.**

State, state. Capitalize *New York State* but not *state of Ohio*, etc., unless the reference is to a state's government: *The State of Ohio brought the suit.* Lowercase references to specific states when standing alone: *The state sued the city. The state government acted.* Capitalize *State* when used with the name of an official agency or with an official title: *the State Education Department, State Comptroller John P. Manley.*

Ordinarily the word *State* is included in references to New York State or Washington State to distinguish them from the cities bearing the same names. But *State* may be omitted when the context makes clear what is meant: *The Governors of California and New York have similar powers. Nebraska's Legislature is smaller than Washington's.*

Lowercase *state* in the general sense: *affairs of state.*

state abbreviations. The abbreviations to be used for states of the United States after the names of cities and towns in stories and, when needed, in datelines are listed separately and alphabetically. Alaska, Hawaii, Idaho, Iowa, Ohio and Utah are not abbreviated. For a list of cities that do not require state names, see **datelines.**

Abbreviations like *N. Dakota* may be used in headlines when absolutely necessary and in tabular and other special matter. Also: *S. Dakota, N. Carolina, S. Carolina* and *W. Virginia.*

State Assembly, the Assembly.

State Capitol (the building), the Capitol.

state chairman of a political party. Joan Manley, Democratic state chairman; the state chairman; the chairman.

State Commission of Investigation (S.C.I.).

state groupings. Capitalize designations like *New England States, Middle Atlantic States, Middle Western States, Southern States, Gulf Coast States, Mountain States, Pacific States*, etc., when referring to the complete groupings.

Statehouse. Capitalize in specific references. In New Jersey it is *the State House.*

State of the State Message. A governor's, if it is formally so called.

State of the Union Message. The President's.

State of the World Message. The President's.

196

state residents and natives. Terms used to denote natives and residents of states of the United States are listed separately and alphabetically, as are terms for natives and residents of many foreign countries and regions, including Canadian provinces, and of many cities of the world.

State Senate, the Senate.

States Marine Lines.

states' rights.

State University of New York. A system of state-supported two-year and four-year colleges and graduate programs. Its units include individual institutions or campuses such as the State University Center at Stony Brook. The State University has its own board and should not be confused with the University of the State of New York (which see). The acronym for the State University of New York is *SUNY,* but in general its use should be restricted to quoted matter. For second references in stories, *the State University* or *the university* is fine, and *State University* or *State U.* suffices for headlines. Also see **City University of New York.**

statewide.

stationary (still), **stationery** (writing material).

station house.

statute mile. See **mile.**

staunch (adj.). Use *staunch* in the sense of steadfast or resolute. Use *stanch* (v.) for stopping the flow of a liquid—blood, for instance—and in similar contexts.

St. Bernard (dog).

St. Catharines (Ontario).

steam(-). steam bath, steamboat, steam engine, steamfitter, steamroller, steamship, steam shovel.

steeplejack.

step-. stepbrother, stepchild, stepfather.

stepping stone.

sterling. See **pounds and pence.**

stevedore. A stevedore, in waterfront usage, is an employer. A longshoreman is a laborer.

stiletto, stilettos.

stimulus, stimuli.

St. James's Palace. Also see **Ambassador to Britain** and **Court of St. James's.**

St. John the Divine, Cathedral of. Not *Cathedral Church.*

St. Louis-San Francisco Railway, the Frisco.

St. Louis Southwestern Railway, the Cotton Belt.

stock-. stockbroker, stockholder, stockjobber, stockman, stockroom.

stock and commodity exchanges. The principal exchanges in the United States are listed separately and alphabetically.

stock market prices should be given in fractions rather than dollars and cents. A stock price of $67.625 should be given as 67⅝. The spell-out-below-10 rule does not apply: *The stock advanced 3 points, to 9.*

Stock Yards (Chicago).

STOLplane, STOLport. *STOL* stands for short takeoff and landing.

stone. As a unit of weight used in Britain, it is equal to 14 pounds.

197

Stone Age.

stop-. stopgap, stoplight, stop-off (n.), stopover (n.), stopwatch.

store-, (-)store. storehouse, storekeeper, storeroom. Also: bookstore, cigar store, department store, drugstore, grocery store.

storm. The National Weather Service defines a storm as having winds of 55 to 74 miles an hour—between a gale and a hurricane—and that is what is meant when a "storm warning" is issued. *Storm,* of course, also has general weather meanings that are not restricted by this definition: *hailstorm, rainstorm, snowstorm, thunderstorm,* etc. See **blizzard, cyclone, gale, hurricanes, tornado, typhoon.**

-storm. hailstorm, rainstorm, snowstorm, thunderstorm, windstorm.

strait (passage) is almost always singular: Bering Strait, Strait of Gibraltar, Strait of Malacca. An exception is the Straits of Florida, although some authorities, but not The Times, make that singular, too.

strait-. straitjacket (n. and v.), straitlaced.

strangle. It means not merely to choke, but to choke to death. Also: *stranglehold.*

strategic arms limitation talks. See **SALT.**

stratum, strata.

streamline.

streetcar.

street-length (adj.).

streets and avenues. In giving the names of streets, avenues, etc., in ordinary reading matter, spell out and capitalize ordinal numerals through the ninth and *Avenue,*

Street, West, East, etc.: *First Avenue, Fifth Avenue, Park Avenue, East Ninth Street.* Use figures for 10th and above: *10th Avenue, West 14th Street, 42d Street, West 113th Street.*

Avenue and *Street* may be abbreviated to *Ave.* and *St.* in headlines and in tabular or other special matter, but not in ordinary reading matter. In headlines, figures may also be used for the ordinal numbers through *Ninth* (except *First*) in the names of avenues: *2d Ave., 5th Ave.,* etc. But *1st Ave.* should be avoided. Also see **Avenue of the Americas.**

Give decades of numbered streets in figures: *the 60's, the East 60's, the West 80's, the 130's,* etc.

Use figures for all house numbers: *1 Fifth Avenue, 510 Broadway, 893 12th Avenue.* Do not use commas in numbers of more than three digits: *1135 11th Avenue.*

Do not use *No.* before a house number except in a sentence like this: *They rented 510 Broadway, but No. 512 remained vacant.*

Street numbers in Queens take a hyphen: *107-71 111th Street.*

In news stories giving an avenue address in Manhattan, also give the nearest cross street. When useful, the nearest avenue may also be specified for addresses that are on streets.

strikebreaker.

strikeout (n. and adj.).

stroke oar.

strong-arm (v. and adj.).

strongman (political).

structure (v.). This overworked verb can often be replaced by *build, construct* or *organize.* Similarly, *restructure* can often be replaced to advantage by *rebuild, recast,* reconstruct, reorganize, revamp or revise.

stumbling block

styles and schools in the arts are listed separately and alphabetically. When dealing with the terminology of art, architecture, music or literature, capitalize the name of a specific historical movement, group or style *(the Impressionism of Monet)*. Lowercase such a term in a more generalized sense *(Joan Manley's paintings are impressionistic in manner)*. The prefix *neo* is lowercased unless specifically adopted by a group or movement as part of its name: *the Neo-Impressionism of Seurat*, but *John Manley works in a neo-Dada manner*.
   In architecture, scholars disagree significantly on the limits and definitions of many styles. In the 20th century, for example, a building designed in a loosely classical vein, like the old Pennsylvania Station in New York, is likely to be called *classical, neo-classical, classical revival* or *romantic classical*. Writers are encouraged in such cases not to use just a style label in describing buildings, but to employ such phrases as *a 20th-century building in the Gothic style*.

sub-. subbasement, subcommittee, subculture, subdivision, submachine gun, subnormal, subzero.

subcommittee. See **Congressional committees and subcommittees.**

subheads. Use single quotation marks for quoted words or phrases in subheads between paragraphs. Avoid time elements like *yesterday, today* and *tomorrow* in subheads in datelined stories.

subpoena, subpoenaed.

sub-Saharan. Use this adjectival form: *sub-Saharan region.* There is no place called the sub-Sahara. See **Sahara** and **Sahel.**

Subtreasury Building. This building in New York City is now called the Federal Hall National Memorial (which see).

subway lines. In New York City, they form three systems: the BMT, the IND and the IRT (all of which see). The abbreviations are nearly always used, even in first references. Also: *the A train, the RR train.*

succah. The tabernacle that symbolizes the Jewish holiday Succoth.

Succoth (Feast of Tabernacles).

such. It is used chiefly as an adjective: *Such men exist.* It may also be used adverbially to indicate degree: *such big pears.*

Sudan, the. The *the* may be dropped only in headlines. In datelines, *the* is not capitalized.

Sudanese (sing. and pl.).

suffixes and prefixes. Words formed from them will be found under the separate and alphabetical listings of the suffixes and prefixes.

suffocate. Its most common meaning is not merely a stoppage of respiration, but a fatal stoppage.

Suffragan Bishop. See **Bishop** (EPISCOPAL).

suite (music). Capitalize in a title: *Bach's Suite No. 1 for Orchestra, Ravel's "Daphnis et Chloé" Suite No. 2.*

sulfate, sulfite. They are not the same thing.

sulfur, not *sulphur,* in all its lowercase forms, but *Sulphur* is not to be changed in proper names.

199

summer, summertime. But: *summer time* for the British equivalent of daylight time.

summit. *A summit conference,* or *a conference at the summit,* but never *a summit* or *the summit* when the reference is to a conference. In general, limit the use of *summit* in this sense to a meeting of the leaders of the world's three or four most powerful nations. Do not use *minisummit.*

sun. For rare instances of capitalization, see **earth, moon, sun.**

SUNY, but generally only in quoted matter, for the State University of New York (which see).

super-. superabundant, superagency, supercarrier, supercaution, supereloquent, superhighway, superindifference, superman, supermarket, supernatural, superpowers, superrefined, superstate, supertanker. But: super-Republican.
  Do not use *super* by itself unless it appears in a name (*Super Bowl,* for instance) or in quoted matter.

Superintendent of Schools. John P. Manley, Superintendent of Schools; Superintendent Manley; the Superintendent.

Superior General (religious). The Very Rev. (or, in certain orders, the Most Rev.) John P. Manley, Superior General of the Jesuit order (or: of the Society of Jesus), the Superior General; Father Manley. But: *a superior general, superiors general* (for capitalized plural exceptions, see **titles**). See **Rev., Most Rev., Rt. Rev., Very Rev., Archbishop** and **Bishop.**

supersede.

supine (lying face up), **prone** (face down).

supra-. supra-auditory, suprafine, supragovernmental, supraintellectual, supranational.

Supreme Court (of the United States). Make it *the Court* in second references. The International Court of Justice (World Court) is the only other court to which this capitalization style applies. See **Chief Justice** and **Associate Justice.**

Surinam, Surinamese (sing. and pl.). Surinam was formerly Dutch Guiana. The adjective is *Surinamese* or *Surinam.*

Surrealism. A movement in art and literature that developed out of Dada in Paris in the early 1920's. It gave priority to irrational images and dreamlike inventions. See **styles and schools in the arts.**

Surrogate John P. Manley, Surrogate Manley, the surrogate.

Surrogate's Court, Surrogates' Courts.

survey should not be used to describe stringer roundups of opinion or man-in-the-street interviews. The term should be limited to scientific soundings of opinion. See **opinion polls.**

Swazi(s). The people of Swaziland. The adjective is *Swazi* or *Swaziland.*

sweatshirt, sweatsuit.

Swedish American Line.

swimming. Times of races are given in figures: *57.6 seconds, 0:57.6.* Unless there is all-electric timing, the order of finish in a swimming race is determined by the judges, not the timers.
  The pool length should be included in all swimming stories.

World records can be set only in pools that are 50 meters long. American records can be set in three categories, according to pool length: 20 yards, 25 yards (known as short course) and 50 meters or 55 yards (known as long course).

Swissair.

syllabus, syllabuses.

symphony. A symphony without a nickname or a special title is capitalized but not quoted: *Brahms's Symphony No. 1,* or *Brahms's First Symphony.* A nickname is quoted: *Beethoven's "Eroica" Symphony.* The whole of a special title is quoted: *"Symphonie Fantastique."* Capitalize the name of a movement: *the Scherzo, the Andante.* Lowercase if the movement is referred to by its place in the sequence: *the third movement, the finale.* If the opus number is cited, it should be within parentheses: *Tchaikovsky's Symphony No. 4 in F minor (Op. 36).* If it is a Mozart symphony, the Köchel catalogue number may be used within parentheses: *Mozart's Symphony No. 40 in G minor (K. 550).*

Synagogue Council of America. It is the umbrella organization of the Reform, Conservative and some Orthodox rabbinical and congregational bodies.

Synod. Capitalize in the name of a church organization.

Synod of Bishops (Roman Catholic).

Syrian Catholic Church. A Roman Catholic church of the Eastern Rite (which see).

Syrian Orthodox Church of Antioch. Separate churches bearing this name belong to two branches of Christianity: Eastern Orthodoxy and Oriental Orthodoxy (both of which see).

syrup.

Szechwan, not *Szechuan,* for the province in China.

T

Tabasco (trademark).

tableau, tableaux.

table d'hôte.

tablespoonful(s). A tablespoonful is equal to three teaspoonfuls or four fluid drams.

taboo.

Taft-Hartley Act.

tailor-made (adj., before a noun).

Taiwan (no longer Formosa) is the name of the island and should be used in datelines after cities and towns. It can also serve, in headlines and news stories, as a synonym for Nationalist China. While many of Taiwan's people are now Chinese (émigrés, or descendants of émigrés, from the mainland), the people native to the island are Taiwanese.

take, bring. *Take* denotes movement away from the speaker or writer, or any other movement that is not toward him; *bring* denotes motion toward the speaker or writer. See **bring, take.**

takeoff (n.), **takeover** (n.).

Talmud. The generic term (literally, *study*) for the legal tradition of Judaism. It consists of the Mishna, which is the written version of the oral tradition, and the Gemara, which is commentaries on the Mishna by later scholars.

tanks (military). Use Arabic numerals in designations: *M-60, M-60's.*

Tan Son Nhut Airport (Saigon).

tape (v.), **tape-record** (v.), **tape recording** (n.). Also: *videotape* (n. and v.).

tapping. Do not confuse with bugging. See **bug, tap.**

taps, the bugle call, is lowercase and not quoted. It is construed as a singular.

target. As a verb, it is trite military and governmental jargon. *Targeted,* for example, should be changed to *set a target, aimed at* or (in the sense of a governmental improvement campaign) *concentrated on.*

Tass is the Soviet Government's official press agency. The name is formed from the initials of the Russian words meaning Telegraph Agency of the Soviet Union.

TB for tuberculosis.

Tbilisi, formerly Tiflis (in Soviet Georgia).

tea-. tearoom, teaspoonful(s), teatime.

team(-). teammate, team play, teamwork.

teamsters. See **International Brotherhood of Teamsters.**

203

tear gas.

teaspoonful(s). A teaspoonful is one-third of a tablespoonful or one and a third fluid drams.

technical sergeant. See **Tech. Sgt.**

Technician John P. Manley (military), Technician Manley, the technician. Also Technician 2d Grade (or 3d, etc.) John P. Manley.

Technicolor (trademark).

Tech. Sgt. John P. Manley, Sergeant Manley, the sergeant.

teen-age, teen-ager. Before a noun, use *teen-age*, not *teen-aged*, except in quoted matter: *teen-age daughter.* Do not use *teen* by itself; *teens* may be used in reference to a span of ages *(sons in their teens)*, but not to the young people concerned, even in headlines. In cap-and-lowercase heads: *Teen-Age, Teen-Ager.*

Teheran (Iran).

telecast (n.), **televise** (v.).

telephone numbers. Use an area code, in parentheses, when the number is outside the New York City calling area: *The Washington police asked that anyone with information call (202) 555-2368.*

Teleprompter (trademark).

Teletype, Teletypesetter (trademarks).

television networks. See **ABC, BBC, CBC, CBS, NBC** and **PBS.** For the sake of consistency, points are omitted in abbreviations of names of networks, stations and network subsidiaries, many of which use abbreviations without points in their official names. In one case (CBS Inc.), the abbreviation is the official name of the parent company.

television programs. In ordinary copy, quote their titles and capitalize principal words: *"Issues and Answers," NBC's "Tonight" show, "The CBS Evening News." Show* is an appropriate word to describe an entertainment broadcast, but *program* is preferred for news and public affairs.

telltale.

temblor, not **tremblor,** for an earthquake.

temperature. Use figures for degrees of temperature: *The temperature was 9 at midnight. Heat of 92.5 degrees was reported. There was a 9-degree drop during the night. It was 10 below at 3 A.M. His temperature was 101.9.* Do not write, *He had a temperature.* Either *He had a high temperature* or *He had a fever.*

The degree mark is available for use in headlines and tabular matter: *60°.* Also: *-10°* for 10 below. In stories and headlines, use figures for an indefinite number of degrees: *The temperature stayed in the 90's for three hours.*

See **centigrade, Celsius,** and **Fahrenheit** and **Kelvin.**

temperature-humidity index. In tables or charts: *T.H.I.*

tempos, not *tempi.*

Ten Commandments (Decalogue). Do not abbreviate or use figures: *First Commandment.* Also *Tenth Commandment* (an exception to the style of using figures for ordinals above the ninth).

Tenn. for Tennessee after cities and towns.

Tennessean(s).

Tennessee walking horse.

tennis. Use figures in scores: *30-15, 30-all, 40-0.* Use *scores* instead of *score* in referring to the result of a match of more than one set: *The scores of the match were 6-1, 3-6, 9-7.*

Players hitting the ball back and forth are rallying, not volleying. A player volleys when he hits the ball before it strikes the ground.

tenpins. Also: *ninepins.*

terrier.

Territory of Afars and Issas (formerly French Somaliland), a French possession in northeastern Africa. The capital is Djibouti.

terror-. terror-ridden, terror-stricken, terror-struck.

testimony. Testimony that is printed verbatim should be indented and should appear without quotation marks. Both instructions apply whether the testimony appears in the body of a story or is used separately. Use the identifiers *Q.* and *A.* except when the questioner and the person questioned are first identified. In most cases, the introduction to the Q. and A. will supply such information. Do not use a dash after *Q.* or *A.* When a speaker's name is given at the beginning of a paragraph of testimony or other transcript material, it should be set in light caps, followed by a colon, not a dash. See **texts.** And, for punctuation of a sentence that trails off or is interrupted abruptly, see **quotations.**

Tet, the Lunar New Year (Vietnam).

tête-à-tête.

Tex. for Texas after cities and towns.

Texan(s).

Texas A & M University. This is the full, official name (with spaces, without points).

Texasgulf Inc., formerly the Texas Gulf Sulphur Company.

texts. Texts are set in the regular body type of The Times, which is 8½-point Imperial, and in three different widths: one column, indented; two columns, indented; and 14-pica measure, without indention. The introductory precedes are accordingly indented or unindented to match the body type. A precede in regular one-column measure is set in 8½-point Imperial italic; the others are in 9-point Imperial italic. Texts and textual excerpts presented in the separate-text format are not enclosed in quotation marks. See next entry.

textual excerpts. When textual excerpts are used, ellipsis should be indicated in important statements or documents if confusion or unfairness may result from the absence of such indication.

Use three points (not asterisks) to indicate an omission in the interior of a sentence, and four points for an omission at the end of a sentence. To indicate the omission of an entire paragraph or more, use a centered line of three points between paragraphs.

Points should also be used in a news article when quoted matter falls into the category described above and is so extensive that the points will not appear to be typographical errors. Quotations in news articles, especially those dealing with sensitive or complicated subjects, must be handled carefully to avoid any distortion that might be caused by putting together statements that were originally not consecutive. In such instances, reattribution and reparagraphing may often provide the solution.

See **texts** (preceding entry).

T formation.

Thai(s).

Thai names. Nearly every Thai uses a given name followed by a surname. But in subsequent references, the given name is used with the honorific. Thus Thanom Kittikachorn is Mr. Thanom, and Thanat Khoman is Mr. Thanat.

Thanksgiving, Thanksgiving Day.

that (conj.). After a verb like *said, disclosed, announced,* etc., it is often possible to omit *that* for conciseness: *He said [that] he was tired.* But if the words after *said* (or after any other verb) can be mistaken for its direct object, the reader may be momentarily led down a false trail, and the *that* must be retained: *The Mayor announced that his party's tax program would be introduced shortly.*

When a time element follows the verb, the conjunction *that* is always needed to make quickly clear whether the time element applies to the material preceding or following: *Governor Manley announced today that he would sign the income tax bill.*

Often a sentence with two parallel clauses requires the expression *and that* in the second part; then the *that* should be kept in the first part also, for balance: *The Mayor said that he might run again and that if he did, Joan Manley would be his campaign manager.*

that, which. *That* is preferred in restrictive clauses: *The university that he admires most is Harvard.* In nonrestrictive clauses, *which* is

mandatory: *Harvard, which is not his alma mater, is first in his affections.*

the. Capitalize when an integral part of a name: *The Hague, The New York Times.* But: *the Netherlands.* See **a, an** and **articles.**

theater, theatergoer. Capitalize *Theater* in names: *the Shubert Theater.*

The Dalles (Ore.).

Thee, Thou, He, Him, His. Capitalize when the reference is to God, Jesus, the Holy Ghost (or the Holy Spirit) or Allah. But do not capitalize *who, whom,* etc.

theft. See **burglary, larceny, robbery, theft.**

The Hague.

theretofore is stilted and should normally be replaced by *until then.* On the rare occasions when *theretofore* is appropriate—perhaps for a formal effect—it should not be confused with *heretofore,* which means until now.

thermos (n. and adj.) for a vacuum bottle.

think tank. This term for an organization engaged in intensive research is slang that rapidly achieved triteness and should be used only in special feature contexts or quoted matter.

third(-). third base, third baseman, third-class (adj.), third degree (n.), third-degree (adj.), third grader, thirdhand (adj. and adv.).

third world. Do not quote or capitalize, but make sure the phrase is used in a context making clear that it refers to underdeveloped or emerging nations.

Thirty Years' War.

thoroughgoing.

thrash (to beat a person), **thresh** (to harvest grain). Also: *thresh out a problem.*

Throgs Neck.

Thruway. This spelling (capitalized) may be used in names of roads. In subsequent references: *the Thruway.* See **Gov. Thomas E. Dewey Thruway.**

thunder-. thunderbolt, thunderclap, thundercloud, thunderhead, thundershower, thunderstorm, thunderstruck.

tidal wave. This term is restricted in scientific terminology to a sea wave due chiefly to the effects of lunar gravity. For the wave induced by an earthquake or submarine landslide, *tsunami* is the correct scientific term. *Tidal wave* remains in general use, a fact that should be explained when *tsunami* appears.

tidelands. The area between the high-tide and low-tide marks. See **offshore oil.**

tidewater.

tie-up (n.).

Tiflis is now Tbilisi, except in certain historical references to the Soviet Georgian capital.

tightrope.

'til. Do not use in place of *until* or *till* unless it appears in a direct quotation from a written or printed source. As for *till* and *until,* they are almost entirely interchangeable, as preposition or conjunction.

tilde. See **accent marks.**

time. Use numerals in giving clock time: *10:30 A.M.* (the preferred form because it is the shortest), *10:30 o'clock, 10:30.* Do not use *half-past 10.* Also avoid the redundant *10:30 A.M. yesterday morning, Monday afternoon at 2 P.M.*

Midnight refers to the end of a day, not the beginning of a new day. Do not say, *The bomb went off at midnight today.* In a morning newspaper, that should be *last midnight.*

The times in the time zones of the United States are: Eastern standard (or daylight) time (E.S.T., E.D.T.), central standard time (C.S.T.), mountain standard time (M.S.T.), Pacific standard time (P.S.T.). Include when pertinent to the story: *10 A.M. yesterday, central standard time.* Also: Greenwich mean time (G.M.T.) and *summer time* for the British equivalent of daylight time.

Clock times in remote time zones may be translated parenthetically, but only if the conversion is truly useful to readers or if the news event is monumental: *The shooting erupted in the Middle East at 10 A.M. (3 A.M. Friday, New York time), and United Nations delegates were awakened for an emergency meeting.* If the story bears the dateline of a city in the same time zone as New York, use *Eastern standard time* or *Eastern daylight time* rather than *New York time.* Within the parentheses, avoid *yesterday, today* or *tomorrow;* name the day instead.

The date of an event is determined by the time in the zone where it occurs. If, for example, an earthquake occurs in California at 11 P.M. on May 1 (when it is already May 2 in New York), subsequent articles should give May 1 as the date of the quake.

In giving elapsed times of voyages, races, etc., do not use commas: *4 days 16 hours 13 minutes.*

See **dates** and **years, decades, centuries.**

time(-), (-)time. time bomb, time clock, timekeeper, time limit, timeout (n.; but: *take time out*), timepiece, timesaver, timesaving, timetable, time-tested, timeworn. Also: full time (n. and adv.), full-time (adj.), longtime (adj.), nighttime, onetime (adj., meaning former), overtime, part time (n. and adv.), part-time (adj.), peacetime, wartime.

Time & Life Building.

Time Inc.

titleholder.

titles. Personal titles of all sorts—academic, business, foreign, governmental, military, religious, etc.—are listed separately and alphabetically, and the style for capitalization or abbreviation is given in each case. Long titles should follow names: *John P. Manley, Minister of Internal Affairs.*

If a title is sometimes capitalized when standing alone, it should nevertheless be lowercased when used generally: *a governor,* or *Pennsylvania will elect a governor.* The plural form for such a title should be capitalized only in reference to a small number of officials individually and specifically identified in the story: *the Governors of New York, New Jersey and Connecticut, the three Governors, the Governors;* but *many states' governors, the governors of the Northeastern states.* Also: *the Bishops of Hartford and Topeka, the two Bishops, the Bishops; Assemblywomen Manley and Jones, the two Assemblywomen, the Assemblywomen.*

Only genuine titles—not mere descriptions, whether lowercase or capitalized—should be affixed to names. Do not, for example, write *harpsichordist Joan Manley* or

Political Scientist John P. Manley. But a phrase in apposition, preceded by *the,* is acceptable: *the sociologist Margaret Manley.* Also see **floor leader, majority leader, minority leader.**

In identifying officials of cities, states or countries, do not make the place name a part of the title: *President Jean-Paul Hommely of France,* not *French President Jean-Paul Hommely; Gov. John P. Manley of California,* not *California Gov. John P. Manley.* But the words *city* and *state* are acceptable in titles: *State Senator Joan Manley, City Comptroller John P. Manley.* Standing alone, without a name, expressions such as *the French President* or *the California Governor* are correct.

A sports title may precede a proper name only when the position is elective or appointive: *Coach Jack Manley, Manager Ralph Houk, Trainer Hirsch Jacobs.* But not *Outfielder Hank Aaron* or *Jockey Eddie Arcaro.*

In the titles of books, plays, speeches, etc., the principal words should be capitalized: *"The Catcher in the Rye," The World Almanac, "A Taste of Honey," "American Prospects and Foreign Trade,"* etc. Separate and alphabetical listings of the categories of titles show whether quotation marks are to be used.

TNT.

toastmaster.

tobacco, tobaccos.

to-do (n.).

Togolese (sing. and pl.). The people of Togo.

toll(-). tollbooth, toll bridge, toll call, toll collector, tollgate, tollhouse cookie, tollkeeper, toll road.

Tolstoy.

Toms River (N.J.).

ton. This unit of weight in the United States and some other countries is equal to 2,000 pounds avoirdupois, or 907.20 kilograms. It is also called a short ton. The long ton, used in Britain, is equal to 2,240 pounds, or 1,016.06 kilograms. The metric ton is equal to 1,000 kilograms, or 2,204.62 pounds. See **metric system.**

tongue-tied.

tonnage (ships). Do not confuse measurements of weight with measurements of freight and passenger capacity: *Displacement tonnage*, a measurement used for naval vessels, is the actual weight of a ship or the weight of the water it displaces. *Deadweight tonnage*, used for freighters, is the cargo capacity of a ship, expressed in long tons. *Gross tonnage*, usually used to describe passenger ships, is a measurement of a vessel's enclosed interior spaces. The figure is derived by allowing one ton for each 100 cubic feet of space.

top(-). topcoat, topgallant, top hat, top-heavy, topknot, topmast, topsail, topsoil.

topsy-turvy.

Torah refers to the Five Books of Moses, the first five books of the Bible, inscribed on a scroll (a Torah) kept in the ark of a synagogue. *Torah* in a generic sense refers to all of Jewish learning. Thus: *The rabbi is a renowned Torah scholar.*

tornado. A violent whirlwind. Do not use *cyclone*, which is ambiguous. The maritime equivalent of the tornado is the waterspout.

Tory, Tories. These are acceptable in headlines or quoted matter referring to the British Conservative Party or its members. In news stories, the words should be avoided, except in special contexts.

totaled, totaling.

touch(-). touch and go (but: *a touch-and-go situation*), touchback, touchdown, touchhole, touch-me-not (n.).

toward, not *towards.*

towboat.

town house.

track and field. Times of races are given in figures: *9.3 seconds, 0:09.3, 3 minutes 58.6 seconds, 3:58.6.*

Spell out mile distances up to 10: *one-mile walk, two-mile run, 10-mile run.* Use figures for all races measured in yards and meters: *60-yard dash, 100-yard dash, 200-meter dash.*

Figures are also used in field events to show height and distance. A pole-vaulter clears 15 feet 4 inches. The next reference to the height should be to 15-4 (eliminating *feet* and *inches*).

In the shot-put, the *shot* is the metal ball and the *put* is the body motion used to propel it. A shot is *put*, not thrown or heaved.

trademarks. Names of products and processes that are patented and are the exclusive property of an individual or company are capitalized: *Coca-Cola* (and *Coke*), *Formica, Frigidaire, Kodak, Polaroid, Technicolor, Xerox,* etc. These and others are listed separately and alphabetically. The use of trademarks can easily be avoided if desirable: *bandage* for *Band-Aid.* But if a trade name is pertinent to a story, use it: *The robbers escaped in a white Cadillac sedan.*

Trailer Train Company.

train-miles.

tranquil, tranquilize, tranquilizer, tranquilizing. But: *tranquillity.*

Tranquillity, Sea of.

trans-. trans-Atlantic, transcontinental, transmigrate, transoceanic, trans-Pacific, transship, transshipment, trans-Siberian.

Trans International Airlines.

Trans World Airlines (T.W.A.).

trapshooting (n.). But: *skeet shooting.*

traveled, traveler, traveling.

treaties, pacts and plans. Capitalize specific names: *Treaty of Ghent, Treaty of Versailles, Versailles Treaty, Pact of Paris, Warsaw Pact.* But: *nine-power treaty, United States-Canadian trade treaty.* Capitalize *Alliance for Progress, Truman Doctrine, Marshall Plan* and similar designations that acquire official or semiofficial stature.

tri-. triangular, tricentennial, tricolor, trilateral, trilingual, trimonthly, tripartite, tristate (see **tristate area**), triweekly.

Triborough Bridge. But: *Queensboro Bridge.*

trigger. As a verb it is overused to the point of triteness and should almost always be avoided.

trillion, in general, should not be used; say, instead, *a million million* or *1,000 billion.* See **numbers, round.**

Trinidadian(s) and Tobagan(s). The people of Trinidad and Tobago.

trio. Capitalize in the title of a musical work: *Mozart's Piano Trio in B flat major (K. 254), Beethoven's "Archduke" Trio.* Capitalize in the name of an ensemble: *Vienna Trio.*

triple crown (horse racing). The Kentucky Derby, the Preakness, the Belmont Stakes.

Tristar, not *TriStar,* for the jetliner.

tristate area, tristate region. Do not use in first references to New York, New Jersey and Connecticut. Instead, name the states. And in second references, *the states* will usually suffice. If a numerical modifier is called for, *three-state* is preferable because it wears better than *tristate.*

triteness. See **clichés.**

Trooping the Color (British ceremony). Not Trooping *of* the Color.

trophies (sports). Capitalize *America's Cup, Davis Cup,* etc.

Truman, Harry S. (with a period, even though the initial does not stand for a name).

tryout (n.).

tsar, czar. The more familiar *czar* is to be used—an exception to our system of transliteration. For a guide to capitalization and non-Russian references, see **Czar, czar, czarist.**

T-shirt.

tsunami (sea wave). See **tidal wave.**

tugboat.

tug-of-war, tugs-of-war.

turboprop may be used, as adjective or noun, in reference to a plane with propellers driven by turbine engines. See **jet, jetliner.**

turn-. turnabout (n.), turncoat, turndown (n.), turnkey (n.), turnout (n.), turnover (n.).

Turnpike, turnpike. Capitalize in names: *New Jersey Turnpike, Pennsylvania Turnpike.* But: *the turnpike.*

TV for television, but only in headlines, quoted matter and special contexts where a colloquial flavor is called for.

TV networks. See **ABC, BBC, CBC, CBS, NBC** and **PBS.**

T.V.A. for the Tennessee Valley Authority.

Twelve Apostles. An exception to the rule of using figures for numbers above nine.

"21" Club (the restaurant). In headlines: *'21'* (provided the context is clear).

tying.

typhoon. The term is used in the western Pacific region to describe a violent storm of the type called a hurricane in the United States. It is often helpful to explain the similarity. See **cyclone.**

tyro, tyros.

Tyrol, not *the Tyrol.*

U

U. for University may be used in headlines when absolutely necessary *(U. of Michigan; Boston U.)* and in tabular and other special matter.

U.A.W. for the United Automobile Workers (which see).

U.F.O.('s) for unidentified flying object(s).

Ugandan(s). The people of Uganda.

UHF for ultrahigh frequency, and **VHF** for very high frequency.

Ukraine, the; Ukrainian.

ukulele.

ultra-. Because it suggests excess, *ultra-* can be pejorative and must be used with care. *Mrs. Manley is ultraconservative*, for example, can in some instances seem to mean that she is more conservative than anyone should really be. As for the hyphen in compounds: *ultra-atomic, ultra-German*, etc. But: *ultramodern, ultranationalistic, ultrasonic, ultraviolet.* See **arch-**.

umlaut. See **accent marks**.

U.N. for the United Nations, but only in headlines, quoted matter or tabular or other special matter.

un-. unaffected, un-American, unbiased, undo, unforgettable, unneeded, un-self-conscious, unsolved, unused, unwed.

under(-). underbid, underclerk, underclothes, underconsumption, underdeveloped, underdog, underdone, underestimate, undergraduate, underground, underhand, underripe, under secretary (which see), undersheriff, understudy, under way (adv.), underworld, underwrite.

Under Secretary of State John P. Manley, the Under Secretary.

undertaker may be used interchangeably with *funeral director.* Do not use *mortician.*

UNESCO for the United Nations Educational, Scientific and Cultural Organization.

UNICEF for the United Nations Children's Fund, even though *International* and *Emergency* have been dropped from the name.

Uniform Code of Military Justice.

Union-Castle Line (Union-Castle Mail Steamship Company).

union names may be shortened, in subsequent references or in headlines, through the use of possessive forms: *the International Brotherhood of Teamsters, the teamsters' union; the United Federation of Teachers, the teachers' union; the United Mine Workers of America,* *the miners' union; the International Ladies Garment Workers Union, the garment workers' union.*

Union of American Hebrew Congregations. A Reform group.

Union of Orthodox Jewish Congregations.

Union of Orthodox Rabbis.

Union of Soviet Socialist Republics (U.S.S.R.). See **Soviet, Soviets, Soviet Union.**

Union Pacific Railroad, a subsidiary of the Union Pacific Corporation.

Union Theological Seminary. In subsequent references: *Union* or *Union Seminary* or *the seminary,* never *Union Theological.*

unique. A dangerous word that should be avoided.

Uniroyal Inc., formerly the United States Rubber Company.

Unitarian Universalist Association.

United Airlines, a subsidiary of UAL Inc.

United Arab Emirates. This is the name of a country incorporating seven emirates: Abu Dhabi, Dubai, Sharja, Ajman, Fujaira, Umm al Qaiwain and Ras al Khaima. A member emirate should not be referred to as a country or a nation. The country name, unlike *United States,* is treated as a plural.

United Arab Republic. Former name for Egypt and Syria when they were united briefly, and a name used by Egypt alone for a time after the union was dissolved.

United Automobile Workers may be used in first references instead of the full name, the United Automobile, Aerospace and Agricultural Implement Workers of America. The abbreviation is U.A.W.

United Church of Christ. A merger of the Evangelical and Reformed Church and the Congregational Christian Churches. Although the name *Congregational* is technically incorrect, it is still used by many individual churches.

United Kingdom. This formal name, a shortened version of United Kingdom of Great Britain and Northern Ireland, is not ordinarily used in stories except in quoted matter or in contexts requiring emphasis on Northern Ireland's status. Otherwise *Britain* suffices.

United Methodist Church. It is a denomination formed by merger of the Methodist Church and the Evangelical United Brethren Church.

United Nations Charter, the Charter. Also: *Chapter IV, Article 9.*

United Nations dateline. The style is:

Special to The New York Times
UNITED NATIONS, N.Y., Dec. 4—

United Nations Economic and Social Council, the Council. This is not UNESCO (which see).

United Nations General Assembly, the Assembly.

United Nations Secretariat, the Secretariat.

United Nations Security Council, the Security Council, the Council.

United Nations Trusteeship Council, the Council.

United Presbyterian Church in the U.S.A. (Northern). But it is *the Presbyterian Church in the U.S.* (Southern). The words *Northern* and *Southern* are not part of the names, but are usually appended for differentiation.

United Press International. Use without an article in references in stories. U.P.I. is the abbreviation, but the periods are not used in datelines: LIEGE, Belgium, May 3 (UPI) —etc. Use a credit line in 5-point Regal type above the dateline on page 1 stories and, when needed, on undatelined stories inside the paper:

By United Press International

United States. Do not abbreviate in stories, except in names, designations of highways and quoted matter. Though *United States* is singular, its possessive is formed as if it were plural: *United States'.*

United States Air Force, the Air Force. But lowercase *air force* in subsequent references to a foreign air force.

United States Army, the Army. But lowercase *army* in subsequent references to a foreign army.

United States Attorney John P. Manley, the United States Attorney, Mr. Manley. Also: *the United States Attorney for the Southern District of New York.* See **assistant.**

United States Catholic Conference.

United States Lines.

United States Marine Corps. For a guide to capitalized and lowercased usage of *marine*, see **Marine Corps, Marine(s), marine(s).**

United States Navy, the Navy. But lowercase *navy* in subsequent references to a foreign navy.

United States Postal Service. It has replaced the Post Office Department. It may be called *the Postal Service* in first and subsequent references.

United Synagogue of America. A Conservative group.

University is often misplaced in names. It is not, for instance, *the University of Indiana;* it is *Indiana University.* It is not *Notre Dame University;* it is *the University of Notre Dame.* If you don't know, check. Do not, however, capitalize *the* in names like *the University of Chicago,* even though the university may follow that style.

University of the State of New York. A formal entity comprising all educational enterprises overseen by the Board of Regents. It consists of all public and private elementary, secondary and higher educational institutions, libraries, museums and all other institutions chartered by the Regents. In addition to degrees granted by individual institutions, the University of the State of New York gives its own degrees through the Regents' external degree program, in which students receive academic credit not only for course work but also for knowledge acquired outside the classroom (on a job or through reading). The president of the University of the State of New York is the State Commissioner of Education. The university should not be confused with one of its components, the State University of New York (which see).

unprecedented. A dangerous word that should be avoided.

up. As a verb it is colloquial, and should be used only in special contexts—*up the ante,* for instance, but not *up the price of sugar.*

up-, -up. upgrade, uphill, upstairs, upstate, up-to-date (adj.), uptown. Also (all n.): breakup, buildup, cleanup, close-up, cover-up (also adj.), crackup, follow-up, frame-up, grown-up, holdup, letup, lineup, makeup (also adj.), mix-up, mock-up, pileup, pushup, roundup, runner(s)-up, setup, shake-up, shape-up, speed-up, tie-up, walk-up, windup.

uppercase. It is one word—noun, verb and adjective—with this exception: *the upper case* for the case in which type is kept.

Upper East Side (of Manhattan).

Upper West Side (of Manhattan).

upward, not *upwards.*

U.S. for United States, but only in headlines, names, quoted matter or tabular and other special matter. Use the abbreviation in road names: *U.S. 40.*

usage, use. *Usage* refers to habitual or preferred practice in such fields as grammar, law, etiquette and diplomacy. *Use* is the preferred noun in references to employment of an object or consumption of a commodity: *the use of energy, gasoline use, automobile use, drug use.*

usherette. Do not use for a woman or a girl serving as an usher. See **women.**

U.S.I.A. for the United States Information Agency.

U.S.I.S. for the United States Information Service. It is used to designate overseas branches of the U.S.I.A.

USLIFE Corporation.

U.S.O. for United Service Organizations Inc.

U.S.S. for a United States ship in Government service. Where it is appropriate in stories make it *the U.S.S. Saratoga,* but *the aircraft carrier Saratoga* is usually better. Use U.S.S. in datelines: ABOARD U.S.S. SARATOGA, off California (or some other locating phrase), May 10—etc.

U.S.S.R. for the Union of Soviet Socialist Republics after cities and towns.

Utah. Do not abbreviate after cities and towns.

Utahan(s).

Utopia, utopia. Uppercase the name of the place in Sir Thomas More's book, but lowercase *a utopia, a utopian enterprise, a utopian* (for a believer in a utopia), *utopianism.*

V

v. and vs. for versus. The former is reserved for the names of court cases and proceedings. Lowercase both abbreviations in cap-and-lowercase headlines. See **versus**.

Va. for Virginia after cities and towns.

V.A. for the Veterans Administration.

Vale of Kashmir.

Valley. Capitalize when part of a name: *Mississippi Valley*. But: *the valley*.

van (the particle). See **personal names and nicknames**.

Van Cortlandt Park (in the Bronx).

variations (music). Capitalize in a title: *Brahms's Variations on a Theme by Haydn*.

varicolored.

Varig Airlines.

Vaseline (trademark).

Vatican I, Vatican II. Use these terms in second references to the First Vatican Council (1869-70) and the Second Vatican Council (1962-65).

VC for Vietcong, but only in quoted matter or special contexts.

V.D. for venereal disease.

vendor.

verbal, oral. Use *oral* rather than *verbal* to convey the idea of words that are spoken. *Verbal* is less precise; its chief meaning is words used in any manner—spoken, written or printed.

Vermonter(s).

Verrazano is the preferred spelling of the name of the explorer: Giovanni da Verrazano.

Verrazano-Narrows Bridge.

verse style. See **poetry**.

versus. Spell out in ordinary contexts: *It was cowboy versus steer, and the steer won*. The abbreviation vs. may be used in headlines in ordinary contexts, and in news stories when the abbreviation seems to be needed in certain nonlegal contexts. But the abbreviation v. should be used in the names of court cases and in reports of court proceedings. In cap-and-lowercase headlines, the abbreviations are lowercased.

Very Rev., the. Used in the Episcopal Church before the name of a dean of a cathedral or, in some instances, the head of a seminary: *the Very Rev. John P. Manley, Dean of the Cathedral of St. John the Divine; Dean Manley; the Dean.* Also, in the Roman Catholic

Church: *the Very Rev. John P. Manley, Superior General of the Jesuit order* (or: *of the Society of Jesus*); *the Superior General; Father Manley.* See **Rev., Most Rev., Rt. Rev., Archbishop, Bishop** and **Superior General.**

vest pocket (n.), **vest-pocket** (adj.).

vet. Do not use for veteran except in AMVETS.

Veterans Day (formerly Armistice Day).

VHF for very high frequency, and **UHF** for ultrahigh frequency.

V.I. for the Virgin Islands after the names of cities and towns in news stories or datelines: CHARLOTTE AMALIE, V.I., Jan. 7 (Reuters)—. The name of the individual island (St. Thomas, in the example shown here) should be omitted from the dateline but mentioned in the story when relevant.

vicar. Lowercase except when part of a title: *Vicar of Christ* (the Pope), *Vicar of Wakefield,* etc.

Vice Adm. John P. Manley, Admiral Manley, the admiral.

Vice Consul Elizabeth Manley, Vice Consul Manley, the vice consul.

vice-consulate.

Vice President, vice president. It is *Vice President Manley* (without first name) in a reference to the Vice President of the United States. First names are used in first references to vice presidents of foreign countries. In subsequent references: *Vice President Manley, the Vice President, Mr.* (or *Miss* or *Mrs.*) *Manley.* In plural references, *vice presidents* is usually lowercase (for capitalized plural exceptions, see **titles**). Also: *a vice president.*

Lowercase *vice president* in references to an officer of a company, a club, a university, etc.

Vice President-elect John P. Manley, Vice President-elect Manley, the Vice President-elect (of a national government; otherwise, lowercase). In headlines: *Vice President-Elect.*

Vice-Presidential, Vice Presidency. Capitalize where the reference is to the office of Vice President of the United States; otherwise lowercase.

vice versa.

vichyssoise.

victoria (carriage).

Victrola (trademark). It will usually be found only in historical references, but it is still a trademark and still capitalized.

videotape (n. and v.).

Viennese (sing. and pl.).

Vietcong. Not two words. The abbreviation *VC* should be used only in quoted matter or special contexts.

Vietminh.

Vietnamese (sing. and pl.) for the people of the unified country of Vietnam. In historical contexts, *North Vietnamese* and *South Vietnamese* may be used.

Vietnamese names. A Vietnamese name usually consists of the family name followed by two given names. Nevertheless widely current Western practice, accepted by the Vietnamese, is to use the last part of the name on second reference as if it were a surname. Thus a Vietnamese named Nguyen Van Hai would subsequently be referred to as *Mr. Hai;* in headlines: *Hai.* His wife, whose given name might be Mai Anh, could be referred to as *Mrs. Nguyen Van Hai*, and in second reference as *Mrs. Hai*. An exception was Ho Chi Minh, who used his pseudonym in Chinese fashion; it is proper to refer to him as *Ho*.

Vietnam War. Not *Vietnamese War*.

vilify.

Village. Capitalize when used alone to mean Greenwich Village. Do not quote, except in headlines when the meaning is not clear.

Virginian(s).

Virgin Islands. Use *V.I.* (which see) after the names of cities and towns.

Virgin Mary, the Virgin.

virtuoso, virtuosos.

visa, visaed.

vis-à-vis.

Viscount Manley of Kent, Lord Manley, the Viscount.

Viscountess Manley of Kent, Lady Manley, the Viscountess.

vitamin A (or *B, G,* etc.). Also: *vitamin A2, vitamin B12,* etc.

Vivian Beaumont Theater (at Lincoln Center).

Voice of America. Capitalize and do not quote, except "Voice" alone and then only if necessary to avoid confusion.

Volkswagenwerk A.G., the German company, can often be referred to simply as *the Volkswagen Company* or just *Volkswagen*. The company's subsidiary in the United States is Volkswagen of America Inc. In headlines, *Volkswagen* is preferred, but *VW* may be used provided the automotive context is unmistakable.

Volstead Act.

von (the particle). See **personal names and nicknames.**

voodoo.

votes. In stories, use numerals in giving the results of votes and of rulings by a court with more than one judge, and use *to* between the numerals: *The vote was 51 to 3, with 3 abstentions. A majority of 9 was obtained. He received 6 votes, 4 of them invalid. The justices ruled 9 to 5 in his favor.* Also: *a 51-to-3 vote, a 9-to-5 ruling.* In headlines, a hyphen may replace *to: 9-5 Decision.*

voting districts. See **district.**

vs. for versus. Lowercase in cap-and-lowercase headlines. Use v. instead of vs. in names of court cases and in court proceedings. Also see **versus.**

Vt. for Vermont after towns.

VTOL for vertical takeoff and landing.

vulgarity. See **obscenity, vulgarity, profanity.**

VW for Volkswagen (the car or the company) in quoted matter. In headlines, *Volkswagen* is preferred, but *VW* may be used provided the automotive context is unmistakable.

vying.

W

Wabash Railroad.

WAC for the Women's Army Corps. But *a Wac* for a member.

WAF for Women in the Air Force. But *a Waf* for a member.

wage earner.

Wailing Wall (Jerusalem). In certain contexts where it is useful or relevant, it should be noted that the Israelis call it the Western Wall.

waistline.

walk-. walk-on (n.), walkout (n.), walkover (n.), walk-up (n.).

wallpaper.

war-. warlike, warpath, warplane, warship, wartime.

War Between the States. Use only in special contexts; otherwise it is *the Civil War*.

Wards Island.

ware-. warehouse, warehouseman, wareroom.

War of 1812.

Warrant Officer John P. Manley (or Joan Manley), Warrant Officer Manley (or Mr., Miss or Mrs. Manley), the warrant officer.

Warsaw Pact.

Wash. for Washington after cities and towns.

wash-. washbowl, washout (n.), washroom.

Washington Heights, the Heights. In first references, there is no article before *Washington*. In headlines: *Washington Hts.*

Washingtonian(s). The people of the state and of the District of Columbia.

Washington's Birthday (holiday).

WASP('s) for white Anglo-Saxon Protestant(s). Use with care, because of its pejorative connotation.

water-. watercolor, watercress, waterfall, waterfront, waterline, waterlogged, waterproof, watershed, waterway, waterworks.

water spaniel.

wavelength(s).

WAVES for Women Accepted for Volunteer Emergency Service. But *a Wave* for a member. The designations are no longer official, but are still used informally by the Navy.

W.C.T.U. for the Woman's Christian Temperance Union.

weather. Storm classifications are given separately and alphabetically. See **blizzard, cyclone, gale, hurricanes, storm, tornado, typhoon.**

Weather Service. Capitalize in second references to the National

Weather Service. It was formerly called the United States Weather Bureau.

week-. weekday, weekend, weekender, weeklong.

weeks. Capitalize officially designated weeks: *Apple Week, Music Week,* etc.

weight lifter, weight lifting.

weights and measures. Many common units of weight and measure used in the English-speaking countries, as well as many metric units, are listed separately and alphabetically. Also see metric system.

weird.

Welfare Island (in New York City), once known as Blackwells Island, is now Roosevelt Island.

well-. well-advised, well-being, well-bred, well-done, well-founded. well-groomed, well-intentioned, well-known, well-mannered, well-nigh, well-read, well-rounded, well-spoken, well-timed, well-to-do, well-wisher, well-worn.

Such forms are hyphenated only when they serve as adjectives before nouns: *He is a well-read man.* The hyphen is not used when the words follow the nouns they modify: *He is well read.*

West, west. Capitalize when referring to that geographic region of the United States, to the Occident or to the grouping of nations opposed to the Communists in the ideological division of the world. Lowercase as a point of the compass.

West Bank, East Bank (of the Jordan River). Continue to capitalize as long as the terms have political significance. Do not hyphenate when used as modifiers in that sense.

West Berlin, East Berlin. Use *West Berlin* or *East Berlin* in datelines, not *Berlin* alone.

Westchester (N.Y.), West Chester (Del., Pa.).

West Coast, west coast. Capitalize when referring to the region of the United States lying along the shoreline of the Pacific; lowercase when referring to the actual shoreline. Also: *the Coast* (but capitalize for West Coast only).

West End (London).

Western, western. Capitalize when referring to the geographic region of the United States, to the Occident or to the grouping of nations opposed to the Communists in the ideological division of the world. But: *western Ohio, western Hungary, western half,* etc. And: *western movie, a television western.*

Western Airlines.

Westerner. Capitalize when referring to a person who was born in the West (United States only) or lives there.

Western Front (battlefront in World War I).

Western Hemisphere, the hemisphere.

Western Maryland Railway, a subsidiary of the Chessie System.

Western Pacific Railroad, a subsidiary of Western Pacific Industries.

West Germany. Use both words, not *Germany* alone, after cities and towns when a locater is required. See datelines.

Westhampton (L.I.).

West Highland white terrier.

West Indies. Do not abbreviate after cities and towns, even in datelines. In most datelines, provided an island is specified, *West Indies* need not be included: ST. GEORGE'S, Grenada, Nov. 7 (Reuters)—.

West Side. Capitalize when regularly used to designate a section of a city. Note: In London it is the West End.

West Virginian(s).

Weyerhaeuser Company.

wharf, wharves.

Wharton School (of the University of Pennsylvania). It is no longer the Wharton School of Finance and Commerce.

whereabouts (sing.).

which, that. See **that, which.**

whimsy, whimsies.

whip (legislative title). Lowercase: *John P. Manley, the Republican whip in the House.*

whippet (small hound).

whisky, whiskies.

white-. whitecap, white-headed, whitewing.

white paper. Lowercase unless it is part of a name: *The State Department issued a white paper on China.*

who, whom. Use *who* in the sense of *he* or *she* or *they: John P. Manley, who was appointed to fill the vacancy. . . . (He* was appointed.) Use *whom* in the sense of *him* or *her* or *them: Joan Manley, whom the board recommended, was finally appointed.* (The board recommended *her.)*

Do not be misled by the verb in a parenthetical phrase between the pronoun and its verb, as in: *John P.*

Manley, whom the police said is the mastermind. . . . (It must be *who*, as removal of the parenthetical *the police said* will demonstrate. Or, to put it another way: The police are saying that *he* is the mastermind.) But *whom* is correct here: *John P. Manley, whom the police described as. . . .* (They described *him.)*

W.H.O. for the World Health Organization.

wholehearted.

Wholesale Price Index (of the Bureau of Labor Statistics).

wide-, -wide. wide-awake, wide-brimmed, wide-eyed, widesought (all adj.). Also: boroughwide, citywide, continentwide, countrywide, nationwide, statewide, worldwide.

widow, widower. In obituaries, say that a man is survived by his wife, not by his widow, just as a woman is survived by her husband, not by her widower. The words *widow* and *widower* can wait for subsequent stories, but even then they should be used only when truly pertinent. See **women.**

Wilkes-Barre (Pa.).

Williamsburg. The Brooklyn neighborhood and the Virginia city (Colonial Williamsburg). Also: Williamsburg Bridge. But: the Williamsburgh Savings Bank.

wilton carpet.

win. Do not use as a noun except in quoted matter.

wind-. windfall, windmill, windstorm.

windup (n.).

wing (hockey player), not *winger.*

Wing Comdr. John P. Manley (British), Wing Commander Manley, the wing commander.

wingspan, wingspread.

wing T (n.), **wing-T formation.**

winter, wintertime.

wire fox terrier (not *wire-haired*).

wiretapping. Do not confuse with bugging. See **bug, tap.**

Wis. for Wisconsin after cities and towns.

Wisconsinite(s).

-wise. Handle this suffix with care. It is fine in traditional forms like *clockwise, lengthwise, otherwise, penny-wise, slantwise.* It is also fine in *weatherwise,* meaning knowledgeable about weather: *He was a weatherwise old mariner.* But this is not so fine: *Weatherwise, it was a terrible day.* That is a faddish coinage, and here are others: *ballotwise, crimewise, energywise, healthwise, wagewise, you-name-it-wise.* Shun such coinages—usagewise, that is.

within, without. A simple *in* is often much better than *within,* which is pretentious in sentences like this: *He had no enemies within the party.* As for *without,* there are many instances in which it is either unclear or not idiomatic, as in: *His critics within and without the industry were seldom silent.* Make it: ... *in* [or *inside*] *and outside the industry.* On rare occasions when more dramatic phrasing is justified, the expression *within and without* is appropriate: *The President denounced enemies within and without.*

woebegone.

women. In referring to women, we should avoid words or phrases that seem to imply that The Times speaks with a purely masculine voice, viewing men as the norm and women as the exception. The principle is similar to that involving certain racial and religious designations, and some of the same questions must be asked: Is the term being used essential to the story? Is it denigrating? Would it be appropriate if applied to someone of another race, religion or sex?

Besides avoiding designations that are obviously disparaging— such as *doll, weaker sex* or *the little woman*—we should be aware of undesirable subtleties of meaning that can be conveyed in some contexts by otherwise innocuous terms like *housewife, comely brunette, girl, grandmother, divorcée, sculptress* and numerous others.

If a woman elected to the State Assembly is characterized initially as *a 34-year-old housewife,* some readers may detect a condescending tone, as well as a seeming exclusion of the subject's obvious participation in civic affairs. Those defects are not present in, for example, *34-year-old Staten Islander.* To take another case, a woman in a supermarket commenting on high prices might suitably be called a customer, as a man might be. In short, the word *housewife* is needlessly overworked as first description or second reference and should be used with care.

As for physical characteristics, they are on occasion pertinent. A profile, or indeed some news stories, may properly note the fact that the subject is unusually tall or short; in some cases weight—of a woman or a man—is a pertinent fact; achievements of strength raise questions of physical capacity. But it is no more appropriate to slide casually into parenthetical references to a woman's appearance—*comely brunette, petite, pert, attractive, bosomy, leggy, sexy*—than it is to speak of *the tiny Councilman.*

It is also inappropriate to refer to a grown woman as a girl—*girl reporter,* for instance. If the sex is truly pertinent, then it can be *woman reporter,* or the information can be given in some other manner. But often the sex distinction will on examination prove not to be important to the reader's comprehension and can thus be omitted entirely. *Coed* is one of the terms most frequently used in instances where it is not really necessary to note the presence of women in groups that are normally mixed by sex. In addition, *coed* as a noun meaning student is virtually obsolete in an age of predominantly coeducational campuses.

Care must also be exercised in using terms that define women by their marital status *(bride, widow, divorcée)* or by their descendants *(grandmother).* Such terms may sometimes be pertinent, and a test of pertinence can be made by asking whether the same information would be used if the subject were a man. Golda Meir has often been called a grandmother in contexts in which Charles de Gaulle would never have been called a grandfather.

Words with grafted feminine endings—*authoress, sculptress, poetess, aviatrix, usherette,* among others—present a further problem. They seem to imply second-rank status, and should in general be avoided. Almost the only words in this category that persist in general usage are *actress* and *waitress.* Even *comedienne,* although still acceptable, is being replaced by *comedian.*

Some terms in which the word *woman* replaces *man* are another matter. *Councilwoman* and *Assemblywoman,* for example, are appropriate. But *chairwoman* (or *chairperson*) should not be used; *chairman* (like *foreman, spokesman* and some similar terms) suffices for both sexes. In the case of a mixed group whose members have similar titles—Councilman and Councilwoman, for example—the best solution in plural references is *Council members* or some equivalent.

Also see related separate entries, including **Assemblyman, Assemblywoman; comedian, comedienne; Councilman, Councilwoman; divorcée; girl; grandmother; housewife; lady; Mr., Mrs. and Miss; Ms.; -person; widow, widower.**

women's liberation. That is the style, lowercase, if the expression must be used at all. But it is outdated and should generally be avoided. And do not use *women's lib,* which many feminists consider belittling. See **women.**

women's wear. But use any variant spellings, such as *Womenswear,* in proper names.

Woodbridge, Wood-Ridge (N.J.).

Woods Hole (Mass.).

woodwork.

woolen, woolly.

work-. workaday, workday, workhouse, workman (or workingman), workout (n.), workshop, workweek.

World Airways.

World Bank may be used in second references to the International Bank for Reconstruction and Development (the official name) and in first references if necessary to avoid a cumbersome sentence. Also, in second references: *the bank.*

World Council of Churches. An organization of more than 250 Protestant and Orthodox churches, including most major ones. Its members are denominations, not countries. Its headquarters are in Geneva, and its chief executive is a general secretary (not *secretary general*). The highest policy-making body is the general assembly, which meets every six or seven years. Interim policy is set by the central committee, which has more than 100 members and meets at intervals of about 18 months.

World Court may be used instead of International Court of Justice (the official name) in second references. Also: *the Court.*

World Series, the Series. Capitalize when referring to the baseball series between the American and National Leagues. Also: *Little World Series* (baseball).

World Trade Center. In subsequent references: *the Trade Center.*

World War I, World War II. *First World War* and *Second World War* may also be used, but the Roman-numeral form is preferred. Also: *a world war, a third world war, the world wars.*

worldwide.

worshiped, worshiper, worshiping.

worthwhile.

wrack. See **rack, wrack.**

wrongdoer.

WUI Inc., formerly Western Union International. It should not be confused with the Western Union Corporation or the Western Union Telegraph Company.

W.Va. for West Virginia after cities and towns.

W. Virginia may be used only in headlines—and then only when absolutely necessary—and in tabular and other special matter.

Wyo. for Wyoming after cities and towns.

Wyomingite(s).

XYZ

Xerox (trademark). Never a verb.

Xmas. Never use.

X-ray (n., adj., v.). X-rays, like gamma rays (which see), lie at the shortwave end of the electromagnetic spectrum. They are generated by processes involving high-energy electrons, whereas gamma rays are emitted by atomic nuclei.

yacht. A sailboat or a powerboat, usually privately owned, that is used for the pleasure of racing or cruising. See the following entry and **pronouns for ships** and **sailboats.**

yachting. Times of yacht and boat races are given in figures: *4 hours 10 minutes 23 seconds, 4:10:23; 10 minutes 54 seconds, 10:54.* In yacht races, when the time of the race and the hour of the day are given, follow this form: *Puritan started at 9:30 and arrived at the stake boat at 2:15:20* (meaning at 15 minutes 20 seconds past 2 o'clock). *She won the race in 4:45:20* (meaning in 4 hours 45 minutes 20 seconds), *beating Priscilla by 6 minutes and Genesta by 9 minutes 15 seconds.*

When possible, stories should carry the direction and speed of the wind. Speed is given in miles per hour or in knots, not *knots per hour.*

Most competition in the metropolitan area is conducted among one-design classes. These classes are referred to as the *Star Class, Thistle Class,* etc. (dropping the *one-design*). Exception: *Manhasset Bay One-Design Class.* Figures are used for metric designations: *5.5-Meter yacht, 12-Meter yacht.*

In predicted log contests, the skipper predicts in writing how long it will take him to cover a given course. His score is based on how close he comes to his estimate. Such events should not be referred to as races.

yard-, -yard. yardarm, yardmaster, yardstick. Also: backyard, barnyard, churchyard, graveyard, lumberyard, schoolyard, shipyard, steelyard, studdingsail-yard.

yarmulke (the skullcap).

yawl. A two-masted vessel in which the mizzen (the small mast aft) is stepped aft of the rudderpost. See **ketch.**

year-. yearbook, year-end, yearlong (adj.), year-round (adj.).

years, decades, centuries. Numerals are used to designate specific years *(1492, 1975, mid-1975)* and decades and centuries *(the 1970's, the 1800's, the mid-1800's).* An apostrophe is used before the numeral when referring to a single year without the century: *the class of '63, mid-'75.* The apostrophe is not used before the numeral in giving decades of years without the century: *the 70's.* In first references in stories, the century should usually be given *(1970, the 1970's),* but the shorter forms *('70* or *70's* or *mid-70's)* suffice for subsequent references and for headlines. Special designations of decades may be spelled out and capitalized: *the Gay Nineties, the Roaring Twenties.*

Spans of years are given as follows: *1861-65, 1880-95, 1895-1900, 1903-4* (not *1903-04*).

Spell out numbers of centuries from first through ninth and lowercase: *the first century, the eighth century.* Use numerals from 10th on: *the 12th century, the 19th century.* Hyphenate the adjectival form: *eighth-century ruins, 17th-century house.*

When years or decades of years begin a sentence, they must be spelled out: *Nineteen sixty-seven* [or *Nineteen hundred sixty-seven*] *was not his lucky year. Nineteen-sixties answers can no longer be accepted.* It may be preferable to recast such sentences: *The answers of the 1960's. . . . The year 1967 was not. . . .*

Commas do not surround a year when it is used with a month alone: *the January 1975 issue of Fortune.* But commas are essential before and after the year when it follows a specific date: *the March 5, 1974, proclamation by the President.* See **dates** and **dates, punctuation in,** and **months.**

Yemeni(s). The people of Yemen (capital: Sana) or of Southern Yemen (capital: Aden).

Yeoman John P. Manley, Yeoman Manley, the yeoman. Also: Yeoman 3d Class John P. Manley, etc.

Yerevan (Armenian capital), formerly Erivan.

yogurt.

Yoknapatawpha County.

Yom Kippur (Day of Atonement).

Yorkshire terrier.

Young Turk(s). When the reference is to insurgents in a political group or other organization, the *Y* is capitalized.

Your Honor. Capitalize when referring to the judge or other presiding officer in a court, but use only in quoted matter.

Yugoslav(s). Noun and adjective. Do not use *Yugoslavian(s).*

Yukon Territory. Do not abbreviate after cities and towns, even in datelines.

Yule, Yuletide. Yule is overworked in headlines and should be the last resort.

zabaglione.

Zaire. Formerly the Democratic Republic of the Congo (former short version: the Congo). The capital is Kinshasa, formerly Leopoldville. But: *the Congo River,* not *the Zaire River.* See **Congo** and **Congolese.**

Zairian(s). The people of Zaire.

zero, zeros.

zigzag (adj., n., v.).

Zim Lines (Zim-Israel Navigation Company).

ZIP code. The first word is all caps, the second all lowercase. Do not use a comma between the name of the state and the ZIP code in giving a mailing address: *New York, N.Y. 10036.*

zoom. In the general sense of rapid movement, the word should be used only to describe upward motion. Zooming sounds and zoom lenses are another matter.

zymurgy. Do not capitalize, quote or otherwise tamper with: *John P. and Joan Manley, who have achieved renown in many fields, have retired to a cabin in a remote hollow in the Great Smokies. There he will continue his research in zymurgy and she will pursue the hobby for which she became known in her girlhood as the Annie Oakley of the Berkshires.*

Standard Proofreading Marks

⋀ Make correction indicated in margin.

Stet Retain crossed-out word or letter; let it stand.

Stet Retain words under which dots appear; write "Stet" in margin.

✗ Appears battered; examine.

≡ Straighten lines.

√√√ Unevenly spaced; correct spacing.

∥ Line up; i.e., make lines even.

run in Make no break in the reading; no paragraph.

no ¶ No paragraph; sometimes written "run in."

out see copy Here is an omission; see copy.

¶ Make a paragraph here.

tr Transpose words or letters as indicated.

ℓ Take out matter indicated; delete.

ℓ Take out character indicated and close up.

ℓ Line drawn through a cap means lowercase.

℔ Upside down; reverse.

⌒ Close up; no space.

Insert a space here.

⊥ Push down this space.

⫠ Indent line one em.

⌐ Move this to the left.

⌐ Move this to the right.

⌐ Raise to proper position.

⌐ Lower to proper position.

//// Hair space letters.

w.f. Wrong font; change to proper font.

Qu? Is this right?

l.c. Put in lowercase.

s.c. Put in small capitals.

Caps Put in capitals.

C&s.c. Put in caps and small caps.

rom Change to roman.

ital Change to italic.

≡ Under letter or word, means caps.

= Under letter or word, means small caps.

— Under letter or word, means italic.

～～ Under letter or word, means boldface.

,/ Insert comma.

;/ Insert semicolon.

:/ Insert colon.

⊙ Insert period.

/?/ Insert question mark.

/!/ Insert exclamation mark.

/=/ Insert hyphen.

\'/ Insert apostrophe.

\"/\" Insert quotation marks.

\/ Insert superior letter or figure.

⁄7 Insert inferior letter or figure.

⌊/⌋ Insert brackets.

(/) Insert parentheses.

$\frac{1}{m}$ One-em dash.

$\frac{3}{m}$ Two-em parallel dash.

Sample of a Marked Proof

By JOHN P. MANLEY
Special to The New York Times

HOUSTON, Monday, Jul 21—Men hve landed and walked on the Moon.

Two Americans, astronauts of Appollo Eleven, steered their fragile 4-legged lunar module safely and smoothly to the historic landing yesterday at 4:17:40 P.M., Eastern daylight time.

Neil A. Armstrong, the 38 year old civilian Commander, radioed to earth and the control mission room here: "Houston, Tranquillity Base here. The *Eagle* has landed."

The fist men to reach the moon, Mr. Armstrong and his co-pilot, Colonel Edwin E. Aldrin Jr. of the Air Force—brought their ship to rest on a level, rock-strewn plain near the southwestern shore of the arid Sea of Tranquility.

Footprints on the Moon

About six and half hours later, Mr. Armstrong opened the landing crafts hatch stepped slowly down the ladder and declared as he planted the 1st human foot print on the lunar crust:

"Thats one small step for man, one giant leap for mankind."